Date Due			
Hensall			
MAR 25			
APR 8			

EARLY
VOYAGES AND NORTHERN
APPROACHES

TRYGGVI J. OLESON

EARLY VOYAGES AND NORTHERN APPROACHES 1OOO–1632

The Canadian Centenary Series

McClelland and Stewart Limited

ACKNOWLEDGEMENTS

We wish to thank the following sources for permission to use their material in the illustration sections.

DET ANTIKVARISKE ARKIV, Oslo: for drawing of Knorr from Norwegian Church wall (Plate 10). NATIONAL MUSEUM OF CANADA: for the artifacts of the Thule and Dorset Cultures (Plates 4 and 5). NATIONAL MUSEUM, Copenhagen: for the Crozier and wooden plates (Plate 2), Crucifix and Kingigtersuaq Stone (Plate 3); Bone combs (Plate 5); the collections of artifacts (Plates 6, 7, 8, 9); and the painting of Eskimos from Godthaab (Plate 16). OLDSAKSAMLING UNIVERSITY, Oslo: for the Gokstad and Oseberg ships (Plate 11). PUBLIC ARCHIVES OF CANADA: for the Maps of the New World (2-5, 7, and 8) and for the photographs of Henry Hudson, Sir Thomas Button, Sir Martin Frobisher, and Thomas James (Plates 12-15). TORONTO PUBLIC LIBRARY: for assistance in obtaining details from the Visscherius map (1) and the map of the Arctic Regions by Willem Barents (6) and "Falconers and their Charges" from The Art of Falconry (Plate 1)

DESIGN: FRANK NEWFELD

The Canadian Publishers
McClelland and Stewart Limited
25 Hollinger Road, Toronto 16

THE
CANADIAN
CENTENARY
SERIES

A History of Canada

W. L. Morton, EXECUTIVE EDITOR
D. G. Creighton, ADVISORY EDITOR

VOLUMES STARRED ARE PUBLISHED

CONTENTS

Early Voyages and Northern Approaches

MAPS AND ILLUSTRATIONS

FACING PAGE 52

An illustration from Frederick II's *The Art of Falconry*—Crozier carved from walrus tusk and wooden plates used for serving food—Crucifix from Western Settlement of Greenland and the Kingigtersuaq Stone—Artifacts of the Thule Culture—Artifacts of the Cape Dorset Culture—Tools and Utensils—Clothes from the Churchyard at Herjolfsnes—Toys and Ornaments—Drawings of ships in Norwegian Church—The Gokstad ship and the Oseberg ship—Henry Hudson—Sir Thomas Button—Sir Martin Frobisher—Thomas James—An old painting of Eskimos

See also Appendix C

FACING PAGE 132

MAPS OF THE NEW WORLD

The Arctic and the Antarctic by Visscherius, 1639—Map of Juan de la Cosa, 1500—From the Contino Chart, *circa* 1500—Map of Johannes Ruysch, 1508—Chart of the North Atlantic, 1570—The Arctic Regions by Barents, 1598—Henry Hudson's Discoveries by Gerritsz, 1612—Jens Munk's representation of his wintering at Hudson Bay, 1619-20

The Canadian Centenary Series

Nearly half a century has elapsed since *Canada and Its Provinces*, the first large-scale co-operative history of Canada, was published. During that time, new historical materials have been made available in archives and libraries; new research has been carried out, and its result published; new interpretations have been advanced and tested. In these same years Canada itself has greatly grown and changed. These facts, together with the approach of the centenary of Confederation, justify the publication of a new, co-operative history of Canada.

The form chosen for this enterprise is that of a series of volumes. The series has been planned by the editors, but each volume will be designed and executed by a single author. The general theme of the work is the development of those regional communities which have for the past century made up the Canadian nation; and the series will be composed of a number of volumes sufficiently large to permit an adequate treatment of all the phases of the theme in the light of modern knowledge.

The Centenary History, then, is planned as a series to have a certain common character and method, but to be the work of individual authors, specialists in their fields. As a whole it will be a work of specialized knowledge, the great advantage of scholarly co-operation, but, at the same time, each volume will have the unity and distinctive character of individual authorship. The result, it is hoped, will be scholarly and readable, at once useful to the student and of interest to the general reader.

The difficulties of organizing and executing such a series are apparent; the overlapping of separate narratives, the risk of omissions, the imposition of divisions which are relevant to some themes, but not to others. Not so apparent, but quite as troublesome are problems of scale, perspective and scope, problems which perplex the writer of a one-volume history, and are magnified in a series. It is by deliberate choice that certain parts of the history are told twice, in different volumes from different points of view, in the belief that the benefits gained outweigh the unavoidable disadvantages.

The Centenary History is a series to be written by individual authors; but it is also planned to have a certain common character and to follow a common method. It has been agreed that a general narrative treatment was necessary and that each author should deal in a balanced way with economic, political, and social history. This varied and comprehensive account will, it is hoped, be presented in a scholarly, interpretative, and readable fashion, so that the student may be informed and the general reader interested.

The editors welcome Tryggvi J. Oleson's volume, the second to be published in the series. Professor Oleson's purpose is to examine how explorers, settlers, and hunters from Norway, part of the great movement of the Vikings in the eighth and ninth centuries, made their way across the north Atlantic and formed contacts with the lands of the Canadian Arctic. These contacts lasted centuries, were known in mediæval Europe, and affected the lives of both the Greenlanders and the Arctic aborigines. This northern route became one by which fishermen, traders, and explorers from England made their way into the Canadian north. Professor Oleson has told a little-known story, but one full of suggestion, of what perhaps is to be termed the pre-history of Canada.

W. L. MORTON,
Executive Editor.
D. G. CREIGHTON,
Advisory Editor.

Early Voyages and Northern Approaches

It is now some twenty-five years since I first became seriously interested in and began the study of pre-Columbian voyages to America, particularly those of the Icelanders, or Norsemen, as they are so often called. Then, about twenty years ago, I read Dr Jon Duason's huge work on the pre-Columbian explorations and settlements of the Icelanders in the western hemisphere. The central part of this work deals with the relations of the Icelanders in Greenland and various parts of the Canadian Arctic with the aborigines of these regions. I found this a fascinating study and undertook to translate all three volumes of the work from Icelandic into English. Since then I have continuously worked with Duason, especially on the problem of racial intermixture between the aborigines and the Icelanders and the fate of both these peoples after they came into contact with one another sometime in the eleventh and twelfth centuries. This problem occupies the central position in this volume. Those who know Duason's work will at once see how heavily indebted I am to him, although we do have our points of disagreement. At times I find it difficult to distinguish between his opinions and mine, for I have consulted all the works he used, in addition to the literature that has appeared since 1947, the year in which the final fascicles of his book appeared. Needless to say, he is in no way, except as explained above, to be held responsible for the views expressed in this book.

Hundreds of works have been consulted over the years. The bibliography appended to this volume is a highly selective one. However, it does, I hope contain at least as many titles that oppose as support the view which I have tried to put forward here. Indeed, that is all but inevitable. Duason is almost the only scholar whose views are largely the same as mine, and support for them is found only indirectly in the many works that deal with the above problem. The authors in setting forth the facts have placed in most cases a different interpretation on them from mine because they have approached the problem of the Thule Culture largely from the standpoint of archæology and have neglected the historical setting of the first half of the second millennium of our era.

The individuals who have been helpful to me in one way or another are far too numerous to mention by name, but I must express my gratitude to a few. I am greatly indebted to the staff of the University of Manitoba Library, particularly Miss K. Coddington, Miss E. Greer, Miss M. Mackenzie and Mrs D. Segal. Dr H. B. Collins of the Smithsonian Institution, Dr Wm E. Taylor and Dr L. Oschinsky of the National Museum of Canada, Mr T. E. Layng of the Public Archives of Canada, Dr Elmer Harp of the Dartmouth College Museum, Dr Moreau Maxwell of Michigan State University, Dr Bruce Chown of Winnipeg, Mr R. A. Skelton of the Map Room of the British Museum, have all assisted me in procuring literature. Professor W. L. Morton, Executive Editor of the Centenary Series, and Professor D. G. Creighton, Advisory Editor, have both made valuable suggestions. Mrs T. A. Saunders of Winnipeg did a superb job in typing a most difficult manuscript. The University of Manitoba made generous research grants to me, and a Faculty Research Fellowship from the Social Science Research Council enabled me to check many sources in London and Copenhagen. I have also to thank Mr Pierre Brunet, the Assistant Dominion Archivist, Colonel G. W. L. Nicholson, former head of the historical section of the Canadian Army, and Dr Helge Larsen of the National Museum in Copenhagen for help in obtaining illustrations.

I may say again that any errors and mistaken interpretations in the book are my own and not those of any of the above.

TRYGGVI J. OLESON

CHAPTER 1

The Northern Approach
to Arctic Canada

One of the most dynamic and dramatic periods in European history opens in the last decade of the eighth century with the attack by certain freebooters from northern Europe on England, Ireland, and France. At this time western Europe had reached a stage of considerable peace and stability after the Germanic invasions of the fifth and sixth centuries, the chaos caused by the internecine quarrels of the Merovingian dynasty, and the raids carried out by the Moslems from Spain in the first half of the eighth century. The war against the Saxons had been pretty well brought to a satisfactory conclusion, and the Lombards had submitted to the Frankish king and their territories in Italy were now parts of his domain. The Moslems were, indeed, a continuing threat to Italy and adjacent islands, but there was a certain tranquillity and a cultural revival which is sometimes known as the Carolingian Renaissance. This movement owed its origins to a great extent to the flourishing culture of England which, although not a unitary state, was marked by a relative freedom from disastrous tribal rivalries and a high level of scholarship and learning. It seemed indeed that the German barbarians who had descended in the fifth and sixth centuries on the various lands of the western part of the Roman Empire were being successfully assimilated into what remained of the classical culture in a rapidly emerging and vigorous Christian society.

But then came the violent irruption from the north. Out of the shadowed fjords of Norway and the glinting sounds of Denmark there descended on Christian Europe the last and fiercest of the Germanic barbarians. We do not know what caused this sudden onslaught. It had no doubt been in preparation for a long time and was preceded by a peaceful exodus of large numbers of Norwegians who settled in the Hebrides, the Orkneys, Shetland, and the Faroe Islands, there to carry on an economy similar to that of the homeland.

Norway has always been a country where "laggard crops are hardly

1

won," and therefore overpopulation is likely to be a problem, much more so than in Denmark where agriculture can be more widely practised. Yet both these people erupt and embark on what we know as the Viking raids at about the same time and to a great extent in the same directions. If over-population was one of the reasons for the raids launched by the Norwegians, fear of Frankish encroachment may have been one of the main reasons why the Danes in the later years of the reign of Charlemagne began their incur-sions against the shores of his realm as well as those of the British Isles. Charlemagne's conquest of the Saxons brought him to the borders of Den-mark and led to hostilities between the Franks and the Danes. Scholars, how-ever, are not in any agreement as to the causes of the Viking raids on the British Isles and western Europe in the early years of the ninth century.

On the other hand, there is no doubt that the Scandinavian peoples had by this time perfected ships which were ideally suited for the carrying out of raids on countries which were not separated by too wide an expanse of water, or which could be reached by coastal navigation as was the case with most of western and southern Europe. These were the so-called and well known longships, long, narrow, low-built, and suited to rowing, excellently adapted to coastal navigation and able to penetrate far inland on the rivers which afford access to the interior of western Europe and the British Isles. Fleets of these superb vessels descended on the Low Countries, France, Spain, England, Scotland, and Ireland during the ninth and tenth centuries. It is usually held that these attacks were, to begin with, solely booty-gather-ing expeditions.

It is doubtful, however, that this was at first the main reason for the irruption of the Scandinavians. The Vikings were cruel and fierce bar-barians, but this was only one side of the coin. Norway and Denmark in the eighth century were highly civilized communities of free-born peasants accustomed to making their living, in Denmark, by an agrarian way of life and, in Norway, by husbandry and hunting. It is very probable that the earliest excursions from Scandinavia which led to the settlement of the Hebrides, Shetland, and the Faroe Islands were prompted by a desire to find new lands in which such a way of life could be carried out when over-population became a problem in the homeland. To these they went quietly year after year, not in longships but in shorter, higher ones, fit to carry family and flocks, herds, and the roof trees of houses, treasured in treeless climes.

Thus by conquest or migration, or both, the Faroes and Iceland, the "Danelaws" of England, Ireland, and France were settled, while the Swedes were settling Russia to the east. In the years between 1016 and 1090, what may be called a handful of Normans carved out a kingdom in southern Italy against the opposition of not only petty Italian rulers but the Byzantine

Emperors, the Moslem rulers of Sicily, and various Popes and Holy Roman Emperors. Here they established a state which in its emphasis on the authority of the ruler and the subordination of the citizen to the state, reminds one more of Nazi Germany than possibly any other state of modern times. The most brilliant embodiment of this absolutism was Frederick II (ob. 1250), known as *stupor mundi* or wonder of the world.

Frederick, out of his abundance of accomplishment, has left us a great masterpiece, his beautiful and incomparable book, *The Art of Falconry*. In it he describes most accurately and in the greatest detail the various kinds of birds used by mediæval man in that most popular of mediæval sports, falconry. Here he describes the noblest of all hunting-birds, the white falcon of Baffin Island. This affords the opportunity of turning to a less well-known episode in the history of the exploits of the Vikings, their expansion westward, their colonization of Greenland, and their fate in what was later to be called the New World. Although certain portions of this period in the history of the expansion of the Vikings, such as the Vinland voyages, are well known, other and later features are less familiar, and it is with these as well that the following chapters deal.

As has been said, there was a peaceful exodus, especially from Norway, to the isles north of Scotland in the late eighth and early ninth centuries. There was a further and much greater migration from Norway in the latter half of the ninth century at the time when Harold the Fair-haired was imposing his rule on Norway. It was at this time, between 850 and 870, that Iceland came within the ken of these Norwegian migrants, and indeed they may have heard reports of it from the Irish, who had been aware of its existence for possibly a hundred years or more. Some Irish hermits had even established themselves there and practised their ascetic way of life under the midnight sun which was bright enough to enable them, we are told, to pick the lice off their shirts. The Norwegians began the settlement of Iceland shortly after 870, taking with them, it would seem, fairly large numbers of Irish slaves or retainers. The settlement of Iceland was completed by 930, and most of the inhabitable parts of that volcanic island, much of it waste with vast expanses of lava and glaciers, had been occupied. Even lands of marginal quality were exploited.

The discovery of Iceland was the first stage in the process which brought Greenland, the Canadian Arctic, Labrador, and even more southerly regions of the east coast of Canada into the orbit of European civilization. Although Greenland must often have been sighted from ships driven slightly off course westward on their way to Iceland, it was not, as far as is known, visited by Icelanders until the ninth decade of the tenth century. Some Icelanders spent a winter on the ice-bound east coast of Greenland around 980, but this wintering there was without consequence. In 982 came Eirikr Thor-

valdsson, commonly known as Eric the Red, the first real settler in Greenland.

What attracted the Icelanders to Greenland was not only the possibility
of following an economy based, as in Iceland and Norway, on husbandry
supplemented by hunting, but even more the great abundance of game.
There were herds of reindeer in the interior; whales, walrus, narwhal, and
bears in the sea and on the ice north of the colonies. Eider ducks were also
to be found in the northern regions, and polar foxes and white falcons,
particularly on Baffin Island. Voyages to the west of Davis Strait and north
and west of Baffin Bay must have begun as soon as the Icelandic colonies
in Greenland were established. These voyages were known as Nordrsetu-
ferdir and these districts as Nordrseta (northern "sitter's" region).

Voyages to the east coast of America also began early. The information
supplied by the two sagas, the *Eiriks saga rauda* and the *Graenlendinga saga*,
which describe the voyages is vague, confused, and sometimes contradictory. As a result, though mention is many times made of visits to
Vinland, it is impossible today to locate the area, although it is not for lack
of trying on the part of scholars. Vinland has been located, for example, on
the west coast of Greenland by a scholar who thought the Icelandic colonies
there were to be found on the east coast. It has been located in James Bay on
the hypothesis that the climate had been much warmer around the year
1000 than it is at present. It has been located on the Great Lakes. It has been
located in Florida, and so one might go on. The truth of the matter is that
any attempt to locate Vinland will be futile until archæological research
has uncovered some evidence of the site of the colony. So far none has been
found in a locality which answers to the mild winter climate that both sagas
agree characterized Vinland.

In 1961, however, the Norwegian explorer and author, Helge Ingstad,
found some house ruins at L'Anse-aux-Meadows on the northern tip of
Newfoundland which he thought might be the houses the Icelanders built
in Vinland. In 1962, further excavations were carried out at this site. These
revealed that the houses might be but were not necessarily Norse structures
from the Middle Ages. Very few artifacts were found, only some iron nails
and quantities of slag, which showed that iron had been smelted there. No
final report has appeared, but Carbon 14 tests appear to suggest a date in
the neighbourhood of 1000. Claims have been made that this was the site of
Vinland, but the climate of northern Newfoundland is such that it can in no
sense fit that of the Vinland described in the sagas, and the grapes from
which Wineland got its name, are not to be found there. Indeed, it remains
a fact that if one is to place any reliance on the accounts of the Vinland
voyages given in the two major sources, the most likely location of it is on

Cape Cod or its environs where, however, in spite of a good deal of amateur archæological work, no trustworthy evidence has been found.

All in all, the Vinland voyages, spectacular and dramatic as they have been made to appear, both in the sagas dealing with them and especially by later commentators, were only a fleeting and unimportant episode in the history of the Vikings in the New World. Their sphere of activity in a period of over five hundred years before they lost their language and religion, was to be confined to Greenland, Labrador, Hudson Bay, and the islands of the Canadian Arctic. It is with this history that the present volume is concerned.

The Icelandic colonies in Greenland were in close touch with the mother country, and especially with Norway after the Archbishop of Trondhjem replaced the Archbishop of Lund as the superior of the Icelandic Church in the latter part of the twelfth century, and after 1262, when the Icelanders accepted the King of Norway as their personal sovereign. Christianity was introduced into Greenland in the year 1000 when the Icelandic National Assembly made it the state religion. Greenland, however, was not made an episcopal diocese until 1123 or 1124, although a missionary bishop, Eirikr Gnupsson, may have been stationed there until he departed for Vinland in 1121. The cathedral was located at Gardar and the bishops of Greenland resided there until 1378. After that date, although bishops continued to be appointed until almost the middle of the sixteenth century, not one reached the country. It is difficult to explain this, for communications with Europe were maintained to at least some extent throughout the fifteenth century. Ties between Iceland and Norway were close. Taxes and tithes of various kinds were paid to both the Church and King. And when the Norwegian king established a trade monopoly in the fourteenth century, the consequences of this policy were serious for both Iceland and Greenland.

Greenland was from the beginning dependent on imports of certain goods from Europe. Driftwood, although fairly plentiful in the northern regions, would not supply all the needs of the farmers and there may have been some importation of this from Norway. It is likely, however, that the great bulk of timber needed came from the abundant forests of Markland or Labrador and that regular voyages were made thither. This is indicated, for example, by an entry in an Icelandic annal for the year 1347 which casually mentions that a ship from Greenland that had been to Markland, evidently a well-known country, was driven off course to Iceland. Wheat and barley may have been imported but likely in small quantities. The thirteenth century King's Mirror, written by an unknown Norwegian, states that the greater part of the population of Greenland had never seen bread. Iron was the most needed import although there is evidence that bog iron was produced in Greenland to a limited extent and there is much evidence that iron was never plentiful even in the farming settlements. Stone and bone implements have been found in ruins dating from almost the earliest days of the settlements.

In return for these imports the Greenlanders exported some of the most valuable articles of mediæval trade. The ivory of the Middle Ages, used for fashioning croziers, chessman, and many other articles, came largely from the tusks of the walrus which were to be found in inexhaustible numbers in the waters north of the farming settlements. The walrus also supplied from its hide, ropes for the rigging of ships which the author of the *King's Mirror* said were so strong that even if sixty men pulled on such a rope they could not break it. From Baffin Island came one of the most valued of the exports of Greenland, the white falcon. It was not only an article of trade but even more a diplomatic instrument, for it was the habit of the kings of Norway to woo other monarchs whose friendship they wished to obtain by presenting them with these birds. Even more valued diplomatic instruments, although much rarer and more difficult to obtain, were live polar bears. These animals the Icelanders captured in special traps, the ruins of which may still be seen throughout parts of Greenland and the eastern Canadian Arctic. The horn of the narwhal was another item much sought after in mediæval Europe for its alleged medicinal value. From the beginning these riches proved an irresistible magnet to many of the Icelandic settlers.

It must not be forgotten that in addition to these more or less exotic products of the north, the seas and rivers abounded in fish and seals, the dietary staples of the inhabitants which were supplemented by caribou meat. Nor should the eider duck be overlooked, although we do not know whether its down was an article of export. The Icelanders erected artificial nesting-grounds for the ducks almost within the shadow of the pole.

Thus from the beginning, hunting was an important supplement to husbandry in the economy of the country and supplied the only articles Greenland was able to export in exchange for foreign goods, with the possible exception of a small quantity of wadmal and cheese. For this and a number of reasons, people left the farming settlements and concentrated on hunting in various parts of Nordrseta, that is, northern Greenland and the eastern Canadian Arctic, including Labrador and the shores of Hudson Bay. These people are the Tunnit of the Eskimo legends.

The Eskimo tradition is that the Tunnit "were a gigantic race formerly inhabiting the north-eastern coast of Labrador, Hudson Strait, and southern Baffin Island. Ruins of old stone houses and graves, which are ascribed to them by the present Eskimo, are found throughout this entire section. Briefly we may say that there is evidence, archæological as well as traditional, that the Tunnit formerly inhabited both sides of Hudson Strait." The Tunnit have been treated as a mystery people, identified as just another

Eskimo tribe, as North American Indians, and recently as the people of the Dorset Culture. None of these views can be sustained. The legends carefully distinguish between them and Eskimos. Indians are well known in Eskimo legends, and the description of the Tunnit cannot possibly fit them. It is the central thesis of this book that the Dorset people antedate the Tunnit; that they were the Skraelings of the sagas, the pigmy, primitive people whose race and origins are unknown; and that the present-day Eskimos are the result of an intermixture between the Dorset people and the Tunnit, that is, the Icelanders who left the farming settlements and adopted what we would call an Eskimo way of life. This amalgam emerged as the Thule Culture, the precursor of the modern Eskimo Culture.

In the following chapters the evidence is traced which points to an early racial intermixture between the Dorset people and the Tunnit, who had come from the farming settlements possessed of iron implements and able possibly for some decades to replace these with fresh iron acquired through trade with the expeditions the farmers are said to have sent annually to the rich hunting-grounds north and west of their farms, who gradually as the supply of iron grew slimmer had to resort to the fashioning and use of bone and stone weapons. Thus, as this fusion of stone-age and iron-age people moved westward, the crude weapons which resulted from the inexperience of an iron-age people in working bone and stone would gradually grow refined and have attained a high quality by the time Alaska was reached.

Most scholars are now agreed that the disappearance of the Icelandic culture which the Vikings had planted in Greenland at the end of the tenth century is the result of racial intermixture. There are, of course, some who cling to older theories as to the disappearance of the settlements. A hoary one that dies hard is that the Icelanders were exterminated by the Skraelings in bloody war, although many have shown that there is not a tittle of evidence of this warfare. Others feel that malnutrition and physical degeneration brought the once sturdy Viking race to an end. Again all recent studies by experts in these fields find no evidence for such a view. Climatic deterioration such as to make husbandry impossible is postulated by some. Although it can be shown that there were some climatic changes toward a colder climate from 500 A.D. on, there is little evidence to show that such changes between the years 1000 and 1500 could have seriously affected the mode of life which the Icelanders adopted on their arrival in Greenland.

Even more untenable is the theory that consanguineous marriages destroyed the vitality of the race. Nor is there any evidence that epidemics and plagues wiped out the people, nor that the worms of a butterfly (Agrotis occulta) destroyed vegetation to any great extent. Many more theories accounting for the disappearance of the Icelandic culture in Greenland could be mentioned but the majority of scholars are now agreed that racial inter-mixture took place. They fail, however, to answer the question: Where are the descendants of this racial intermixture to be found today or where do we find evidence of their existence, say, from the thirteenth century on? There can only be one answer. The Thule Culture, with its typically Icelandic structures, hunting-installations and methods, and various other features which have disappeared in the present-day Eskimo culture, is the result of an intermixture between Icelanders and the Dorset people, a cul-ture which begins with the former people the dominant partner but which sees the gradual submergence of the dominant partner and the triumph of the more primitive one, the loss of European culture and language and a decline in both the intellectual and material culture in the course of the centuries.

The pattern that emerges from the evidence which this book presents indicates then that the Icelanders had thus helped to create the first of Canadian peoples other than the aborigines. They had also brought Arctic Canada into the orbit of mediæval Europe, and had made it a remote and shadowy, but by no means unknown, frontier of mediæval Christian civilization.

Moreover, by their shipping and their settlement, they built across the waters and islands of the north Atlantic an approach to Arctic and southern Canada that English and French traders and explorers were to use in the search for Asia and the exploitation of the lands and islands intervening. Out of these men's efforts were to come the Newfoundland fisheries and the Canadian fur trade; out of their efforts were to come the New France of Champlain and the Rupert's Land of the Hudson's Bay Company.

CHAPTER 2

The Norwegian Occupation of
the Atlantic Islands

Canada is one of the nations belonging to what is often called the circum-polar complex.[1] To it belong, in addition, Sweden, Norway, Russia and, in Alaska, the United States of America. The history of Canada before the seventeenth century is largely the history of the penetration of the Canadian regions of the circumpolar complex by the ancestors of the present-day Eskimo, by the mediæval Scandinavians and, in the fifteenth and sixteenth centuries, by the Portuguese, French, and English.

The recorded history of Canada thus begins, as far as this work is concerned,[2] with the first ventures of Europeans into the North Atlantic. We do not know precisely when these voyages began. The Greek Pytheas of Marseilles seems to have sailed north from Britain in the fourth century A.D., visited either Norway or Iceland, and come into contact with the polar ice pack, possibly north of Iceland.[3] Of more certain knowledge are the voyages of the Irish, who were among the earliest Europeans to venture upon the north Atlantic. There is no doubt that the Irish monks reached and took up abodes in the Faroe Islands and in Iceland as early as the eighth century, but there is no proof that they went beyond Iceland to Greenland and America, as is often argued.[4] When and under what circumstances they discovered Iceland is not known, but it is almost certain that their vessels were skin boats known as *curraghs*.[5] There is no doubt, also, that they occupied parts of Iceland early in the eighth century, albeit in small numbers and perhaps not continuously, until about 870 when the Norwegians began to settle it.[6] No written record survives, and no archæological artifact, to prove what is, however, a distinct probability, that the Irish visited America.[7]

From contacts with Iceland, the Norwegians may have learned of the existence of islands in the North Atlantic.[8] It is with their ventures that the first major steps were taken which were to lead to the discovery of North America and the founding of settlements there. The irruption of the Vikings

11

on the European scene in the eighth and ninth centuries is one of the best-known chapters in history. Less well known are the reasons for this tremendous burst of energy which was to carry the Scandinavians to almost the four corners of the world.[9] As with many migrations in human history, it is difficult to know all the reasons that moved these vigorous people to explore unknown portions of the world but, as we have mentioned, over-population must have been one of the most powerful incentives for the Viking excursions in the search for new lands in which the Scandinavians might settle.[10] However that may be, it is certain that at the beginning of the ninth century the Norwegians were establishing themselves in the island chain north of Scotland. In the course of the ninth and tenth centuries Norwegians of all classes emigrated to Ireland, the Isle of Man, the Hebrides, the Shetland Islands, the Orkney Islands, the Faroe Islands, and Iceland. In all these lands, they were to a greater or lesser extent able to carry on the type of life they had been accustomed to in Norway, a type of life which could later be adapted to conditions in Greenland and Canada.

In Norway the main aim of agriculture was to produce fodder for as many domestic animals as possible, and in order to do this in a relatively barren country it was necessary to resort to the exploitation of all kinds of natural fodder crops. It has often been pointed out that twigs, leaves, moss, lichen, pine tufts, and even horse manure might be mixed with chaff and used as fodder for cattle. The plough was little used, and furrows were normally turned with spades. The whole aim of this husbandry was to maintain an adequate supply of domestic animals, especially cattle. Less attention was paid to cereal crops, so that men trained in an economy of this kind were well fitted to cope with conditions in Iceland and Greenland where cereal crops are almost impossible to grow.[11]

Nor were the Norwegians less acquainted with the other chief means of livelihood in these two countries: fishing and the hunting of sea and land mammals. In Norway, salmon-fishing was widely practised; seals were taken in large numbers; and deer were an important element in the diet of the people. All the skills necessary in the pursuit of hunting and fishing the Norwegians brought with them to Iceland, Greenland, and the Canadian Arctic, which were so rich in game and fish.

Add to these skills another in which the Scandinavians of the eighth century surpassed all other peoples in the world, and the stage is set for expansion whenever conditions in the homeland made this necessary. In seamanship and boat-building, the Norwegians had no peer. Archæologists have traced the evolution of the boat in Scandinavia through many centuries[12] until, by the Viking Age, the longship – long, narrow, low-built, and suited to rowing – enabled the Vikings to carry out their raids on neighbouring countries. The longship, however, is not a type of ship suitable for voyages to Iceland and later to Greenland and America. It is not suitable for pelagic navigation and may never have been used for the voyage to Iceland.[13] For such voyages, the Norwegians used much higher-built ships than the longship, ships which are generally referred to as *kaupship*, but were more particularly designed by such terms as *knorr, buza,*[14] or *byrdingr*. They were broader than the longship, had a rounder form and much deeper draught. There were permanent decks fore and aft, and the mast seems to have been fixed. Unlike the longship which was rowed, the *kaupship* was normally driven by sail.[15] These ships with a crew of only fifteen to twenty men were completely seaworthy and could carry a large cargo and many passengers. On them the art of pelagic navigation was to be mastered by the Icelanders.

Trained in an economy of husbandry and hunting, the Norwegians were by the ninth century ready to undertake the voyages which brought Greenland and the northern parts of Canada into the orbit of European and Christian civilization.[16]

The Scandinavians made their first recorded visits to Iceland in the period 850-870.[17] Whether these visits were the result of accidents, such as storms at sea, or whether the seafarers were searching for a land which was already known in the Western Isles, is not known. The early voyages occurred at a time when there was considerable emigration from Norway to the British Isles, Shetland, the Orkneys, and the Faroes. It was not, however, until around 870 that the Norwegians began the settlement of the country – a movement greatly accelerated by the disturbed conditions in Norway, where King Harold the Fair-haired was breaking the power of the petty kings and nobility in his effort to become sole master of the land. The Age of Settlement in Iceland lasted from 870 to 930. By the latter date, all the inhabitable parts of the island had been occupied and a national state or republic erected – the last Germanic *Volkerstaat* to be established. This contained all the familiar institutions of the Old Germanic states with a national assembly known as the Althing,[18] where all important questions – political, judicial, military, and legislative – were settled. This Icelandic Commonwealth was generally referred to by its members as a *her* (army), or *log* (laws)[19], in the Old Germanic fashion. All its members were subject to its authority until death or outlawry severed the tie.[20]

In Iceland the Norwegians found a land not dissimilar to the one they had left – possibly a little poorer in that no cereal crops could be grown there[21] and deer were not to be found. It could, however, well support an economy based on husbandry for a limited population, and the wealth of the sea, which grew ever in importance, was, as today, immense.[22] The population in 930, although it cannot be accurately estimated, may have been as high as thirty thousand. By that date, lands of marginal productivity were already being utilized by the latest settlers to arrive, and the population continued to increase.[23]

With the settlement of Iceland, the last step leading to the discovery of the New World[24] was taken. It could only be a matter of time until Greenland was sighted. From Horn, on the northwest coast of Iceland, the distance to the east coast of Greenland is only 190 miles, and under abnormal refraction the mountains of Greenland may be seen from the mountains of Iceland.[25]

Ships plying the sea from Norway to Iceland could easily be driven to the vicinity of Greenland. It is not surprising, therefore, that a sighting of Greenland sometime before 930 is recorded. A certain Gunnbjorn Ulfsson was driven west from Iceland and reported that he had seen some skerries (rocky islets), which were henceforth known as Gunnbjorn's Skerries.[26] It appears that many sailors had similar experiences,[27] but it is not until the last quarter of the tenth century that the Icelanders set foot on Greenland. Hrolfr Thorbjarnarson and Snaebjorn Holmsteinsson, with a company of some two dozen men, went in search of Gunnbjorn's Skerries in 980-81. They made their way to some point on the east coast of Greenland, where they wintered.[28] Snaebjorn and others of his company were slain by Hrolfr and his men, who then returned to Iceland by way of Norway.[29]

It was from the west coast of Iceland that these early contacts with Greenland were made. They cannot fail to have come to the ears of the man who was destined to found the Icelandic colonies there, which were to serve as the basis for the first penetration by Europeans of the Canadian Arctic, where racial intermixture was to produce a uniform and widespread culture on the Canadian mainland and the islands of northern Canada.

Eric the Red was the son of Thorvaldr Asvaldsson, one of the settlers of Iceland.[30] Thorvaldr had been outlawed from Norway for homicide and had made his way to Iceland where he had taken land at Hornstrandir, in the northwest corner of Iceland. His farmstead, known as Drangar, was a poor one on an inhospitable coast.

His choice of this land indicates that he came to Iceland in the last years of the Age of Settlement, or just before 930. If this date is correct, Eric the Red must have been born in Iceland,[31] at Drangar, where he lived until his marriage to Thjodhildr Jorundardottir, at which time he moved south to Haukadalr.

Like his father, Eric was frequently involved in disputes and litigation. Before long he was forced to leave Haukadalr and move to Brokey, and again from there to Oxney.[32] In 982, on a charge of homicide, he was sentenced to outlawry for three years. He was, of course, obliged to serve this sentence abroad, and only after having done so would he regain his rights and citizenship in the Icelandic Commonwealth. Faced with this necessity,

he chose to go in search of Gunnbjorn's Skerries. Making his way west to
Greenland, he encountered the ice pack off its coast, sailed south, and rounding Cape Farewell made his way north along the west coast until he
reached the vicinity of present-day Godthaab, where he wintered.[33] The
following summer he sailed farther north, exploring widely what were later
to be known as the "wastes" of Greenland. In the autumn he sailed
south and wintered near the southern tip (present-day Ikigait). The
third summer he sailed as far north as Melville Bay, returning south to
winter in what became known as Eiriksfjordr (Tunugdliarfik). In 985 he
returned to Iceland.

Eric had, while on his explorations, become convinced of the feasibility
of Greenland as the site of an Icelandic colony, and in order to entice others
to follow him thither, he gave to Greenland the name by which it has since
been known. Nor was his effort in vain. A colonizing company was organized in Iceland and a flotilla of twenty-five ships was required to carry
those who were prepared to embark on this venture. Most of these people
came from the west coast of Iceland and did not, it seems, consist of the
nobler or wealthier families.[34] This circumstance indicates that population
pressure was making itself felt in Iceland and that the living to be made on
marginal land was so precarious that many were prepared to seek their fortune farther west in an uninhabited land, whose riches – great indeed – were
painted in glowing colours by the intrepid explorer who had probed its
fjords and valleys.

In 986, fourteen of the twenty-five ships safely reached Greenland,[35] the
others either being lost at sea or driven back to Iceland. Eric himself settled
in Eiriksfjord and gave his farmstead the name of Brattahlid (Kagsiarsuk).
Some of his partners in the colonizing venture settled in other fjords of the
Julianehaab district and the remainder farther north in the region of the
Godthaab fjords. Thus were laid the nuclei of the two farming settlements
which were to be known respectively as the Eastern (Eystribyggd) and the
Western (Vestribyggd). Thence the Icelanders were destined to expand into
the whole of the eastern Canadian Arctic and tap its resources.

In the years following 986, considerable numbers of settlers must have
arrived from Iceland and established themselves in the Eastern and Western
Settlements. Both literary sources and archæological research reveal that
there were about three hundred farmsteads[36] in the two settlements, and
recent investigations have shown that in the so-called "wastes" separating
the two districts there were at least twenty-two farmsteads.[37] The actual
population is difficult to determine but the ruins of the farmsteads enable
one to conclude that on the smaller farms were to be found at least ten
people and on the larger, twenty to thirty or even more. It may be confidently asserted that the population of the farming districts in Greenland

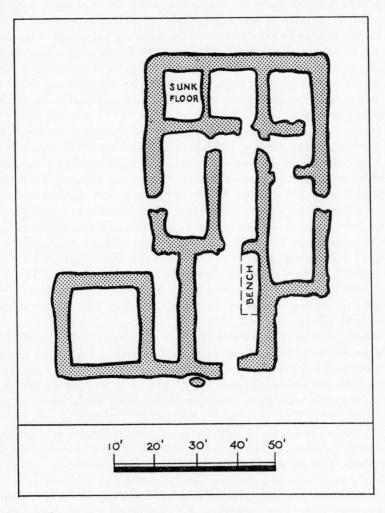

Floor plan of Brattahlid house

was not less than five thousand and more likely about ten thousand in the thirteenth century.[38]

The land to which the Icelanders came was not the bleak, inhospitable, ice-covered waste that Greenland is often imagined to be. On the contrary, the ice-free tracts between the coast and the inland ice on the southern part of the west coast of Greenland were fully as luxuriant as most parts of Iceland. Here, surrounding the fjords, grass grew in abundance and shrubs and dwarf trees were to be found,[39] providing fodder for domestic animals. The ruins of stables at the various farms in Greenland amply testify to the large number of cattle kept by the Icelanders.[40]

In addition to husbandry, Greenland offered its settlers vast opportunities for hunting by land and sea. The sea was filled with an unlimited supply of seal, and herds of reindeer roamed over the land. The importance of the seal in the economy of Greenland is evident from the start. More than half of the bone material collected at Brattahlid consists of seal bones,[41] and reindeer bones are found in considerable numbers in both settlements.[42]

The walrus and the whale also played a large part in the economy of the Greenlanders. Walrus bones have been found among the ruins of the Western Settlement, indicating that the hunting-grounds extended far north along the west coast and as far south as Godthaab. This is not to say that the inhabitants of the Eastern Settlement were any less accustomed to hunt the walrus than those of the Western Settlement, but that only the head and meat were transported home from the hunting-grounds.[43]

The habitat during the Middle Ages of various species of whales whose bones are found in the Norse ruins is difficult to determine. There can be no doubt that, as is the case with the walrus, the Greenlanders hunted these mammals in the waters far north of the Settlements as well as, to a much lesser degree, off the Settlements themselves. Here again, whale bones are found in much greater numbers in the ruins of the Western Settlement.[44]

In later chapters all these matters will be dealt with more fully in an examination of the migration of large numbers of the Icelanders, who had colonized Greenland, to the islands of the Canadian archipelago and northern continental Canada, and the eventual disappearance of the European-Christian culture of the Icelandic settlements in Greenland. In the meantime, we shall examine the voyages of the Icelanders to continental America, although they did not lead to any permanent settlement south of Labrador.

CHAPTER 3

The Elements of Fact in
the Icelandic Sagas

The first explorations by Europeans in the western hemisphere were undoubtedly those of Eric the Red, delineated above. They would seem to have
been confined to the west coast of Greenland, although it is not impossible
that they included parts of the Canadian archipelago. There is, however, no
evidence for this, but there is irrefutable evidence that the shores of continental America and Baffin Island were seen by Europeans in the very year
in which Greenland was settled.

The two chief sources on the voyages of the Icelanders to the shores of
America are the *Graenlendinga saga*, written about 1200, which records six
voyages, and the *Eiriks saga rauda*, written in the second half of the thirteenth century, which records only three. In many cases the two are irre-
concilable, and scholars have given more weight now to one, now to the
other, without much of a basis for their preference. It would be going
beyond the limits of this work to try to assess which is the sounder.[1]

In fact it must be said that the *Graenlendinga saga* and the *Eiriks saga*,
although they both contain much information which is based on old and
sound tradition, include much that is only fantasy or tradition which has
been preserved in an extremely muddled form. Yet because they are the only
or almost only literary and historical sources on the voyages made to
Vinland by the members of the family of Eric the Red, or those closely connected with it, they must not be neglected. They must, however, be treated
with caution. Above all, the pitfall must be avoided of regarding one of the
sagas as completely reliable and the other as totally worthless. At the same
time this need not mean that one version is not more solidly grounded in
fact than the other. It should be remembered that both in these matters and
in the later history of the fate of the Icelandic colonies in Greenland, the
surest evidence is that which is revealed by archæology combined with a
judicious use of the written sources. The validity of these observations will,

it is to be hoped, emerge in the summary of the two sagas which follows.

Both sagas deal with expeditions undertaken from Greenland to three regions lying west and south. No matter which version is accepted, there can be no question that Leifr Eiriksson, the son of Eric the Red, was the first European to set foot on American soil, but whether he was by accident driven to lands hitherto unknown, or whether he was deliberately seeking the lands already sighted, must be an unanswered question at the present stage of our knowledge.

The three regions visited by the Icelanders are called in the sagas Helluland (Flagstoneland), Markland (Woodland), and Vinland (Wineland). It appears that at the time the sagas were written, they were well-known places. Both sagas agree that it was Leifr who gave these lands their names and first set foot thereon around the year 1000. There can be no doubt as to the location of Helluland and Markland. The former is described as a land with glacier-covered mountains. Huge flagstones, devoid of any vegetation, stretched from the foot of the mountains to the sea; many polar foxes were observed there. This land can only be Baffin Island. South of it lay a level, heavily wooded region in which numerous deer were to be seen. There were also extensive stretches of white sand on its shoreline. Again there can be no doubt that this was a part of the coast of Labrador – very likely the region south of Hamilton Inlet.

The third region, Vinland, is more difficult to locate. It is described in similar terms in both sagas, as a region with a temperate climate, so temperate in fact that there was scarcely any frost in winter and cattle could forage for themselves the year round. Grapes were found in abundance, and self-sown wheat. The dew on the grass was very sweet. An island lay north of the country and a river ran from a lake into the sea. Salmon were very plentiful. Day and night were of more equal length than in Greenland. This was the region Leifr Eiriksson called Vinland and where he built a number of houses. It was this region also where a settlement was formed which endured for three years, and where the first white child was born in America.

What then have the sagas to tell us in detail about this region which has so tantalized both scholars and laymen, especially since 1837, when C. C. Rafn published all the relevant texts in his *Antiquitates Americanae*?

The *Graenlendinga saga* gives an account of the Vinland voyages radically different from that of the *Eiriks saga*. Whereas three voyages are given in *Eiriks saga*, six are recounted in *Graenlendinga*. These are those of (1) Bjarni Herjulfsson; (2) Liefr Eiriksson; (3) Leifr's brother Thorvaldr; (4) Thorsteinn's abortive attempt; (5) the expedition of Thorfinnr Karlsefni Thordarson; (6) Freydis's expedition. An account of these six voyages follows.

FIRST VOYAGE

Among those who accompanied Eric the Red to Greenland in 986 was Herjulfr Bardarson.[2] His son Bjarni, a travelling merchant whose habit it was to spend alternate years with his father in Iceland, returned home in 986 to find that his father had left for Greenland. Determined to spend the winter as usual with his father, he sailed for Greenland with his crew, but three days[3] out they were caught in a storm from the north and driven for several days far south off their course. When the storm abated and it was possible to take bearings, they sailed for a day until they sighted land. It was not mountainous, but forested and hilly. Leaving it on the port, they sailed for two days until they came to a level, wooded land, which they again bypassed, continuing the voyage in a northerly direction. After three days a high mountainous land with glaciers was seen and left behind. Four days later, after a stormy voyage, a land Bjarni recognized from descriptions previously given him as Greenland was reached. Here they landed at a ness which proved to be Herjulfsnes, the site of Herjulfr's farmstead.[4]

This voyage of Bjarni has often been rejected as pure fantasy,[5] but in itself it bears all the marks of authenticity.[6] His course may be conjectured to have been as follows: he set out to sea from Eyrarbakki near the southeast corner of Iceland. He sailed for three days on a westerly course making for Cape Farewell in Greenland at a speed of approximately seven miles an hour for a distance of 510 miles. This would bring him into the East Greenland current which flows south off the east coast of Greenland. This current divides into two branches just east of Cape Farewell. One flows around the Cape and north off the west coast, bringing with it the ice which in the spring prevents access to the sea from the parts of the west coast where the two mediæval farming settlements of the Icelanders were located. The other branch flows on south to the Newfoundland banks where it joins the southward-flowing Labrador current. Not far from here, the Gulf Stream is encountered and the notorious fogs in the region off Newfoundland are born.

When the weather worsened, Bjarni was in the East Greenland current and was swept far south of his intended course by the strong current and the northwest wind, in such foggy weather that all sense of direction was lost. Bjarni ran before this storm for "many days." Finally, when the fog lifted, he could get his bearings and very likely judge by the altitude of the sun how far off course he was. Then, after a day's sailing, land hove in sight. Here for the first time Europeans looked upon the shoreline of a part of Canada.

From the description given in the saga, it could have been either New-

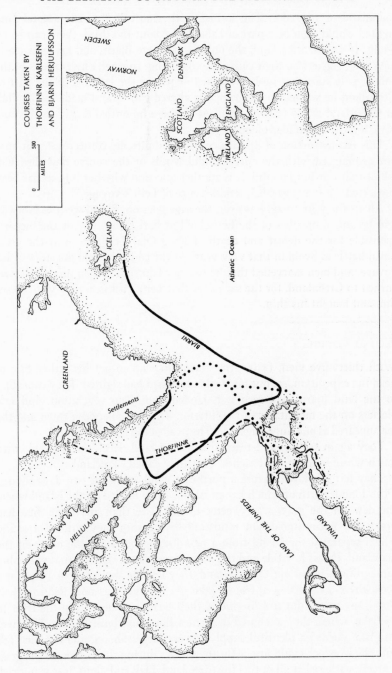

B

foundland or Labrador. The former is the more likely. The second land sighted would then be a part of Labrador. About the third, there can be no doubt. It was Baffin Island, the only land where Bjarni and his crew could have seen glaciers on their course. Recognizing, through observations of the sun or pole star, that he had reached or passed the latitude of the part of Greenland he wished to reach, Bjarni altered course and made his landfall in Greenland at his father's farmstead, where he settled down, so the saga says, for the remainder of his days.

This reconstruction of Bjarni's course is admittedly conjectural, but any-one acquainted with the currents and winds of the course described will admit that it is not fanciful. It is another question whether it is, as has been suggested, "a faint, garbled, reminiscence of Leifr's voyage."[7]

About the year 1000,[8] however, the saga goes on, Bjarni went to Norway and became a member of the household of Earl Eirikr, one of the men re-sponsible for the defeat and death of King Olaf Tryggvason at the great naval battle at Svold in that very year. At the court, he told the story of his voyage, and men marvelled that he had not landed. He then presumably re-turned to Greenland, for the saga says that Leifr Eiriksson now went to see him and bought his ship.

SECOND VOYAGE

With thirty-five men, Leifr, after trying in vain to get his father Eric to head the expedition, set out for the lands Bjarni had sighted. They came first to the land Bjarni had seen last, landed, found no vegetation, and saw glaciers on the mountains in the interior. The space between them and the sea appeared as one huge flagstone. They called the land Helluland.

They again set sail and reached a second land, level and wooded, with much white sand on the beaches. This they called Markland.

They left Markland before a northeast wind and after two days sighted a third land, north of which lay an island. They landed on the island where the dew on the grass was sweeter to the taste than anything they had previously encountered. On returning to the ship they entered a sound which separated the island from a ness jutting out from the north of the mainland. It was low tide and the water here was so shallow that their ship ran aground. Impatient to reach land, they left the ship and ran ashore at a spot where a river flowed from a lake. As the tide was now floating their ship, they rowed out to it in one of their boats and took it up the river to the lake, where they anchored it, went ashore, and built booths. The river and lake yielded a plentiful supply of very large salmon, and the men felt sure the livestock could forage for themselves during the winter, as the grass scarcely withered at all in this frost-free land. Day and night, it was noticed, were of more equal length there than in Greenland. So they prepared to winter there and proceeded to build large houses. After these were completed, Leifr divided his force in two – one half to explore the neighbourhood and the other to remain in camp. He himself alternated between the two.

One evening Leifr's foster father, Tyrkir, was missing. When they found him, they learned that he had found grapes. Leifr commanded his men to pick the grapes and hew vines and other trees to take back to Greenland, and in the spring they returned to Greenland with a heavy cargo. On the voyage back Leifr rescued some sailors shipwrecked on a skerry and was henceforth known as Leifr the Lucky. The following winter Eric the Red died.

THIRD VOYAGE

The next year Leifr's brother, Thorvaldr, borrowed his ship and with thirty men sailed for Vinland. They reached Leifr's houses in Vinland without incident, beached the ship, and spent the winter there. In the spring Thorvaldr sent a few men west up the river in the ship's boat to explore the land, which they found to be attractive – wooded almost to the shoreline which was characterized by extensive white sands, off which were many islands and shallows. They encountered no men or animals, but came upon a granary made of wood on a westerly island. In the autumn they returned to the settlement.

The next summer the company took the ship and travelled east along the northern coast. Rounding a ness, they ran into a gale that tore the keel off the ship, forcing them to land in order to repair it. Before they departed Thorvaldr suggested that they erect the keel on the ness and call it Kjalarnes. This they did and then made their way east into a region heavily indented with fjords where they anchored off a wooded headland and put out the gangway. Thorvaldr was entranced with the beauty of the spot and said that he would wish to make his home here. On their way back to the ship they saw three hillocks which on examination proved to be three skin boats with three men under each. They killed eight of these, but one escaped with his boat. At the head of the fjord they thought they discerned a settlement but, overcome with drowsiness, they fell asleep before investigating it. Suddenly they were awakened by an unknown voice warning them to leave. Skin boats were then seen approaching on the fjords, and Thorvaldr ordered his men to prepare to defend themselves behind a *vigfleki* (a defensive wall made of willows and wood and placed at the edge of a ship during battle). The Skraelings, as the saga calls the natives, were repulsed, but Thorvaldr had been fatally wounded by an arrow during the engagement. At his request he was buried there, and on his grave his men erected two crosses and called the headland *Krossanes* (Crossness).[9] They then returned to Leifr's houses, spent the winter there, and loaded the ship with grapes and vines for their return to Greenland in the spring.

FOURTH VOYAGE

The news of Thorvaldr's death prompted his brother Thorsteinn to set out for Krossanes, accompanied by his wife Gudridr and twenty-five men, to bring back his brother's body. The expedition ran into foul weather and was storm-tossed all summer. Finally when winter was setting in they managed to get back to Greenland, landing at Lysufjord in the Western Settlement. Here they spent the winter during which Thorsteinn died. On his deathbed he prophesied that Gudridr would marry an Icelander and from the union would issue a "noble lineage." Gudridr returned to Leifr in the spring and made her home with him at Brattahlid.

FIFTH VOYAGE

That summer there came from Iceland to Brattahlid Thorfinnr Karlsefni Thordarson. By the following winter he was married to Gudridr. One of the favourite subjects of conversation at Brattahlid was Vinland, and Thorfinnr became caught up in the excitement, with the result that an expedition of sixty men and five women was planned for the spring. In their enthusiasm the little group had every intention of settling in Vinland, and they took along a good supply of livestock of all kinds. The voyage was uneventful, and they reached Leifr's houses with little difficulty. A stranded whale supplied them with excellent food on their arrival, and soon they were able to supplement this diet with grapes and game, which they found in abundance. Thorfinnr set the men to felling trees and hewing them into timber, which was placed on a cliff to dry.

During the following summer there appeared out of the woods a large band of Skraelings, come to trade. At first, terrified by the bellowings of Thorfinnr's bull, they ran off with the grey furs, sables, and various peltries they had brought, and later attempted to get into the houses, but were beaten off by Thorfinnr and his men. At length, however, although neither side could understand the language of the other, the Skraelings put down their bundles and trading began. They wanted weapons, but Thorfinnr would not give them any. Instead he had the women bring out milk for which the Skraelings eagerly bartered their furs. After their departure Thorfinnr caused a stockade to be built around the houses, and the little colony settled down. It was at this time that Gudridr gave birth to the first white child to be born in America. They called him Snorri.

Early in the winter the Skraelings appeared again with the same kind of wares, and milk was once more offered in exchange. While the trading was going on, a Skraeling, in the attempt to carry off weapons from the Icelanders, was slain by one of Thorfinnr's housecarles. The entire group of Skraelings then fled. Thorfinnr, however, expected them to return and assigned his men to battle stations. Return they did, with a fine figure of a man as leader, but the Icelanders were ready for them, and they were completely routed.

In the spring the expedition returned to Greenland with a very valuable cargo of vines, grapes, and furs. Thorfinnr stayed that year in Greenland, and next summer sailed for Norway where he spent the winter selling his furs. While there he also sold to a German for a high price his *husasnotra* ("house-neat," a decorative carving used both on the gables of a house and the stems of ships) which was made of the wood *mosurr* (maple) found in Vinland. The following summer he returned to Iceland where he settled in Skagafjord.

SIXTH VOYAGE

Talk continued about the huge profits to be made in Vinland. The same summer as Thorfinnr returned to Greenland, two brothers, Helgi and Finnbogi, arrived in Greenland from Norway. Freydis, the illegitimate daughter of Eric the Red, proposed that they join her in an expedition to Vinland. They agreed, and Leifr allowed them the use of his houses. Each party was to consist of thirty men and some women, but Freydis secretly took with her thirty-five men. The brothers did not discover this secret until the expedition reached Vinland. Dissension arose almost immediately for Freydis would not let the brothers use Leifr's houses, and they had to build their own. During the winter Freydis treacherously encompassed the slaying of Helgi and Finnbogi and all their party, including the women, whom she slew herself when her men proved reluctant to do so. She swore all her party to silence about these evil deeds. In the spring the brothers' ship was loaded with all the products obtainable and the party returned to Greenland. There, eventually, their crimes became known and, although Leifr could not get himself to punish Freydis as she deserved, she and the members of her expedition were shunned by everyone.

Eiriks saga rauda records, however, only three voyages to Vinland: (1) Leifr's accidental discovery of Vinland when he was returning from Norway to Greenland in the year 1000; (2) the abortive attempt of Leifr's brother Thorsteinn to visit Vinland; (3) the expedition of Thorfinnr Karlsefni. In both sagas it is this voyage that commands the greatest attention.

Eiriks saga gives the following account of these three voyages.

FIRST VOYAGE

The account of an accidental discovery by Leifr of what would appear to be Vinland, gives the following information. In the year 1000 Leifr set sail for Greenland from Norway. After a lengthy voyage, in which he must have been blown off course, he came upon a strange land of which he had had no previous knowledge. Self-sown wheatfields were there, and grape vines grew profusely in this smiling land. Forests of maple trees, called *mosurr*, were also found, and plenty of timber from which Leifr constructed his houses. On the voyage back to Greenland he rescued some shipwrecked sailors and brought them back with him, which act, the saga says, showed his magnanimity, and he was thereafter know as Leifr the Lucky.

SECOND VOYAGE

The expedition was storm-tossed for weeks, sighting Iceland and birds from Ireland. At the beginning of winter they managed to return to Greenland. It is uncertain whether Eric the Red took part in this voyage. In any case it was a complete failure.

THIRD VOYAGE

Thorfinnr's expedition consisted of three ships which carried 160 men and women, as well as livestock. They set out from the Eastern Settlement, sailing north to the Western, and thence farther north to Disko Island. Here they altered course and sailed southwest for two days until they came to a land characterized by huge flat stones and a great number of Arctic foxes. They named it Helluland. Leaving it, they again sailed for two days before a north wind until they came upon a heavily wooded land whereon were many animals. This they called Markland. An island lay off to the southeast. Here they killed a bear and called the island Bjarney (Bear Island). They then continued south until they came to a ness lying on their starboard. To it they gave the name Kjalarnes (Keelness) because they found the keel of a ship on it. The long coast with its white sand, along which they had been sailing, they called Furdustrandir (Wonder Strands).

The land now became indented with bays. Sailing into one of these they put ashore a couple of Scots, Haki and his wife Hekja, with instructions to run inland, for they were fleet of foot, and to explore the land. When the two returned, one carried a bunch of grapes and the other an ear of self-sown wheat.

The next stop was a bay which had an island at its entrance. It was covered with the eggs of innumerable eider ducks. They named the island Straumey (Current Island) and the bay, Straumfjord. In this beautiful mountainous country they disembarked with the livestock and spent a severe winter, during which food ran short.

It was at Straumfjord that Thorhallr, a trusted though rough retainer of Eric the Red, ran off. He was a great hunter, well acquainted with the "wastes" of Greenland and adjoining lands, and may have accompanied the expedition as a guide, at least for the early stages of the course to Vinland. Three days later he was found lying on his back, muttering incantations and invoking Thor, who sent a whale to the famished people. All those who ate of its flesh became ill, and an appeal was made to God, whereupon both the hunting and weather improved.

In the spring disagreement arose between Thorfinnr and Thorhallr as to whither to sail in search of Vinland. The latter wished to go north of Furdustrandir and the former south. The upshot was that Thorhallr, with eight men, left the expedition. Before he departed he composed two stanzas, one deploring the lack of wine and the other taunting those who remained for eating whalemeat while they praised the unpraiseworthy Furdustrandir. Thorhallr never reached Greenland.

Thorfinnr and his companions then sailed south for a long time, until they reached a spot on the coast where a river flowed from a lake to the sea, accessible only at high tide because of sand banks. They called this place Hop (landlocked bay), and found there grapes and self-sown wheat, fish in every stream, and many kinds of wild animals in the woods. They also encountered the aborigines one morning, coming towards them from the sea in skin boats propelled by some kind of stick. They were swarthy, evil-visaged men, with coarse hair, large eyes, and broad cheeks. After staring at the Icelanders for some time from the boats, they departed. Thorfinnr spent a pleasant winter there, for there was no snow and they had good grazing for the cattle.

The aborigines returned in the spring in their skin boats, and this time barter took place. The Icelanders gave them red cloth in return for skins and furs, but refused them weapons. At the height of this trading, a bull owned by Thorfinnr charged from the woods and so terrified the natives that they fled to their boats and departed southward. Some time later they returned, this time in a bellicose mood and carrying weapons in the form of slings with some kind of "bomb" which may have been launched from them. In the ensuing battle the Icelanders were almost routed, but Freydis, the daughter of Eric the Red, rushed out to the battlefield, exhorted the men in the best tradition of Germanic women, and when the natives approached

her, slapped her naked breasts with a sword. The tide turned and the Skraelings, as the Icelanders termed the natives, fled.

This encounter seems to have unnerved the Icelanders. They abandoned
their "paradise" and sailed north again. During the voyage, they killed
five Skraelings, whom they found sleeping in skin doublets, and discovered
an island covered with animal dung. At length they reached Straumfjord,
where there was no lack of all necessities.

Having rested there, Thorfinnr and a number of his men began a search
for Thorhallr the Hunter. Their course took them north of Kjalarnes and
then west. They sailed far with land to port, past a wilderness with few
open spaces, until they reached the mouth of a river which flowed from east
to west. Here they made camp on its south bank. One morning Thorvaldr,
the son of Eric the Red, was shot by a uniped, or one-legged man, who stole
out of the woods and caught him unaware, and who escaped under chase.
Not wishing to take further risks, they left shortly thereafter and in the
course of their voyage back to Straumfjord, thought they caught sight of
the Land of the Unipeds. It also seemed to them that the mountain range,
at the spot where Thorvaldr was slain, was a part of that at Hop and that
Straumfjord lay halfway between these two places.

During the third winter, which was spent at Straumfjord, dissension
arose over women, and in the spring the expedition set out for Greenland[10]
before a south wind. On the way they stopped at Markland, where they
encountered five Skraelings – a bearded man, two women, and two boys.
The man and the women escaped, disappearing, it is said, into the ground.
The two boys were captured and taken to Greenland, where they were baptized and taught Icelandic. From them the Icelanders learned the names of
the boys' parents – Vethildi and Ovaegi – and those of two kings who
ruled the Skraelings – Avaldamon and Avaldidida. The boys also told of a
land opposite their own, whose inhabitants wore white clothes, carried
standards, and yelled loudly. The author of the saga says that this was
believed to be White Men's Land or Ireland the Great.

The above is a brief summary of what our two chief sources tell us of
Vinland and the course thither from Greenland. They leave many questions
unanswered, but they do furnish irrefutable evidence that the Icelanders
visited the eastern waters and shores of America and even attempted
settlement there. If we go beyond this, and try to pinpoint the places
mentioned, we tread on treacherous ground, as will appear from the discussion in the next chapter. The sagas are, however, not the only sources.
In addition, reference is made elsewhere to the parts of America known
to the Icelanders, and some of these are older than the two chief sagas.

The earliest mention of Vinland is probably that on a rune stone found at Honen in Ringerike, Norway, about 1817. It has since disappeared but an unsatisfactory copy of the inscription exists. A rough translation of the runes reads: "They came out and over wide expanses, and needing cloth to dry themselves on and food, away towards Wineland, up into the ice in the uninhabited country. Evil can take away luck, so that one dies early."[11] The inscription is believed to be an epitaph on a young man. All it tells us is that Vinland seems to have been well known in Norway about 1050, the date assigned to the inscription.[12]

The next mention of Vinland is to be found in the works of Adam of Bremen. He writes (ca. 1075):

> He [the king of the Danes, i.e., Sveinn Ulfsson] spoke also of yet another island of the many found in that ocean [i.e., the one in which Greenland lies]. It is called Vinland because vines producing excellent wine grow wild there. That unsown crops also abound on that island we have ascertained not from fabulous reports but from the trustworthy relation of the Danes. Beyond that island, he said, no habitable land is found in that ocean, but every place beyond it is full of impenetrable ice and intense darkness.[13]

Adam's authority here would seem to be of the best[14] although his accounts of distant lands are often out of touch with reality.

In the *Islendingabok* (*The Book of the Icelanders*), written by Ari Thorgilsson about 1122 or 1123, Vinland is mentioned incidentally in connection with the establishment of the Icelandic colony in Greenland:

> Both east and west in the country they found human habitations, fragments of skin boats and stone implements from which it was evident that the same kind of people had been there as inhabited Wineland and whom the Greenlanders called Skrellings.[15]

This is the earliest mention of Vinland in Icelandic literature.

Landnamabok,[16] *Kristni saga*,[17] and other thirteenth-century sagas in Iceland mention Vinland, but only incidentally and in a manner which tells us nothing except that its existence was known. More interesting is a notice in various Icelandic annals – a historical genre which the Icelanders began to cultivate late in the thirteenth century. *Sub anno* 1121, it is noticed that Bishop Eirikr *upsi* (Pollack) Gnupsson of Greenland went in search of Vinland.[18]

Geographical treatises which probably date from the fourteenth century mention lands in America. An interpolation in the *Leidarvisir* (*Itinerary*) of Abbot Nikulas Bergsson of Munkathvera[19] reads as follows:

> From Bjarmaland [Russia] uninhabited lands stretch north until Greenland is reached. South of Greenland is Helluland. Then Markland from which it is not far to Vinland the Good which some men think is a projection of

Africa. It is said that Thorfidr [sic] Karlsefni made a *husasnotratre* and then went in search of Vinland the Good and came to where they thought that land to be but could not explore it nor avail themselves of its products. Leifr the Lucky was the first to discover Vinland, and at that time he found merchants in distress on the sea and gave them life by the mercy of God; and he introduced Christianity in Greenland where it grew so that a bishopric was established at the place called Gardar.[20]

Similar geographical descriptions of the lands west of the Atlantic are to be found in other Icelandic sources from the thirteenth and fourteenth centuries. They do not necessarily indicate that contact with Vinland had been maintained from the time of its discovery or that it was maintained in the fourteenth century. They are, however, an indication that the discovery of Vinland was still remembered, and possibly the attempts of the Icelanders to settle there were still fresh in the minds of Icelanders in the centuries subsequent to the so-called Vinland voyages. More than this we cannot say.

CHAPTER 4

The Location of Vinland

Where were these lands that were discovered in America by the Icelanders? We have established the location of Helluland and Markland, as Baffin Island and some part of the coast of Labrador, possibly the regions north and south of Hamilton Inlet. Both these lands were to be visited by the Greenlanders for centuries and eventually settled after a fashion by them and by the Eskimos.

Of the location of Vinland there is no such sure ground. All that is certain is that this land lay south of Markland and was even considered an extension of Africa. Here one must bear in mind the geographical concepts of both mediæval man and the Icelanders.[1] For them, the world was divided into three great land masses: Europe, Asia, and Africa. All lands must belong to one of these three continents. Vinland could, of course, be considered an island, as Adam of Bremen considers it, but if it were part of a continental land mass, then it must be part of Africa, which would make of the Atlantic an inland sea. In the same way Greenland was thought to be an extension of Asia, joined to the continent by a land-bridge extended north of Iceland, east to Asian Russia. Greenland was never considered an island by the Icelanders.

The *Graenlendinga saga* and *Eiriks saga rauda* are, as the summary of their contents shows, impossible to reconcile. Both contain a good deal of information concerning the region known as Vinland but in a form which baffles any attempt to locate the exact region of the American coast on which it lay. At the same time, the information supplied by these two sources is not sufficient to establish the chronology of the voyages made from Greenland to America in the eleventh century. In fact, the sagas record only a few of the voyages that must have been undertaken from Greenland, as soon as the Icelanders established themselves there, to Baffin Island, Labrador, and the region known as Vinland. It is impossible to understand

31

the role assigned to Thorhallr the Hunter in *Eiriks saga* except on the presumption that he had already journeyed at least to the north part of the west coast of Greenland, to Baffin Island, and very probably to parts of Labrador. This is patent in the statement: "He had a wide acquaintance with uninhabited regions."[2] Again, the granary found by Thorvaldr points to a visit or visits by an unknown expedition.[3] But these earlier or possibly contemporary voyages have not been recorded, or the record has perished. Family pride is responsible for the preservation of the accounts we possess of the Vinland voyages, which were all carried out by the family of Eric the Red or those connected with it. Let us examine the account in *Eiriks saga* of Leifr's accidental discovery.

According to the saga, Eric the Red colonized Greenland in 986, but it was not until fourteen years later that his son, Leifr, went to Norway. On his way thither there occurred a romantic episode in the Hebrides. Leifr fell in love with a highborn maiden and by her fathered a son, of whom the author can tell us little, except that his name was Thorgils, that he came to Greenland, and was accepted by Leifr as his son. Some say that the boy came to Iceland in the summer of the year in which the marvels occurred at Froda,[4] and that strange things happened to him later in life. Clearly the author knew nothing factual about Thorgils, and the whole episode is probably apocryphal.

From the Hebrides Leifr sailed to Norway in the autumn of 999 and spent the winter at the court of King Olaf Tryggvason. He was baptized and undertook, at the urging of the king, the Christianization of Greenland. Here again the saga would seem to depart from the truth. There is no evidence that King Olaf played any part in the introduction of Christianity to Greenland. Dr Jon Johannesson has shown[5] that all the oldest and most trustworthy authorities state that King Olaf Christianized five lands: Norway, Iceland, and the Shetland, Orkney, and Faroe Islands. Greenland is not mentioned. Nor would one expect it to be. As a colony of Iceland it would *ipso facto* become Christian when the Icelandic Althing adopted Christianity. Indeed, the *Historia Norwegiae*, written about 1200, says that the Icelanders found and settled Greenland, and buttressed it with the Catholic faith.[6]

The whole tale of Leifr's voyage from Norway to Greenland in the year 1000 then becomes suspect. Indeed, the account in the saga is so short and terse that one can hardly avoid the conviction that the author knew little or nothing of an accidental discovery of lands west of the Atlantic by Leifr at this time:

> Leifr put to sea and had a lengthy voyage and met with lands of which he had previously no knowledge. Self-sown wheatfields were there and grown vines. There were also trees, called mosurr. They took samples of all this

and some timbers so large that they were used in the construction of houses. Leifr found men on a wreck and brought them home with him. In this he demonstrated his magnanimity and nobility of mind on this as on many other occasions for he introduced Christianity into the country and was ever thereafter known as Leifr the Lucky.[7]

The saga then goes on to record that Leifr introduced Christianity into all parts of the country and told the people of King Olaf's wishes in this matter and of the benefits and glory that would accrue from the acceptance of the true faith. Eirikr is said to have been very reluctant to change his faith, but his wife Thjodhildr did so immediately and had a church built at some distance from the farm buildings.[8] From then on she refused to live in the marriage bond with Eirikr and this displeased him greatly.

If we accept the fact that the story of the Christianization of Greenland at the instigation of King Olaf is groundless and that the author of the *Graenlendinga saga* had no knowledge of such a missionary venture, it follows that the author of the *Eiriks saga* must have taken this from the saga of King Olaf Tryggvason which Gunnlaugr Leifsson (ob. 1219), a monk at the monastery at Thingeyrar, wrote in Latin. If one grants also that the *Graenlendinga saga* is older than the *Eiriks saga*, then there is a strong indication that the whole account of Leifr's accidental discovery of Vinland is based on Bjarni Herjulfsson's accidental discovery of America. It would also follow that the description of the three lands visited by Thorfinnr Karlsefni as related in the *Eiriks saga* is a transference from the *Graenlendinga saga* of the voyage to America by Leifr as related therein. When one also considers that the *Eiriks saga* includes in Thorfinnr's voyage almost all the personnel who took part in the first five distinct voyages recounted in *Graenlendinga saga*, it becomes difficult to avoid the conclusion that the *Eiriks saga* is a very untrustworthy document. Furthermore, one can hardly avoid believing that the author of the *Eiriks saga*, because of insufficient information or because of a desire to glorify Thorfinnr Karlsefni, has taken four or five voyages and lumped them into one. He has also through ignorance or deliberation omitted any reference to Bjarni Herjulfsson. The *Eiriks saga* is therefore not to be relied on when it conflicts with the older *Graenlendinga saga*.

It must, of course, be admitted that all these matters are to some extent conjectural and that both sagas contain accounts that are so confused and often so vague that definite conclusions cannot be drawn. Nevertheless, one can hardly escape accepting the *Graenlendinga saga* as the source which comes nearer the truth in the matter of the voyages undertaken by the family of Eric the Red and those most closely connected with it. Again, one should emphasize that both sagas are family sagas and no doubt on that account omit mention of many voyages made to Vinland by others. They are like mediæval law codes which record only a small percentage of the bulk of the law of the community.

In holding these views on the *Eiriks saga*, it would be pointless to try to trace the location of the various places mentioned in the account of Thorfinnr's voyage to and sojourn in Vinland, nor is the account in the *Graenlendinga saga* of the course followed by the various expeditions to Vinland such as to enable one to identify with any certainty the localities mentioned. This, of course, has been abundantly demonstrated by the great discrepancy shown in previous attempts to locate Bjarney (Bear Island) off Markland, Furdustrandir, Kjalarnes, Straumfjord, Straumey, the Land of the Unipeds, and Vinland itself. Even the passage about the length of day in Vinland:

> Day and night were more equal there than in Greenland and Iceland; during the skammdegi [i.e., the period *circa* November 20 to January 20] the sun was in *eyktarstadr* [i.e., the place on the horizon over which the sun is at 3 : 00 or 3 : 30 p.m.] and in *dagmalastadr* [i.e., the place over which the sun is at about 9 : 00 a.m.]

has proved a broken reed for there is no agreement as to what *eyktarstadr* and *dagmalastadr* mean.

Picking and choosing from the numerous conjectures that have been made as to the location of the above-mentioned places, one may give, for what it is worth, an opinion as to where they were located.

> Bjarney – Newfoundland
> Furdustrandir – the south coast of Labrador
> Kjalarnes – some southerly point on the east coast of Labrador
> Straumfjord – Seven Isle Bay
> Straumey – one of the islands at Seven Isle Bay
> Vinland – the region of Cape Cod
> Einfaetingaland – up the St Lawrence River (if not wholly legendary)

It must be realized, however, that nothing but archæological discoveries will ever enable us to locate these places with any certainty.

To sum up, we may say that our two sagas enable us to conclude only that the voyages described therein were made from Greenland to Baffin Island (Helluland), Labrador (Markland), and some point on the east coast of the United States in the vicinity of New England or farther south (Vinland). It cannot even be asserted that the Icelanders sailed far up the St Lawrence, for surely such a mighty river would have made an impression whose traces would be found in the literary sources.

Vinland failed to attract the Icelanders after the abortive attempt of Thorfinnr Karlsefni to colonize it. It is true that Freydis made a voyage thither, and no doubt there were a few others who made their way to it but they cannot have been many. That an Icelandic colony flourished there for a score of years or even centuries is one of the many myths of pre-Columbian history. Even the location of Vinland seems to have been forgotten early for, as has been mentioned, in 1121 Bishop Eirikr Gnupsson had to search for it as a lost country.

It is often asked why the Icelanders, having found such a paradise, should then have failed to settle there. Why did they not leave the ice-covered mass of Greenland? One reason is that Greenland was not as inhospitable as it has often been painted. Its ice-free coastal lands and valleys provided lush vegetation and fodder for the husbandry of the Icelanders for at least the first two or three centuries. As we have seen, the sea teemed with marine life and the regions adjacent to the farming settlements were even richer than the settlements in the products which commanded profitable prices in the markets of mediæval Europe. These areas acted as a magnet, as we shall see, to draw any surplus or indigent population away from the settlements and, of course, overpopulation never became a problem. Again, Vinland with all its fabled wealth would seem to have had a native population more hostile than that of the northern regions.

The Vinland voyages, although they have been so dramatically depicted in the sagas, were never more than a brief and accidental episode in the life of a people who were more than content to carry on their wonted way of life in the countries they had settled, as long as this could be done without undue hardship. The energies of the Icelanders in Greenland found ample outlet in the exploitation of the riches which were so easily to be acquired in the peaceful lands which we know today as Ellesmere[9] and Baffin Islands, Labrador, and the regions washed by Hudson Bay. To this task the Icelanders increasingly turned their attention in the centuries following the founding of the colonies in Greenland. In the course of this, their paths crossed with an aboriginal people with whom it was their destiny to become intermixed and subsequently bear a new culture beyond even the uttermost bounds of the Canadian Arctic.

CHAPTER 5

The Expansion of Greenland

As soon as the Icelanders settled in Greenland they began to make voyages and settlements outside of the farming districts. They made their way to the east coast of Greenland, especially to the Angmagssalik region where Krosseyjar were located and polar bears were numerous, and also to Finnsbudir, farther south. The most favoured regions were the southerly ones: Greipar, that is, the fjords in the Holsteinsborg-Sukkertoppen region; Karlbudir, that is, the south part of Disko Bay; and Kroksfjardarheidi, that is, the district which begins at Umanak Bay and runs possibly as far north as Melville Bay. Frequent voyages were also made to the north, as far as Smith Sound and possibly Kennedy Channel. Just south of Umanak at Nugssua Peninsula lay Eisunes, which draws its name from the coal deposits found there, and farther north Aedanes, named for the eider duck.[1] That they explored the region between Melville Bay and Inglefield Land is evident, as they called it Skaginn or the Peninsula, and regarded it as the western extremity of the land-bridge that joined Greenland to Russia. Again, Landsendi *hinn nyrdri* is probably the peninsula at Etah.

To the west, expeditions were made to Ellesmere, Devon, and Baffin Islands, through Hudson Strait to the region around the Melville Peninsula and Southampton Island, and possibly farther into Hudson Bay. All these regions, although more particularly north Greenland, were known as Nordrseta. Labrador may have been included as voyages were frequently made there for timber.

The *locus classicus* on voyages to Nordrseta is an entry in the *Graenlandsannall* of Bjorn Jonsson which reads as follows:

> All the great farmers in Greenland possessed large ships and small craft, built to make voyages to Nordrseta to procure all kinds of game and trimmed timbers; sometimes they themselves went along as is often mentioned in accounts both in the saga of Skald-Helgi and also in this tale of Thordis. There . . . seal hunting was much greater than at home in the settlements

. . . . Driftwood is there but no trees growing; this northern peninsula of Greenland especially receives the wood and jetsam from the bays of Markland.

Furthermore, it is said:

The Greenlanders must constantly sail north to the wastes on the northern land's end or peninsula, both for wood and the procurement of game. The regions there are called Greipar and Kroksjardarheidi. It is a long and arduous course, as the saga of Skald-Helgi distinctly attests. The following lines were composed about these voyages: "Heroes went north to Greipar which is the end of the settlement of Greenland."[2]

It was, of course, the wealth of these regions that prompted voyages to and settlement in all the lands of Nordrseta. They were far richer in all kinds of marine and land animals than were the farming settlements. Here whales sported and walrus abounded. Seals, which were a staple of the diet, were found in inexhaustible quantities. Polar bears were plentiful and were taken both alive and dead. White falcons, the most prized bird of the hunting circles of the Middle Ages, were plentiful on Baffin Island. There was no dearth of narwhal or eider ducks. Driftwood from the great rivers of Siberia was to be found in abundance. All this explains not only the annual voyages to these regions but also the rise of more or less permanent settlements in the whole of Nordrseta.

This exodus from the farming districts is to be explained in several ways. The lands north and west of the settlements were rich in game and attracted many people who either found husbandry irksome or had arrived too late to secure good farms. Those who had been convicted of breaking the law, through desire or necessity frequently had to leave the area either for a term of years or permanently. Another factor may also have been the increasing acquisition by the Church of the farms in both the Eastern and Western Settlements. As is well known, by the fourteenth century the Church owned all the land in both these regions. In the earliest years, too, attachment to paganism may have prompted some to leave when Christianity became the only accepted religion in the older settlements.

As has been mentioned, voyages were made to the east coast of Greenland in spite of the difficulties posed by the almost permanent ice barrier off this coast. Navigation, however, is possible between the coast and the inner edge of the ice pack, and there are numerous references in the sagas and other writings to men who visited these regions and even spent some years there.[3] Ivar Bardarson mentions four places where hunting was carried on. In addition to Finnsbudir and Krosseyar, which have already been mentioned, he notes the fjord called Ollumlengri (the longest of all) which is to be identified with Scoresby Sound and Berufjord, likely Lindenows Fjord. This

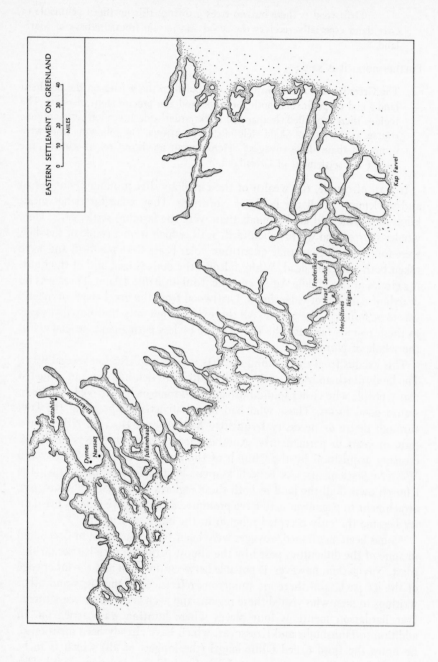

EASTERN SETTLEMENT ON GREENLAND

MILES
0   10   20   30   40

Kap Farvel

Frederiksdal
Hvat Sandur
Herjolfsnes
Ikigait

Einliksfjordur
Brattahlid
Dymes
Narssaq
Julianehaab

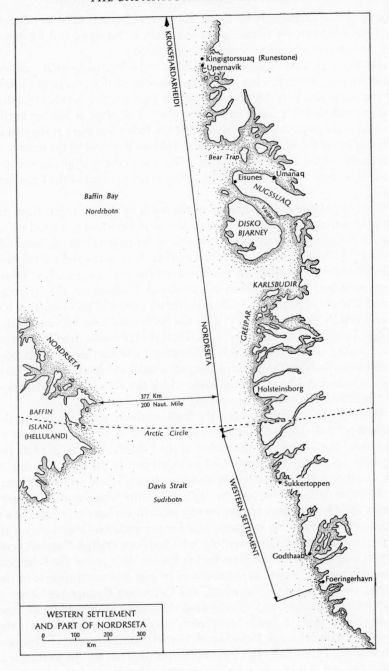

KROKSFJARDARHEIDI

• Kingigtorssuaq (Runestone)
• Upernavik

Bear Trap

Eisunes • • Umanaq
NUGSSUAQ

Baffin Bay

Nordrbotn

DISKO
BJARNEY

Vaigat

KARLSBUDIR

NORDRSETA

NORDRSETA

GREIPAR

• Holsteinsborg

377 Km
200 Naut. Mile

BAFFIN
ISLAND
(HELLULAND)   Arctic Circle

Davis Strait

Sudrbotn

WESTERN SETTLEMENT

• Sukkertoppen

Godthaab •

• Foeringerhavn

WESTERN SETTLEMENT
AND PART OF NORDRSETA
0   100   200   300
Km

last he praises exceedingly for the great number of whales to be found there and the inexhaustible abundance of fish. Both in Berufjord and Krosseyar the bishop had a monopoly on hunting rights.[4]

On the west coast of Greenland, Greipar and Kroksfjardarheidi were the chief hunting districts. Here permanent hunting settlements seem to have arisen early and here possibly the earliest intermixture between the Icelanders and Skraelings may have taken place. Bear traps at Eisunes testify to temporary or permanent settlement of the Icelanders there as they do in Krosseyar, on the Melville Peninsula in Hudson Bay, and in the regions of Lancaster, Jones, and Smith Sounds.[5] The ruins of the ship shelters and various relics in all these regions also testify to the presence of the Icelanders here.[6]

Further proof of the penetration of the north by the Icelanders from the farming settlements is offered by rune stones and cairns. On a small island named Kingiktorsuak, north of Upernivik in latitude 72° 58' N, longitude 56° 14' W, the Eskimo Pelimut found in 1824 three cairns and a small rune stone. Roughly translated, the inscription on the rune stone reads: "Erling Sigvatsson and Bjarne Thordsson and Enridi Oddsson on the Saturday before Gangdag [April 24][7] made this [these] cairns." This inscription has been dated by runologists as 1333. Its inscribers must have wintered in this region, judging by the date, April 24. Therkel Mathiassen, who has carried out so much archæological work in Greenland and northern Canada, also found hereabouts on the island of Inugsuk a small wooden doll with a long, narrow robe and a hood over the head, which can only be a representation of a mediæval Icelander in Greenland.[8]

This is by no means, however, the most northerly point reached by the Icelanders, and their penetration was not confined to the west coast of Greenland but extended to the islands of the Canadian Arctic. In 1876, the explorer, Sir George Nares, who led an expedition to the Polar Sea, found, on a small but high islet called Washington Irving Island on the east coast of Ellesmere Island in latitude 79° 35', two cairns whose evident age precludes their having been erected by any modern explorer or whaler.[9] Two other cairns were found by the second *Fram* expedition (1898-1902). This expedition was led by Otto Sverdrup, who had been Fridtjof Nansen's companion and Captain of the *Fram* on her famous drift across the Polar Sea. The object of the second expedition was to map unknown regions of the Arctic, west of northern Greenland, and Lieutenant Gunnar Isachsen was the cartographer. Both in 1898 and 1899 the *Fram* was stopped by ice from sailing north through Smith Sound and, therefore, in the second year the expedition sailed through Jones Sound. Here the southern coast of Ellesmere Island showed luxuriant vegetation and plentiful game, but the weather was inclement and it was only with the greatest difficulty that the expedition made its way to Hell Gate. It was on this voyage that the two cairns were discovered on the south shore of Ellesmere Island in longitude 88° or 89°, showing that the mediæval Icelanders had penetrated that far westward, for their construction was obviously not Eskimo and their age again unquestionably mediæval.[10]

There is other evidence, too, for the presence of Icelanders in these regions. Dr Edward L. Moss, the physician of the Nares expedition, found on Norman Lockyer Island (*circa* latitude 79° 28′ N and longitude 74° 50′ W) a bird shelter which he describes as follows: "It consisted of four stones piled together like a miniature 'Druid altar', so as to form a chamber large enough to shelter a nest. Generations of eider duck had been hatched in it in security since the last wild hunter left the shore."[11] Then, about 1900, Sverdrup and Isachsen found, far west on Jones Sound, on St Helena (89° 20′ W, 76° 29′ N) and Devil Islands (90° 45′ W, 76° 29′ N), numerous bird shelters of the same kind. If these are indeed eider-duck shelters, and there seems to be almost unanimous agreement that this is so, they could only have been erected by the mediæval Icelanders in Greenland.

It has often been pointed out, but never more cogently than by Vilhjalmur Stefansson, that there is a vast difference in the Nordic and Eskimo ideas on the present and the future. In discussing Sverdrup's finding of the artificial eider duck shelters, he writes:

> The Norse are husbandmen, only secondarily hunters; the Eskimos (with the sole exception of their relation to the dog) are hunters only. The Eskimos own no birds and protect none; the Norse own barnyard fowl and protect the eider duck. The Eskimos use the skins of dead birds for clothes; the Norse use the down of live birds for quilts, and in other ways. Eskimos kill eider ducks if they can; they may or may not eat their eggs. The Norse sometimes kill eiders when they are on a journey; but when they live in eider districts they kill no birds and gather no eggs, for to them the down of present and prospective birds is of more value than the meat and eggs would be as food. In Norse communities it is anti-social, if not a crime, to kill eiders or destroy their eggs.
>
> But in order that you may gather down successfully you must make your locality attractive to the ducks and you must protect the down from being carried away by the wind. Therefore you build shelters for the nests. These, called "houses," have been consistent in form, though of more than one type, in Scandinavian lands for a thousand years, perhaps much longer.

Although Sverdrup was skeptical of the Norse origin of these nests, Isachsen came to share Stefansson's views and Duason has advanced much the same arguments, with some new material on the method of laying out nesting-grounds and types of nests.[12]

As has been mentioned, the white falcon was the most prized hunting-bird of the Middle Ages in that most popular of all sports, falconry. Its habitat is predominantly Baffin Island although it is occasionally found as a bird of passage in Greenland and Iceland. It is, therefore, reasonable to assume that most of the white falcons of the Middle Ages must have been taken on Baffin Island. As will be seen, later ruins also attest to the visits and settlements of the Icelanders there.

Prized as the falcon was, its lustre was overshadowed by that of the polar bear. European monarchs seemed to have regarded these animals almost as status symbols, and anyone who could present a king with a live polar bear could retire on the gifts which the grateful monarch showered on the donor. When the Icelander, Audunn, gave a polar bear to King Sveinn Ulfsson of Denmark (*circa* 1060), he was rewarded with the money for a pilgrimage to Rome, an ocean-going vessel loaded with fine cargo, rings and silver. The kings of Norway presented other rulers with live polar bears in order to gain their favour or support. In the thirteenth century King Hakon Hakonarson presented Henry III of England with a polar bear which was treated royally and allowed to fish in the Thames daily. Hakon also gave a polar bear to Emperor Frederick II, who in turn seems to have given this or another bear to the Egyptian Sultan, El Kamil.

The only regions in which polar bears could be taken are Greenland and the Arctic regions of Canada. There the Icelanders erected bear traps far and wide. Although traps for adult bears could not be utilized in the farming settlements as it would have been too dangerous to allow the bears to wander about in the hope that they might enter the trap, traps for bear cubs have been found at the settlements. The ruins of a standard-type adult bear trap are to be found on the Nugssuaq. It is built of huge and carefully chosen stones, is rectangular, 1.15 × 2.28 metres. There is an entrance passage 1.5 metres long and 0.55 metres wide at the entrance and narrowing to 0.47 metres at the point where it enters the trap itself. It seems to have been six or seven feet in height. The trap was roofed with either flagstones or wood beams covered with turf and stones.[13]

These bear traps have been found at Angmagsalik (Krosseyar) in the regions of Jones, Lancaster, and Smith Sounds and as far west as the Melville Peninsula. They attest to the presence of the Icelanders in all these regions, not just temporarily but over a prolonged period of time. The Eskimos assert that not they but the Tunnit built these traps, and indeed it is certain that the Eskimos have never taken polar bears alive.

One must not forget also, when discussing the emigration of the Icelanders from the farming settlements, the evidence offered by various Icelandic artifacts found in different parts of Greenland and the Canadian Arctic. In the course of his investigations into the regions penetrated by the Icelandic farmers of Greenland in search of permanent or quasi-permanent hunting settlements, Dr Jon Duason, who has devoted his whole life to a study of

Icelandic contacts with Greenland and America in the Middle Ages and early modern period, lists a number of these relics, found before 1940 in various parts of the Arctic. It would be tedious to list here all the articles found but it may be mentioned that among them are fragments of a bronze kettle found in the Julianehaab district, a brass horse used as a weight on silver scales near Sukkertoppen, elaborate styles and another bronze kettle in the vicinity of Disko Island, a cask made of staves at Inugsuk, along with iron articles and dolls which clearly depict Europeans. As far north as the Thule region, numerous articles of Norse origin have been excavated. In eastern Greenland, Norse relics have also been found.[14] All these articles stem from purely Nordic and not Eskimoized culture and are far too numerous and widely scattered to allow one to entertain the idea that they were obtained in trade by the Eskimos or carried off by them on visits to the Icelandic farming settlements.

It may, in fact, be stated definitely that the Icelanders roamed throughout the whole of Greenland and the eastern Canadian Arctic. On these travels they certainly met the aborigines to be found in these regions, to whom they gave the name of Skraelings. What manner of men were these natives? What information do we possess about these people at the time the Icelanders met them?

CHAPTER 6

The Folk Known as the Skraelings

The *Islendingabok* tells us that when Eric the Red and the other colonists explored Greenland, "Both east and west in the country they found human habitations, fragments of skin boats and stone implements from which it was evident that the same kind of people had been there as inhabited Wineland and whom the Greenlanders called Skrellings."[1]

The word Skraeling has as its root *skral*, which means small, wizened, or shrivelled. The Skraelings whom the Icelanders met in America are described in both the *Eiriks saga* and the *Graenlendinga saga*. In the former, the encounter is described as follows:

> Then one morning early, when they looked about them, they saw a multitude of skin-canoes, on which poles were being waved which sounded just like flails – and waved sunwise.
>
> "What can this mean?" asked Karlsefni.
>
> "Maybe it is a token of peace," Snorri Thorbrandsson told him, "so let us take a white shield and put it out towards them."
>
> They did this, and their visitors rowed towards them, and were astonished at what they found, then came ashore. They were dark, ugly men who wore their hair in an unpleasant fashion. They had big eyes and were broad in the cheeks. They stayed there for a while, astonished at what they found, and afterwards rowed off south past the headland.
>
> Karlsefni and his men had built themselves booths up above the lake; some of their houses were near the waterside, and some farther away. They now spent the winter there. No snow fell, and the whole of their stock found its own food by grazing. But when spring came in they saw early one morning how a multitude of canoes came rowing from the south round the headland, so many that the bay looked as though sown with charcoal, and this time too poles were being waved from every boat. Karlsefni and his men raised their shields, and as soon as they met they began trading together. Most of all these people wanted to buy red cloth, in return for which they had furs to offer and grey skins. They also wanted to buy swords and spears,

but this Karlsefni and Snorri would not allow. The Skraelings were taking a span's length of red cloth in exchange for an unblemished dark skin, and this they tied round their heads. Their trading continued thus for a while, when the cloth began to run short for Karlsefni and his men; they then cut it up into such small pieces that they were no wider than a finger-breadth, but the Skraelings even so gave just as much for it as before, or indeed more.

The next thing was that the bull belonging to Karlsefni and his mates ran out of the forest bellowing loudly. The Skraelings were terrified by this, raced out to their canoes, and then rowed south past the headland, and for three weeks running there was neither sight nor sound of them. But at the end of that period they saw a great multitude of Skraeling boats coming up like a stream from the south. This time all the poles were being waved anti-sunwise, and the Skraelings were all yelling aloud, so Karlsefni and his men took a red shield and put it out against them. The Skraelings ran from their boats and then they clashed together and fought. There was a heavy shower of missiles, for the Skraelings had warslings. Karlsefni and his men could see the Skraelings hoisting up on to a pole a very large ball, closely comparable to a sheep's paunch, and a deep blue-black in colour, which they let fly from the pole inland over Karlsefni's troop, and it made a hideous noise where it came down. A great fear now struck into Karlsefni and all his following, so that they had no other thought in their heads than to run away and make their escape up along the river, for they had the impression that the Skraeling host was pouring in upon them from all sides. They made no stop till they reached some rocks, but there made a brave defence.

Freydis came out of doors and saw how they had run off. "Why are you running from wretches like these?" she cried. "Such gallant lads as you, I thought you would have knocked them on the head like cattle. Why, if I had a weapon, I think I could put up a better fight than any of you!"

They might as well not have heard her. Freydis was anxious to keep up with them, but was slow on her feet because of her pregnancy. Yet she kept moving after them to the forest, but the Skraelings now attacked her. She found a dead man in her path, Thorbrand Snorrason – he had a flat stone sticking out of his head. His naked sword lay beside him; she picked it up and prepared to defend herself. The Skraelings were making for her. She pulled out her breasts from under her clothes and slapped the naked sword on them, at which the Skraelings took fright, and ran off to their boats and rowed away. Karlsefni's men came up to her, praising her courage. Two of Karlsefni's men had fallen, and a multitude of Skraelings. Karlsefni's men had been overrun by sheer numbers. Now, after this, they returned to their booths and bandaged their wounds, and puzzled over what force that could have been which attacked them from inland. It looked to them now as though there had been only one host, which came from the boats, and that the other army must have been a delusion.

Further, the Skraelings had found a dead man whose axe lay beside him. One of them picked up the axe and cut at a tree with it, and so they did one after the other, and thought it a treasure, and one which cut well. After-wards one of them set to and cut at a stone, so that the axe broke, and then they thought it useless because it could not stand up to the stone, so threw it down.

It now seemed plain to Karlsefni and his men that though the quality of the land was admirable, there would always be fear and strife dogging them there on account of those who already inhabited it. So they made ready to leave, setting their hearts on their own country, and sailed north along the land and found five Skraelings in fur doublets asleep near the sea, who had with them wooden containers in which was beast's marrow mixed with blood . . . they killed them.[2]

It is impossible from this description to determine whether the aborigines encountered here were Indians or "Eskimos." The employment of skin canoes and the method of propelling them suggests kayaks. The physical description, however, could fit either Indians or "Eskimos" – although the failure to make any comment on a dwarfish stature of the natives might be held to rule out the possibility that they were "Eskimos," or Skraelings. The use of the catapulted ball, which so terrified Karlsefni and his men, has led some to think that Indians are indicated, but there is no agreement on this. All in all, the identification must remain doubtful, but on the whole the description of the physical characteristics of the attackers would seem to fit "Eskimos" more aptly than Indians.

In the *Graenlendinga saga*, the encounter with the Skraelings is described as follows:

In the summer succeeding the first winter, Skrellings were discovered. A great troop of men came forth from out the woods. The cattle were hard by, and the bull began to bellow and roar with a great noise whereat the Skrel-lings were frightened and ran away, with their packs wherein were grey furs, sables, and all kinds of peltries. They fled towards Karlsefni's dwelling, and sought to effect an entrance into the house, but Karlsefni caused the doors to be defended [against them]. Neither [people] could understand the other's language. The Skrellings put down their bundles then, and loosed them, and offered their wares [for barter], and were especially anxious to exchange these for weapons, but Karlsefni forbade his men to sell their weapons, and taking counsel with himself, he had the women carry out milk to the Skrellings, which they no sooner saw, than they wanted to buy it, and nothing else. Now the outcome of the Skrellings' trading was, that they carried their wares away in their stomachs, while they left their packs and peltries behind with Karlsefni and his companions, and having accomplished this [exchange] they went away. Now it is to be told, that Karlsefni caused a strong wooded palisade to be constructed and set up around the house. It was at this time that Gudrid, Karlsefni's wife, gave birth to a male child, and the boy was called Snorri.

In the early part of the second winter the Skrellings came to them again, and these were now much more numerous than before, and brought with them the same wares as at first. Then said Karlsefni to the women: "Do ye carry out now the same food, which proved so profitable before, and nought else." When they saw this they cast their packs in over the palisade. Gudrid was sitting within, in the doorway, beside the cradle of her infant son, Snorri, when a shadow fell upon the door, and a woman in a black nam-kirtle entered. She was short in stature, and wore a fillet about her head; her hair was of a light chestnut colour, and she was pale of hue, and so big-eyed, that never before had eyes so large been seen in a human skull. She went up to where Gudrid was seated, and said: "What is thy name?" "My name is Gudrid; but what is thy name?" "My name is Gudrid," says she. The housewife, Gudrid, motioned her with her hand to a seat beside her; but it so happened, that, at that very instant Gudrid heard a great crash, whereupon the woman vanished, and at that same moment one of the Skrellings, who had tried to seize their weapons, was killed by one of Karlsefni's followers. At this the Skrellings fled precipitately, leaving their garments and wares behind them; and not a soul, save Gudrid alone, beheld this woman. "Now we must needs take counsel together," says Karlsefni, "for that I believe they will visit us a third time, in great numbers, and attack us. Let us now adopt this plan: ten of our number shall go out upon the cape, and show themselves there, while the remainder of our company shall go into the woods and hew a clearing for our cattle, when the troop approaches from the forest. We will also take our bull, and let him go in advance of us." The lie of the land was such that the proposed meeting-place had the lake upon the one side, and the forest upon the other. Karlsefni's advice was now carried into execution. The Skrellings advanced to the spot which Karlsefni had selected for the encounter, and a battle was fought there, in which great numbers of the band of the Skrellings were slain. There was one man among the Skrel-lings, of large size and fine bearing, whom Karlsefni concluded must be their chief. One of the Skrellings picked up an axe, and having looked at it for a time, he brandished it about one of his companions, and hewed at him, and on the instant the man fell dead. Thereupon the big man seized the axe, and after examining it for a moment, he hurled it as far as he could, out into the sea; then they fled helter-skelter into the woods, and thus their intercourse came to an end.[3]

Here again it is really impossible to determine whether the natives were Indians or Eskimos. The one thing that might indicate that we are dealing with Indians and not Eskimos is the description of the chief of the Skraelings who is described as being of "large size and fine bearing" but it is difficult to say whether this was so. Were one able to localize the scene of these encounters with the aborigines, which of course cannot be done, one might arrive at some tentative conclusion.

But it is not the Vinland Skraelings that occupy the centre of the stage.

They are only peripheral figures, just as the voyages to Vinland itself occupy only an interlude in the five-hundred-year history of the Icelanders in Greenland and the Canadian Arctic. It was the Skraelings of the Arctic who have found a place in the literary sources of the Middle Ages. What have the sources to tell us of the people who bear this derogatory name?

One of the earliest references to the Skraelings occurs in the *Historia Norwegiae*, written in the early part of the thirteenth century:

> On the other side of the Greenlanders to the north-west hunters have met with a dwarf-sized folk, whom they call Skraelings. If they are struck with weapons, no clotted blood appears but the wounds become white. When they are dead, however, the blood flows continuously. They have no iron whatsoever but use the teeth of marine animals for missile weapons and sharp stones for knives.[4]

All mediæval commentators on the Skraelings are agreed that in stature they were very small. The *Inventio Fortunata*, written about 1364, calls them "Pygmies which are not at the uttermoste above four foote high."[5] On his map of the northern lands in 1569, Gerhard Mercator has the inscription, "Here lived pygmies, at the most four feet in height, like those who in Greenland are called Skraelings."[6] On a globe from 1541, Mercator has indicated: "Here live pygmies, in the vulgar tongue called Skraelings."[7] Mercator's source was no doubt the *Inventio Fortunata*. The *Navigatio Brendani*, based probably on information from the Icelanders, is referring to the Skraelings when it says: "instantly the harbour was filled with imps in the image of pygmies or dwarfs."[8] The anonymous author of the letter to Pope Nicholas V, *circa* 1448, writes:

> and when men journey to the mountains of that land [Greenland] they find pygmies living there, small in stature, only an ell in height. When they see human beings they run together and conceal themselves in holes in the ground like a colony of ants. It is impossible to gain a victory over them as they do not wait to be attacked.[9]

The Archbishop of Nidaros, Erik Walkendorff, who was tremendously interested in the past history and the rediscovery of Greenland, in a description of Finnmark, the northern part of Norway, wrote the following about 1500:

> Northwest from Finnmark is a folk, which is small and puny in stature, i.e. one and a half ells, who are commonly called Skraelings. They are an unwarlike nation, for fifteen of them do not dare to approach one Christian or Russian, neither for battle or conversation. Their abodes are subterranean, so it is impossible to investigate them or capture them . . .[10]

Akin to this description is that written by Sigurdur Stefansson, rector of the Latin school in Skalholt, whose mediæval archives were still intact in 1590:

> But there is another land near this Vinland, whose correct name is Helluland, but because of the dwarfs, i.e. the human pawns who lived there, is called the land of the Skraelings. For in the Norse language, Skraeling has almost the same meaning as a courageless (and peaceful), weak man (feeble). The inhabitants of this territory have been a source of much misfortune to the Greenlanders, as the Icelanders learned from conversation with bishops who were often sent from Greenland – I do not know on what business – to Norway. But now we are in the dark concerning the condition of all these territories and will be forever probably, unless most gracious God, for the glory of his name, by the preaching of the Gospel, will call this miserable folk to communion with his holy church . . .[11]

Claudius Clavus Swart writes in the fifteenth century:

> After them [the wild Lapps] occur, still farther west, the little pygmies, one ell in height, whom I saw after they had been captured on the sea in a small skin boat, which now hangs in the cathedral at Nidaros. There is also a long skin boat, which was once taken with such pygmies aboard.[12]

Again, Paulus Jouius von Nouocomen writes:

> Truthful witnesses have related that in a land to the northwest of the Lapps are to be found Pygmaei, who dwell in eternal darkness, so that when they are full grown, they are only as big as our children are when ten years of age. They are a fear-filled people.[13]

Michael Beheim obtained some information about the Skraelings when he travelled to Norway and Denmark in 1450. He describes them in terms similar to the above in a poem which he wrote about his voyage.[14]

Eskimo legends also tell of the Skraelings, and it was from an Eskimo girl whom he took captive in 1717 that Courtemanche heard of them.[15] They are described in these legends as a black dwarf nation who lived in subterranean dwellings, were poor hunters who could not build hunting traps or other installations, and had no dogs. Just as in the Icelandic sagas, it is said that these dwarfs often disappeared into the ground.[16]

The abodes of these earth pawns are often described by early explorers and have been excavated by archæologists. In Icelandic records, they are called vistir and are only round, subterranean excavations or natural caves. They contain no built-up walls or other evidence of constructive ability.[17]

Dr Duason, the foremost living authority on the Skraelings, has come to the conclusion that the Skraelings were a dwarf people, three to four feet in height.[18] In this connection he quotes the nineteenth-century explorer, George Francis Lyon, who around 1824 found a 2′ 4″ long corpse, buried in an ancient mount on Southampton Island.[19] He also cites Luke Fox, self-styled "North-West Fox," who claims to have found about five hundred burials on an island in Sir Thomas Roes Welcome. None of the corpses was more than four feet in length.[20] The Skraelings, according to Duason's information, were black, evil-visaged, had coarse hair and no beards; their eyes were coal-black and the nasal bone low and very narrow; the front of the nose was broad and the nostrils prominent; their cheek bones were high, the chin pointed, and the forehead low; their legs were short and stout but their trunks long in proportion. Their abodes were holes in the ground and they had no idea of how to build stone structures. They ate their food raw, had no acquaintance with metals and possessed no dogs – but possibly had hand sleds. They were not Eskimos, as we know that people. Indeed the Eskimos themselves have a name for them – Inuarudligkat – which designates a black-complexioned race of dwarfs who lived subterraneously in holes.

As to their relation to other peoples, little can be said. Nor can their language, which is now spoken by the Eskimos, be shown to be related to any known language. Our sources of information on the Skraelings are reduced considerably by the theory, maintained by Duason, that they practised sea burial, so that it will be only by a fortunate accident if the bones of a pure Skraeling are found. With what people inhabiting the regions of the Arctic penetrated by the Icelanders in the centuries following the tenth are the Skraelings to be identified?

CHAPTER 7

The Character of the Dorset Culture

In the regions south of the Gulf of St Lawrence and in Newfoundland, the Icelanders might have come upon Indians as well as so-called Eskimos but, except in the case of the Vinland voyages around the year 1000, the Indians cannot be the people described in mediæval and early modern works as the Skraelings. North of the Gulf of St Lawrence, on the other hand, there is only one people whom the Icelanders could have encountered in the regions they inhabited or visited. These people are the bearers of the so-called Dorset Culture and must indeed be identified as those to whom the Icelanders gave the name of Skraelings.

The Dorset Culture was first identified in a brilliant piece of detective work by the eminent Canadian anthropologist, Diamond Jenness, in 1925.[1] On the basis of a number of artifacts found at Cape Dorset on Baffin Island, he has traced the origin of this culture to the first millennium, B.C., and shown it to have existed into the second millennium, A.D.[2] Since 1925 Dorset Culture sites have been found in many parts of the Canadian archipelago as well as in Labrador and Newfoundland. Especially important are the sites in the Thule and Disko Bay districts of Greenland, in Peary Land, and northeastern Greenland. The Sermermiut site near Jakobshavn in Disko Bay first enabled archæologists to conclude beyond doubt that the Dorset Culture was older than the Thule Culture, but had itself been preceded by older and distinct cultures in western Greenland, particularly the Sarqaq Culture.[3] Again, the Danish American expedition to Arctic Canada in 1954 found an extremely important Dorset Culture site at Igloolik, off the east coast of the Melville Peninsula. The Igloolik site is, however, not a pure Dorset Culture site, but a combination of Dorset and Thule cultures.[4]

There can be no doubt that the Skraelings were the bearers of the Dorset Culture. All the information afforded by archæology confirms the fact that they are the only people who were to be found in the Canadian Arctic at the time the Icelanders arrived there. The eminent anthropologist at the

Smithsonian Institution, Henry B. Collins, summarizes our information on their culture as follows:

> At the Dorset sites, there is no trace of such typical Eskimo elements as whalebone mattocks and sled shoes, harness toggles, bone arrowheads, the throwing board, and harpoon sockets and finger rests. Completely ignorant of the bow drill, the Dorset Eskimo cut or gouged out the holes in their implements. Rubbed-slate artifacts, so common among other Eskimos, were very scarce as compared with implements of chipped stone. Distinctive types of harpoon heads, small ivory carvings and a simple geometric art style are other features that characterize the Dorset Culture. The Dorset people hunted walrus, seal, polar bear, caribou, hares and foxes, but not the narwhal, beluga or right whale. They had no knowledge of dog traction, though small hand sleds were used. As yet there is no definite information regarding their houses.[5]

It is to be noted, too, that the implements of the Dorset people were smaller than those of the succeeding Eskimos.

Unfortunately, so far no skeletons of the Dorset people have been found. This is understandable, for it would seem, if we accept Dr Duason's view, that the Dorset people did not bury their dead but cast them into the sea or, when old age approached, even committed suicide by hurling themselves off cliffs.[6] The two recently discovered human mandibles from Dorset Culture sites on Sugluk and Mansel Islands in Hudson Bay and Hudson Strait may possibly be those of Dorset people, but it would be very difficult to assert that they are not from a mixed race. Even if they are not pure Dorset, however, they would seem to confirm the accounts of the dwarfish character of the Dorset people, for while they are both said to be comparable with present-day Eskimo mandibles, they are somewhat smaller.[7]

As to the houses of the Dorset people, there can be no doubt that they did not possess houses in the true sense of that word, that is, buildings constructed of turf, sods, or stones. Their abodes were, as mentioned above, simply subterranean pits, often connected by tunnels. These are sometimes very difficult to identify. The *vistir* of the Skraelings are now only small circular depressions in the level surface of the ground. Large numbers of them have, however, been noticed and often described,[8] but in many cases the discoverers have been unaware that these were *vistir*. One of the best descriptions is to be found in the account of Frobisher's second voyage in 1577:

> Upon the maine land ouer against the Countesses Iland we discouered, and behelde to our great maruell, the poore caues and houses of those countrie people, which serue them (as it shoulde séeme) for their winter dwellings, & are made two fadome vnder grounde, in compasse rounde lyke to an Ouen, being ioyned fast one by another, hauing holes like to a Foxe or Conny

PLATE 1

PLATE 2

PLATE 3

PLATE 4

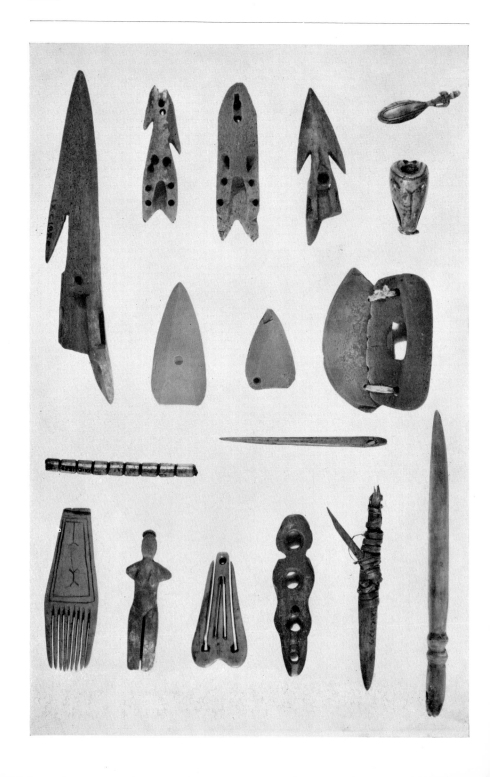

PLATE 5

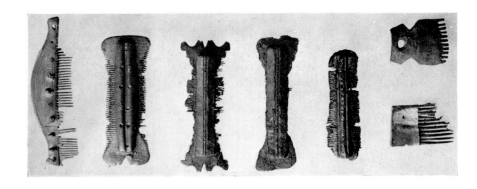

PLATE 6

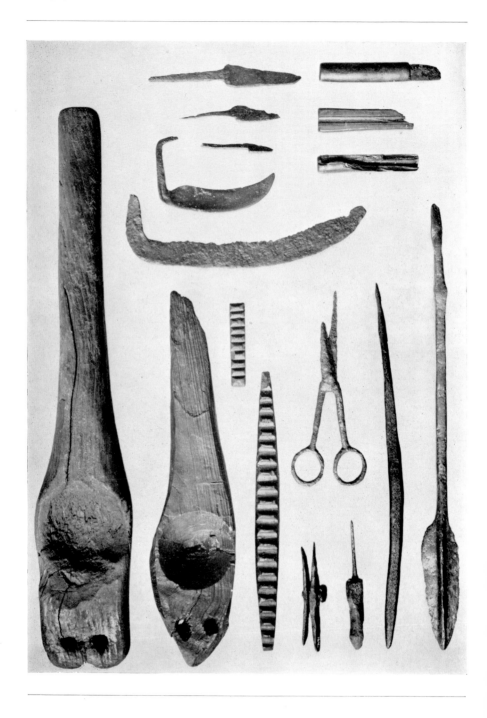

PLATE 7

PLATE 8

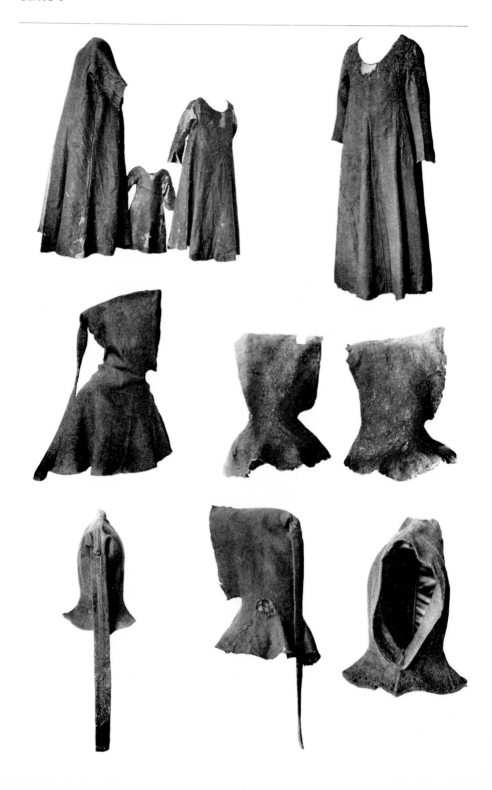

PLATE 9

PLATE 12

PLATE 13

PLATE 14

PLATE 15

PLATE 16

berrie, to kéepe and come togither. They vndertrench these places with gut-
ters so, that the water falling from the hilles aboue them, may slide awaye
without their anoiaunce : & are seated commonly in the foote of a hil, to
shielde them better from the colde winds, hauing their dore and entrance
euer open towardes the South. From the ground vpward they builde with
whales bones, for lacke of timber, whiche bending one ouer another, are
handsomly compacted in the toppe togither, & are couered ouer with Seales
skinnes, whiche in stead of tiles, fenceth them from the rayne. In eache
house they haue only one roome, hauing the one halfe of the floure raysed
with broad stones a fote higher than y other, whereon strawing Mosse, they
make their nests to sléepe in. They defile these dennes most filthylie with
their beastly féeding, & dwell so long in a place (as we thinke) vntill their
owne sluttishnesse lothyng them, they are forced to séeke a swéeter ayre, and
a new seate, and are (no doubt) a dispersed and wandring nation, as the
Tartarians, & liue in hords and troupes, withoute anye certayn abode, as may
appeare by sundry circumstances of our experience.[9]

Therkel Mathiassen found similar house ruins at Disko Bay in 1933. He
describes this *vist* as follows :

House VI is a small, round house, dug rather deep into the gravel, there were
only few stones in it, some of them set on edge in the passage, others floor
stones and those forming the edge of the platform. The roof construction lay
in the bottom of the house, it consisted of eight large pieces of whale rib up
to 1½ m. long, several with notches or cuts made when cutting them up,
and a piece of a caribou antler.[10]

The rectangular houses which have been found in various areas where the
Dorset Culture has flourished are almost certainly to be dated to a period
where the Dorset Culture was no longer a pure or primitive one but had
become or was in the process of becoming the Thule Culture.[11] How did this
come about?

C

The Identity of the Tunnit

Before we can discuss the Thule Culture proper, we must first deal with another people whose destiny became linked with that of the Dorset, as forerunners of Thule. These are the Tunnit of Eskimo legend. Much has been written about this people but usually without reference to the historical circumstances that prevailed at the time.[1] They are generally described as a variant of the aboriginal people who preceded the bearers of the Thule Culture in the Canadian Arctic. Only recently, it has been suggested that they are to be identified with the Dorset Eskimos.[2] Who, then, were the Tunnit?

Our information about them comes largely from the Eskimo legends, folk tales in which a good deal of historical information is to be found. Many of the legends tell of a people of large physique who were to be found in Labrador and parts of the Canadian Arctic before the coming of the Eskimos. In Baffin Island and in West Greenland, they are called Tornit; in Labrador, they are sometimes called Greenlanders, but more often Tunnit (the plural form of the singular *Tuneq*) as they are also referred to in the regions west of Hudson Bay. The word is thus formed of the two words, *tun* (reindeer) and *it* (men). They are thus "the men of the reindeer."[3]

The Eskimo legends in Greenland assert that the Tunnit were the earliest inhabitants of that country. In Baffin Island and in Labrador, they are said to have come from Greenland. In the western Arctic, they are said to have come from the east.

As an example of the legends about the Tunnit preserved by the Eskimos, one may cite the following, which Boas collected among the Baffin Islanders:

> In olden times, the Inuit [that is, the Skraelings or Eskimos] were not the only inhabitants of the country in which they live at the present time. Another tribe similar to them shared their hunting-grounds. But they were on good terms, both tribes living in harmony in the villages. The Tornit were

much taller than the Inuit and had very long legs and arms. Almost all of them were bleareyed. They were extremely strong and could lift large boulders which were by far too heavy for the Inuit.

The Tornit lived on walrus, seals and deer, just as the Eskimos do nowadays, but their methods of hunting were different. The principal part of their winter dress was a long and wide coat of deerskins similar to the jumper of the Eskimo, but reaching down to the knee and trimmed with leather straps. When sealing in winter they wore this garment, the lower edge of which was fastened on the snow by means of pegs. Under the jacket they carried a small lamp called tuminiang (literally, resembling a footprint) or quming, over which they melted snow in a small pot. Some Eskimo say that they opened the seals as soon as they were caught and cooked some meat over the lamps. When the seals blew in the hole they whispered, "kapatiparu" (I shall stab it), and when they had it, "Igdluilik". Frequently they forgot about the lamp, and in throwing the harpoon upset it and burned their skin.

All their weapons were made of stone. For the blades of their knives they used green slate (uluqsaq, literally, material for women's knives), which was fastened by ivory pins to a bone or ivory handle. The points of their harpoons were made of bone, ivory or slate, those of their lances of flint or quartz which was also used for drillheads, but they made neither kayaks or bows.

Their method of hunting deer was remarkable. In a deer pass, where the game could not escape, they erected a pile of cairns across the valley and connected them by ropes. Some of the hunters hid behind the cairns, while others drove the deer towards them. As the animals were unable to pass the rope, they fled along it, looking for an exit, and while attempting to pass a cairn were lanced by the waiting hunter, who seized the body by the hind legs and drew it behind the line. This tale is related as a proof of their strength and it is said that they were able to hold a harpooned walrus as the Eskimo holds a seal.

The Tornit could not clean the sealskins so well as the Inuit, but worked them up with part of the blubber attached.

The old stone houses of the Tornit can be seen everywhere. Generally they did not build snow houses, but lived the whole winter in stone buildings, the roofs of which were frequently supported by whale ribs. Though the Eskimo build similar structures, they can be easily distinguished from one another, the bed of their huts being much larger than that of the Tornit.

Though both tribes lived on very good terms, the Inuit did not like to play ball with the Tornit, as they were too strong and used large balls with which they hurt their playfellows severely.

Tornit did not build any kayaks, but as they were aware of the advantage afforded by their use in hunting, they stole the boats from the Inuit, who did not dare to defend their property, the Tornit being by far their superiors in strength. Once upon a time, a young Tuneq had taken the kayak of a young Inuit without asking him and had injured it by knocking in the bottom. The Inuit got very angry and ran a knife into the nape of the

Tuneq's neck while he was sleeping. (According to another tradition, he drilled a hole into his head.) The Tornit then became afraid that the Inuit would kill them all and preferred to leave the country for good. They assembled at Quernivtung (a place in Cumberland Sound, Baffin Land) and in order to deceive any pursuers, they cut off the tails of their jumpers and tied their hair into a bunch protruding from the crown of the head.[4]

This hairdress, which the Eskimos wear to this day, is thoroughly Icelandic, according to Duason.

In these legends we are obviously concerned with three peoples: the present-day Eskimo who have preserved the legends, the Tunnit, and the Skraelings. The Tunnit can be no other people than the Greenland Icelanders, much taller, as they were, than the Skraelings, with much longer arms and legs. Through intermixture between the Icelanders and the Skraelings, who were the bearers of the Dorset Culture, the memories of both the Icelanders and the Skraelings became confused, and sometimes the qualities or behaviour which belonged to one people were assigned to the other. Thus the statements that the Tunnit could not clean seal skins as well as the Eskimos, and that their way of preparing meat was disgusting, were probably transferred from the Skraelings to the Tunnit. Again, when it is said that the beds of the Tunnit were smaller than those of the Inuit (Eskimos) the Tunnit are again being confused with the Skraelings, but in the main there can be discerned in these legends recollections of both the early Icelandic hunters who moved into regions where the Skraelings were to be found and with whom the former intermingled. An example of this is the statement that the Skraelings or Eskimos were reluctant to play ball with the Icelanders, for as is well known, the old ball game of the Icelanders was exceedingly rough.[5] Another example of the recollection of the early days when intermixture began, is the accurate description of the houses, which were characteristic of the Thule Culture before integration had culturally and materially reached such proportions that the Skraeling element had become the predominant one, as indeed it remains to the present day.

The Eskimos in Labrador have virtually the same to say about the Tunnit as have those on Baffin Island. E. W. Hawkes collected many legends there and came to the following conclusion:

Tunnit (Tornit in Baffin Land) according to tradition were a gigantic race formerly inhabiting this northeastern coast of Labrador, Hudson Strait, and southern Baffin Land. Ruins of old stone houses and graves which are ascribed to them by the present Eskimo are found throughout this entire section, penetrating only slightly, however, into Ungava Bay. Briefly we may say that there is evidence, archæological as well as traditional, that the Tunnit formerly inhabited both sides of Hudson Strait. The oldest Eskimo of northern Labrador still point out these ruins, and relate traditions of their having lived together until the Tunnit were finally exterminated or driven out by the present Eskimo.

Just as the Baffin Island Eskimos had done, the Labrador Eskimos related that the Tunnit stole kayaks from them, that they were stupid and slow-going but so powerful that the Eskimos had to resort to all kinds of treachery. They also relate that the Tunnit built their houses of such heavy rocks that the Inuit could not lift them and that they used whale ribs and shoulder blades in the construction of their houses (an obvious reference to the houses of the Thule Culture). The confusion of the Tunnit with the Skraelings occurs also in the Labrador legends.[6]

Knud Rasmussen, who probably understood the Eskimo mentality better than any man in the present century, obtained the following information about the Tunnit on King William Island:

It was the Tunit [sic] who made our country inhabitable, who discovered where the caribou crossed the water and made hunting grounds there, found the fish in the rivers and built salmon dams, built fences here and there and forced the caribou to follow certain paths. They were strong but timid and were easily put to flight and it was seldom heard that they had killed others. They caught caribou (where they crossed the water) and rowed the kayak on the sea; at Avertoq, Bellot Strait, one can see remains of the animals they caught, whales, walruses and narwhales; they were also skilful hunters of the musk ox and bear. Once they had land at Netsilik, Willersted Lake; then they killed an Eskimo's dog at his request, by throwing a spear at it with the foot, but became frightened and fled. By Lake Qipkiaq, at Netsilik, ruins can still be seen of their stone houses with the doorways surrounded by large, yellow, sappy flowers with thick stalks.

Once the Tunit lived at Qingmertoq (Adelaide peninsula); there the land was taken from them by the Ugjulingmiut. The Tunit fled eastward to Saitoq but, when they reached Naparutalik, they threw off all their clothes and swam over Kingarsuit. On the little island Pagdlagfik, they reached land, but they were so exhausted that they fell forward and died.[7]

Obviously, in all these legends fantasy is mixed with fact, but the salient facts are easy to point out and may be summarized as follows. The Tunnit were a much larger race than the present-day Eskimo. They were able to build stone structures which the Eskimo did not or could not attempt. They were much stronger and the charge of cowardliness is, probably, a piece of face-saving on the part of the Eskimos. They were great hunters and their mode of life as it emerges from the legends can only be described as mediæval European. Their original homeland was Greenland and they migrated from the farming settlements there to the Arctic lands of Canada. They are, in other words, Icelanders who, for one reason or another, found it more congenial or advisable to leave the farming districts and to adopt what we know as an Eskimo way of life, bringing to it, however, many of the features of the material culture of Scandinavia in the Middle Ages.

Indeed, when we consider the historical background of Greenland and Canada in the centuries after 1100, there is no people other than the Icelanders who could have played the role assigned to the Tunnit in the Eskimo legends. Duason has even pointed out that the names of the two Tornit champions of whom Boas obtained information on Baffin Island are, in origin, Icelandic: Koodlowetto (in Icelandic, Gudleifr), and Eyeeyvolwalow (in Icelandic, Eyjolfr).[8] It is also to be noticed that the Tunnit must have spoken a language other than that of the Skraelings, for the Eskimo legends tell us that they barked like dogs and spoke an unelastic tongue.[9]

Nor can the Tunnit have been Indians, for the Eskimos are well acquainted with the Indians, calling them Erkilik and describing them in their legends. It may be that the Skraelings mentioned in the Vinland sagas are either the Beothuks or Micmacs of the Maritimes and Newfoundland, or both. What relations, if any, existed between these people and other Indians of the interior and the bearers of the Dorset Culture is not known, and various opinions have been advanced. It may be confidently asserted, however, that the Tunnit were not Indians. Indeed, the material and intellectual culture of the Indians does not bear even a superficial resemblance to what we know of the Tunnit Culture.

The greatest living authority on the Tunnit, Jon Duason, has concluded:

> The Tunnit were Icelandic sitters. There is nothing in the legends that cannot very well apply to them, and there are many things that can apply to no other people or folk than them. This cannot be a coincidence. Nor would it have been possible to fabricate this, and indeed what could have been the purpose in so doing? The legends would not be so true to reality were they not true, and had not the Tunnit, in reality, been Icelandic boothsitters.[10] There can be no doubt here. Everything fits. According to the legends the Tunnit are, undoubtedly, Icelandic sitters (setar) and no other people.[11]

CHAPTER 9

The Origins of the Thule Culture

It is sometimes forgotten that until the twelfth century at the earliest there was no such thing as a genuine Eskimo culture diffused throughout the Canadian Arctic. Until then the north was peopled with small, localized groups such as the old Bering Sea, Punuk, Birnirk, Ipiutak, and even the Dorset Cultures, none of which can properly be described as Eskimo.[1]

As soon as the Icelandic hunters or boothsitters, that is, the Tunnit, began to migrate from the farming settlements, they came upon the aborigines in Northern Greenland and the islands of the Canadian archipelago. These aborigines were the Dorset people of whom we have spoken. The intermixture between the Icelanders and these more primitive people, which must have begun as early as the eleventh century, was to lead to the development of a new and distinctive culture and the evolution of a new people – the true Eskimos who spread from Greenland in the east to Siberia in the west. This development, from which the modern Eskimo culture has evolved, is known as the Thule Culture.

The Thule Culture was first discovered by the Dane, Therkel Mathiassen, the brilliant and gifted archæologist of the Fifth Thule Expedition,[2] which explored Arctic North America in the years 1921-1924 under the leadership of Knud Rasmussen. Mathiassen excavated Thule sites at Chesterfield Inlet, Southampton Island, the Melville Peninsula, and Baffin, Bylot, and King William Islands. Since then, he and the Danish archæologists, Erik Holtved and Helge Larsen,[3] have excavated numerous Thule sites in west and east Greenland. Collins has investigated sites on Baffin Island and Cornwallis Island.[4] J. Alden Mason found a Thule Culture site at Point Barrow in Alaska, and other discoveries of a similar nature have been made,[5] that have established beyond the shadow of a doubt that the Thule Culture extended even beyond the limits of Greenland and the Canadian Arctic.

It is the contention of most scholars that the Thule Culture originated in Alaska and gradually spread eastward until it reached Greenland. There is

59

little evidence for this assertion. The oldest Thule sites are to be found in Greenland and the youngest in Alaska. In fact it is true that an attempt has been made to link the Thule Culture with the Birnirk Culture, but this can hardly be regarded as successful.[6]

Because the Thule Culture, as well as many of the pre-Eskimo cultures, has been studied in a historical vacuum, only the odd scholar has realized the intimate connection between it and the Icelandic colonies in Greenland. Collins has correctly pointed out that in northwest Greenland,

> The earliest stage of the Thule culture there – apparently the earliest Thule stage known in the Eastern Arctic – was no longer a stone age culture. Iron, obtained either directly or indirectly from the Norse settlers in west Greenland, had already replaced stone as blades for harpoons, knives and adzes. This would mean that the first Thule Eskimos arrived in Greenland after the establishment of the Norse settlements towards the end of the 10th century. As the Dorset Eskimos had been in Greenland for an undetermined period prior to this, the stone implements found by Eric the Red in southwest Greenland in A.D. 982 were probably Dorset.[7]

He then goes on to state that, as Fridtjof Nansen[8] and Vilhjalmur Stefansson[9] contended, there must have been contact between the Norsemen and "Eskimos" as early as the eleventh and certainly not later than the twelfth century, and his views are buttressed by studies which K. Fischer-Moller[10] made on skeletons disinterred in the graveyards of the West Settlement.

Collins has pointed out also that the Polar Eskimos, one of the more primitive branches of the Eskimo family in modern times, but one who knew how to utilize meteoric iron, did not do this as an improvement or a substitute for the stone tools of their ancestors. On the contrary, their ancestors had used iron obtained from the Norsemen with whom they intermingled (a circumstance which Collins fails to emphasize). When this source of supply was cut off, the Polar Eskimos turned to meteoric iron as a substitute not for stone implements but for forged iron ones. Again Collins points out that in northeast Greenland the Eskimos have used rubbed slate implements since the seventeenth century or later and that the slate blades have been made in imitation of European iron implements when these were no longer available to them.[11]

From the above, it is evident that the Thule Culture in its earliest known sites must have been in contact with the Icelanders who travelled north from the farming settlements of Greenland. It is also known that the Thule and Dorset Cultures existed contemporaneously to begin with in many places and that gradually the Thule Culture replaced the hitherto predominant Dorset Culture, that is, a stone age culture is replaced by an iron age culture.[12] The simplest explanation for this state of affairs is the inter-mingling and racial intermixture of a stone age people with an iron age people, and the latter can only have been the Icelanders from south Greenland, that is to say, the Tunnit.

In his painstaking analysis of the material culture of the Thule Eskimos, Therkel Mathiassen has observed that "the art of the Thule Culture manifests a steady degeneration gradually as it spreads from Alaska eastwards."[13] This is an amazing and almost inexplicable development. On the other hand, if the Thule Culture originated as an iron age culture in Greenland and gradually spread westward to Alaska and Siberia, there is no problem in explaining the increasing excellence of its arts and artifacts. An iron age people increasingly cut off from sources of iron is driven to the manufacture of stone and bone implements and in the course of generations, masters this new technique.

Thus the Thule Culture, whose bearers were an intermixture of the Dorset people and the Tunnit Icelanders, spread across the whole of the Canadian Arctic. As we have mentioned, scholars who believe in the Alaskan or western origin of the Thule Culture are forced to posit a "later return movement"[14] within the past few centuries which brought to northern Alaska a number of traits which the Thule Eskimo had acquired in the Central regions. But there is no need to believe in an original migration of Thule people eastward to Greenland and, in fact, there is no evidence for it. It is significant, too, that skeletons excavated at Point Barrow, which undoubtedly belong to a people of the Thule Culture, resemble to the point of identity the physical type of the present-day Eskimo of southern Greenland and Labrador.[15]

CHAPTER 10

The Material Culture of the Thule Eskimos

The discoverer of the Thule Culture, Therkel Mathiassen, has this to say of it:

> The Thule culture, as we know it from these old finds [his excavations on the Fifth Thule Expedition] show us *a highly developed and remarkable Eskimo culture*. It presents to us a people, living in permanent winter houses by the coast, in conical tents in summer, hunting the whale, the walrus, the seal, the bear and the caribou, trapping foxes, catching birds and salmon, all by means of a highly developed implement technique. They had all the typical Eskimo forms of weapons and implements: the dog sledge, the kayak, the women's boat, the harpoons with moveable foreshaft, loose head and bladder; the ice-hunting harpoon, the bladder dart, lance, bow and arrow, fox trap, bola, bird dart, throwing board, salmon dam, salmon trap, salmon spear, leister, snow knife, men's and women's knives, the mattock, adze, bow drill and hand drill, scrapers, needles and needle cases, the blubber pounder, soapstone cooking pot, pottery, combs; they mastered a highly developed proficiency in ornamentation and carving and were also familiar with the snow house. It is an Eskimo culture which, in many respects, is richer and more developed than that met with among the present day Central Eskimos. The Thule culture is by no means a primitive culture.[1]

It will be seen from Mathiassen's words that in the Thule Culture, we are confronted, materially speaking, with a far higher civilization than that of the Dorset people. It was far better equipped to exploit the resources of the Arctic. Also, from the beginning, it utilized iron implements, a fact of which Mathiassen was not fully aware but which later evidence has revealed.

It is quite true, as Mathiassen says, that the Thule Culture is richer and more developed than that of the present-day Central Eskimos, who are an off-shoot or outgrowth of the Thule Culture.[2] The only reasonable explanation of the more advanced state of the Thule Culture is that it enjoyed, to begin with, the ability and technical skill of a people at a higher cultural level than that of any of the aborigines of the polar regions. Only one such people existed in the relevant regions in the years 1000-1300 – the Icelanders in Greenland, large numbers of whom early became boothsitters and brought with them to the aborigines whom they met and with whom they intermingled, an iron culture and far superior techniques in the hunting of land and marine animals. But as time went on, the superior Tunnit were gradually swamped by the inferior Skraelings and were, so to speak, barbarized, losing in the process much of the skill and technique they once possessed, not to mention the spiritual and intellectual culture which depended for its existence on the retention of the Icelandic tongue and contacts with Christendom. This process is a familiar one. The children of the mixed marriages learned the language of the mother and in the vast majority of cases she will have been a Skraeling, for not many Icelandic women will have accompanied the boothsitters into the hunting-regions of the Arctic. Thus we may presume the loss of first, the Christian faith; second, the language; and third, the technical skill; in a geometrical progression. Finally, the extreme degeneration is reached among the physical heirs of the Thule Culture – the Sadlermiut.[3]

The views set out above and in the foregoing chapter will, no doubt, seem radical to many, yet they are borne out by an examination of the material culture of the Central Eskimos in the mediæval phase of Canadian history.

Let us first examine a somewhat obscure phase of the Thule Culture, that is, the type of house characteristic of it. We have seen that the houses of the Dorset Culture may be described as almost circular holes in the ground but, over vast regions where the Thule Culture spread, we find square or rectangular houses which are in every way the same as the Icelandic dwelling house known as *skali*. The square Tunnit house and the later square Eskimo house are simply the Icelandic dwelling-house or booth. The description given by David Cranz and W. A. Graah could be descriptions of Icelandic *skalar* and indeed William Thalbitzer, M. Mauss, and H. Beuchat remark on the resemblance of the square Eskimo house to the Icelandic *skali*.[4]

The whole question is vastly complicated by the fact that both the circular or oval whalebone house which Mathiassen regards as typical of the Thule Culture and the square house of the Tunnit and later Eskimos have no doubt been rebuilt often in the course of the centuries. One may conjecture that the whalebone type of house was built by the Dorset people after they had come into contact with the Tunnit and whaling had become a much more important part of their culture than previously, and that contemporaneously, the Tunnit were building their square houses which gradually superseded the whalebone house. But it should be emphasized that this is only conjecture.

Concerning houses found on Ellesmere Island, Mathiassen writes:

There is thus hardly any reason to doubt that at any rate the earlier houses [whalebone houses] at these settlements are of the Thule type; the later houses, which in the sketches have become regularly rectangular, are possibly of the Cape York type.[5]

The whalebone and square houses were the permanent winter houses of the Tunnit and Thule people, but the Icelanders also had temporary summer dwellings in Nordrseta on their summer hunting-expeditions. These were tents, and there are still to be found the stones which the Tunnit placed around the edges of these. They differ markedly from the tent rings of the Eskimo (the Dorset people do not seem to have used tents). As Mathiassen points out, it is not known with certainty what type of tent was most common.[6] The fact, however, that the stones usually lie in a circle, indicates that the tents used were cone-shaped (topptjald) or bell-shaped (knapptjald), types known from Iceland and from the Eskimo regions in modern times.

The "tent site rings" are sometimes square and the tent may have been a beam or ridge-pole tent. Mediæval Icelanders used the beam tent but it does not seem that the Eskimos have used them. Mathiassen found a rectangular one with rounded corners at Igdlutalik, an island just south of Umanaq in the vicinity of Kangamiut.[7] Others (square tent "rings") have been found in the vicinity of latitude 74° 40′ on the east coast and in the vicinity of Danmarks Havn (latitude 76° 46′). This latter site was rectangular and the tent likely a ridge-pole type. The tent circle is made of extra large stones.[8] Mathiassen found such tent rings in the region north of Repulse Bay, in southern Baffin Island, on the Rae Isthmus, and on King William Land. They are reported also from Labrador, the Melville Peninsula, Southampton Island, Lyon Inlet, and elsewhere.[9] The size of the stones distinguishes all these tent rings from later Eskimo rings and shows that they were erected by the Tunnit.

A hunting aid used by the Icelanders is a lookout from an elevated rock known as vardberg. On these vardberg, little shelters were built to shield the hunter against the elements. From them, the hunters or lookouts searched the sea with their eyes for whales, jetsam, wrecks, ships, or whatever they could see. Vardberg are very common in Greenland, both in the farming settlements and in the wastes, but they are also to be found on high peaks along the coast of Labrador. The Eskimo do not mention them in their legends, and their construction and the stones employed are such that they can only be Icelandic. Akin to these are cairns which were erected both inland to guide travellers and also on the coast for the guidance of mariners. The three found in the vicinity of the rune stone of Kingigtorsuaq have already been mentioned. They were no doubt sea marks (the runic inscription proves this) and all are agreed that they are the work of the Icelanders.[10]

The Sverdrup Expedition in 1899 found "two regularly built round cairns . . . a short distance west of Bjorneborg, in longitude 80° W, in a westerly part of Jones Sound." These are undoubtedly also the work of Icelandic hunters or the Tunnit.[11] Sir George Nares found in 1875 two unquestionably Icelandic cairns on the summit of Washington Irving Island off the east coast of Grinell Land, latitude 79° 35′ N, and longitude 73° W.[12] Again, these must be the work of the Tunnit.

As the Icelanders must needs traverse the sea to reach north Greenland and the Arctic lands of Canada, they had to have harbours or landing-places. Those who wintered or were permanent boothsitters there would require ship shelters of one sort or another. Are these to be found in the Thule Culture region? The Putnam Expedition discovered in 1927, on an islet which at low tide is connected by land with the island of Sculpin near Nain in Labrador, a harbour of the type found in mediæval Iceland and Scandinavia. Various Tunnit ruins are said to be found here, some of which resemble Icelandic ship sheds. The harbour is described as a "protected landing place for small craft, with some indication of a partially artificial breakwater." The shore seems also to have been cleared of large stones.[13] Väino Tanner later investigated some of the ruins on Sculpin Island and was led to believe that some of them were ship shelters such as the mediæval Icelanders built.[14] These ship sheds were known as *hrof* when unroofed and *naust* when roofed. The Icelandic sagas mention such sheds in Greenland but none has been identified there, although such structures may have been mistakenly identified as store houses. They have, however, been found in Labrador and are described by G. M. Gathorne-Hardy as follows:

> A large specimen measured 17 feet 6 inches by 10 feet, another, 15 feet by 9 feet 6 inches internally. Most were somewhat smaller. Many are of a strictly rectangular plan. The floor has been levelled by clearing away the large stones. The walls seen were about 2 feet high and did not appear ever to have been much higher. I heard, however, of one on a small island near Port Manvers, . . . which must have been at least 4 feet 6 inches in height. . . . The walls had evidently never consisted of any other material besides the stones, and great care and experience must have gone to the construction of such dry stone walls, seeing the excellent condition in which many of them remain at the present day. In no case was there a trace of any dwelling with the characteristic passage entrance.[15]

Again, George Palmer Putnam found some on Sculpin and other islands in the vicinity of Nain, which he describes in similar terms. The Eskimo at Nain were said to refer to these structures as "the houses built by strange people."[16] Therkel Mathiassen, while denying that these structures are *hrof*, indirectly confirms by his description that they are such and mentions several in other parts of Arctic Canada. He writes:

It is most probably the large square stone erections in particular which have been the basis of the Norse theory. What is the meaning of these oblong, low stone structures? As houses, the walls seem to be too low, and they never seem to have been higher. The interior is smooth and cleared of stones, consequently without remains of a broken-down roof. Quite similar stone buildings I have seen in several places on Melville Peninsula. From Cape Welcome near Naujan in Repulse Bay I have described one. It is an irregular square building of heavy stones, 4-5 m. square, the maximum height of the walls being 1 m. By the local Eskimo it is regarded as a festival place, where eating, dancing and feasting took place on days of good hunting, possibly it is a remnant of the square dancing house of the Alaska Eskimo. Similar structures I have seen on the neighbouring Tent Island (5 × 6 m., the walls' maximum height being 1½ m.), and on the island Ugli and Iglulik. These festival places are all of them situated on the summer camping sites.[17]

His contention that these were built as festival places is completely un-acceptable, although they are now used as such by the Eskimos. The Eskimos do not know who built them and they are not found inland. As a matter of fact, stone structures of which he writes in another connection are probably *hrof*:

Kayak supports of stone have been seen, especially in Repulse Bay, in close proximity to Thule ruins, as at Naujan and Simiutaq; some of them are very broad, as if for two kayaks or a women's boat. Kayak supports are mentioned from Lyon Inlet and Southampton Island, from Ellesmere Land and North-east Greenland where, however, classification of these remains is uncertain. The Western Eskimo use wooden scaffolding for kayak supports.[18]

The size of some of these structures is such that they are more suited for storing, in an inverted position, the boats of the Icelanders rather than the kayaks of the Eskimos, but their origin and use are uncertain.

Dome-shaped, hollow stone structures (borg), which are to be found throughout the eastern part of the Thule Culture region, are certainly another creation of the Tunnit. The Eskimos do not know to what use these were put. When Knud Rasmussen asked his countrymen what these struc-tures were used for, they told him they were fox traps. In *Gronland langs Polhavet* Rasmussen explained their use and published a diagram showing one fox after another leaping high into the air to fall into the so-called "tower" trap. As has been pointed out, this must have been quite a feat, for the *borgir* originally had no opening at the top.[19]

These structures were no doubt used by the Tunnit for the same purpose as they were used in Iceland, that is, for the drying and storing of meat and possibly as shelters for the hunters during the summer. They are found in all parts of Greenland and the eastern Canadian Arctic, and as far west as Victoria Island. In 1609 Hudson found them being used as store houses on

Digges Island. He describes them as "some round Hills of stone, like Grass cockes, which at the first I tooke to be the worke of some Christian." He took off the uppermost stone and found them hollow and "full of Fowles hanged by their neckes."[20] G. F. Lyon describes very well the *borgir* he found on Southampton Island:

> We passed several small store-houses, of about six feet in height by ten in diameter, built of rough slabs of lime-stone, rudely but regularly piled up, and Neeakoodloo opened one to show me that it contained a quantity of split salmon, suspended by the tails in such a manner that no small animals could reach them.[21]

Many others have described these *borgir* in various parts of the Arctic. They are built of very large and heavy stones, and their construction requires considerable skill and craftsmanship. They are certainly not the creation of the Eskimos.

Nor can there be much doubt that the V-shaped walls, into which the caribou were driven and which are found throughout the Thule Culture regions, were constructed by the Tunnit. As we know both from archæology and from written sources such as the *King's Mirror*,[22] caribou hunting was one of the principal sources of food for the Icelanders in the farming settlements of Greenland. When they moved into the wastes of Canada, they took with them their method of ambushing the caribou. As far as we know the Skraelings did not employ this method of hunting reindeer.

Structures much more peculiar than the caribou fences are the polar-bear traps mentioned above, which are to be found throughout the Thule Culture regions. These traps are constructed of very large and carefully selected stones. The workmanship is of the best. They were not, of course, to be found in the farming settlements, for it would be too dangerous to allow polar bears to roam there until by chance they entered a trap, but they are found in northern Greenland and in various parts of the Canadian Arctic as far west as the Melville Peninsula. There can be no doubt that these traps were constructed by the Icelanders or the Tunnit, for the Skraelings and later Eskimos could have had no interest in the capturing of polar bears alive. Only the Icelanders, who knew how prized these bears were in mediæval Europe and who had the means of transporting them thither, would have had an interest in raising these structures. These traps are one of the most impressive proofs of the wide-ranging activity of the Icelanders in the Canadian Arctic.[23]

Akin to the polar-bear traps are the eider-duck nests. As has already been noticed, these have been found on Norman Lockyer, Devil Island, and St Helena Island. They are exactly the same as the nests used in Iceland in mediæval times and to this day. Unquestionably, they are not the work of

the Skraelings or the modern Eskimo. They are again another incontro-
vertible proof of the presence of Icelandic boothsitters in the regions where
they are found.[24]

All these above-mentioned installations supply us with proof that the
Thule Culture was predominantly an Icelandic one, very distinctly set apart
from the aboriginal cultures of America. There are also many Icelandic
features which have not been mentioned but which have Icelandic counter-
parts. There are, for instance, protective fences built of stones much larger
than the ones used by the Eskimos, the shelters to sleep in (skygni), fireplaces or pits (eldgrofir) and hearths (hlodir), burial cairns, drying posts
(therristolpar), stone sheds for drying (grjothjallar), fish walls (fiskigardar),
whale creeks (hvalvagar), whale pits (hvalgrafir) and meat pits (kjotgrafir),
hunting blinds (stilli), fishing places (veidistodvar), fishing pits and weirs
(stemmur), chests (ker) and creels (teinur), ambushes (satir), fox traps
(skollagildrur), large boulders (tables) placed upon stones (grettistok), stones
on a hearth (raufarsteinar), Hel-bridges or hopping stones (heljarbryr),
stone rows for the game of "rowing to seal" (stone rows in the shape of a
kayak), geese-folds (gaesarettir).[25] All these structures, installations, and
games have their prototypes in Iceland, and the Icelandic language has
names to cover them all. There can be little doubt that their introduction
into the Thule Culture stems from the Icelandic boothsitters who met and
intermixed with the Dorset Eskimos. They all date from the period
1000-1500.

As Duason has pointed out, all these works and installations can be
ascribed only to the Icelanders from the farming settlements of Greenland,
that is, to the Tunnit. In other words, the ruins of the Thule Culture are
"Tunnit ruins and the Tunnit structures are the work of the Icelandic
boothsitters, hunters and voyagers to the Northern Booth Dweller's
Region."[26] The very fact that evidence of the use of iron is to be found at
most Thule Culture sites proves that we are here dealing with two peoples
who have intermingled. The stone and bone implements show that one of
these was a stone-age people who can only have been the bearers of the
Dorset Culture. The iron tools can only have come from the Icelanders, for
the Skraelings and other earlier aborigines of the Canadian Arctic did not
know or use iron. We are thus forced to the conclusion that the Thule
Culture is an amalgam of the culture of the aborigines of America circa 1000
and the Icelandic settlers of Greenland, who came thither in the years around
1000 and spread from west Greenland to almost all parts of the eastern
Canadian Arctic. This amalgam constitutes the Thule Culture which is the
ancestor of the modern Eskimo race and culture.

Before leaving this subject, it should be stated that in the ruins of the
Thule Culture, the most common inscriptions on articles were two runes.

Most frequently found is the symbol of the hammer of Thor, T, but as is well known, Thor was the most popular god in the Icelandic pantheon. The other rune found on many articles across the Canadian Arctic was the so-called man rune, represented usually as Y, but with variants. To suggest as Mathiassen does that this represents a tree, verges on the ludicrous.[27] Both runes attest the heavy intermixture of the Icelanders and the Skraelings to form the Thule Culture.

CHAPTER 11

The Disappearance of
the Greenland Colonies

When Greenland was visited by Europeans in the latter half of the sixteenth century, the Icelandic settlements as such had disappeared and were now occupied by a mixed population, some of whom had European features and others features which we now regard as characteristic of the Eskimo. All these people spoke the Eskimo language and were not Christians but pagans. In other words, the Icelandic language had disappeared, an economy based on husbandry and hunting had been replaced by one based exclusively on hunting, and the European physical characteristics had been replaced by the quasi-Mongoloid characteristics which we have come to associate with the Eskimo. These same circumstances prevailed in Baffin Island, Labrador, and indeed throughout the whole of the eastern Canadian Arctic. What had happened here?

Numerous answers have been given to this so-called mystery. It would be both tedious and irrelevant to discuss these theories at any great length but brief mention may be made of the more prominent ones.

One of the most popular theories is that the Icelanders were exterminated by the Skraelings or by pirates in bloody warfare. For this theory there is no evidence, as we have seen. The Skraelings were certainly not a warlike race, and there is no indication in all the extensive ruins that have been excavated in the farming settlements of Greenland that warfare, robbery, plundering, or any such activities took place. Indeed, Nansen, Stefansson, and Duason have shown conclusively that this explanation for the disappearance of the Greenland colonies is pure fantasy.[1]

Another theory states that malnutrition and physical degeneration brought the race to an end. This explanation, when it is not based on pure speculation and *a priori* reasoning, is largely based on the disinterment of a number of skeletons in the churchyard at Herjolfsnes in the Eastern Settlement, which was carried out in 1921 by the eminent Danish archæologist, Dr Poul Norlund.[2] In the churchyard, he dug up some two hundred graves and recovered some clothing (the only clothing of the common people in the Middle Ages that has been preserved), about thirty coffins, and skeletal remains of some twenty-five bodies of both children and adults. Practically nothing was left of some of these bodies, but others were fairly well preserved. None of the skeletons had, however, been buried in the coffins which were exhumed. The bones of those inhumed, which had been dignified by a burial in a coffin, had all disintegrated.

These skeletal remains were transported to Denmark where they were subjected to a painstaking anatomical examination by Dr Fr. C. C. Hansen, professor of Anatomy at the University of Copenhagen. He found in most of the remains unmistakable signs of disease, malnutrition, excessive wear of teeth, and other deficiencies. Dr Hansen also measured the empty coffins, which varied in inside length from 154 to 204 cm. (*circa* 60 to 80 inches), and attempted to determine the approximate height of the individuals who had once been buried in them. On the basis of his examinations and measurements, he concluded:

> The vigorous northern race that originally colonized Greenland degenerated in the course of the centuries under the influence of the hard and at last constantly deteriorating life conditions and other unfavourable conditions, especially isolation both intellectually, materially and as regards race hygiene. It became a race of small people, little powerful, physically weakened, with many defects and pathologic conditions.

Of the twenty-five bodies, in eight cases the remains were so few that nothing of importance could be deduced. Of the remaining seventeen bodies, sixteen were found in the northeast or northwest corners of the churchyard and one in the southeast corner. This last was a well-preserved find, the bones of a powerful individual whose health had been good. Now, it is well known that in mediæval times only the lowest and most poorly nourished classes in the community – beggars and paupers – were buried in the portion of a chuchyard north of the church. This consideration does not seem to have weighed at all with Dr Hansen who, in his eagerness to postulate a general deterioration among the inhabitants of Greenland, even ventures the suggestion that the remains of the powerful individual found in the southeast corner of the yard were probably those of a foreign visitor. No real attempt was made by him or Dr Norlund to determine the age of these burials. Duason has shown on the basis of Norlund's own report that some of them at least were not from the last days of the colony but from the thirteenth century. Again, in measuring the coffins, Hansen has adopted the arbitrary standard of subtracting 15 cm. (*circa* 6 inches) from the length of the coffin to arrive at the theoretical maximum length of the individual and has then, on the basis of the width of the coffin, calculated the probable height of the individual. In the case of the coffin whose length was 204 cm. (*circa* 80 inches), this method results in a probable height for the buried individual of 181 cm. (*circa* 71 inches). Such a method does not inspire confidence, especially when it is considered that wood must have been fairly scarce and that coffins would probably be made as small as possible, that some of the excavated ones had been used more than once (Norlund deduces this from the absence of a lid in five cases), and that little is known of the age of these burials. It would indeed seem that seldom have such sweeping generalizations been made on the basis of such small evidence and with so little consideration of various factors which would affect the results. Dr Hansen makes no allowance for the difference in stature between mediæval and modern man, which was, as is well known, considerable. In any case, the skeletal remains from the paupers' corner and the coffins exhumed at Herjolfsnes cannot possibly be regarded as a representative sample of the physical condition of the Icelanders in Greenland at the close of the fifteenth century.[3]

Indeed, more recent skeletal remains in Greenland have been found to show no signs of degeneration. K. Fischer-Moller writes in 1942 :

> On examining the skeletons from the West Settlement I have found no sign of degeneration, nor of any chronic disease except for chronic rheumatism; the finding of such a disease, however, is not at all surprising in severe and cold natural conditions, where protection against cold and damp would be very imperfect, especially as regards the houses. But neither among adults nor among children is there any sign of rickets or tuberculosis, and the teeth, while displaying hard wear as do those of all people living under primitive conditions, are not worn more than those of Nordic people in the Middle Ages; and finally, the teeth are completely free of caries. If life was so short, and we find so many who died young, it must be remembered that this was usual everywhere in the Middle Ages, though this high mortality must have been due mostly to acute epidemic diseases.[4]

Nor is the situation different as far as the Eastern Settlement is concerned. K. Broste and Fischer-Moller found none of the signs of physical degeneration and chronic disease which Hansen believed to be exhibited by the skeletal remains from Herjolfsnes. Only arthritis, an extremely common disease in the Arctic, was revealed in skeletal material which they excavated at Gardar. These bones also revealed that these people were no dwarfs but of a stature comparable to that of European mediæval man and that they did not die at an unexpectedly early age. These scholars conclude :

> The skeletons from Gardar provide us with a cross-section of a population of pure Nordic type, with well developed individuals displaying no sign of degeneration, whereby they make a valuable addition to the previous investigations into the anthropology of the mediæval Norsemen.[5]

In his writings, based largely on the evidence from the churchyard at Herjolfsnes, Norlund has emphasized that there was a gradual deterioration in the climate of Greenland in the later Middle Ages. Others have also advanced this theory which, according to them, helps to explain the abandonment of husbandry and the degeneration which brought the Icelandic race to an end in the country. This is still a very much disputed question, but the evidence for a deleterious change in climate from 1300 on is very slim, and the flourishing condition of the Eastern Settlement, as attested by the buildings erected toward the end of the fifteenth century, would seem to contradict any argument based on this hypothesis. Icelandic weather records from the later Middle Ages again do not suggest any serious worsening of the climate.[6]

It has been argued that consanguineous marriages destroyed the vitality of the race. There is, of course, no evidence that such marriages took place, unless we are to believe that a letter to the archbishop of Trondhjem from Pope Alexander III refers to Greenland.[7] In his letter he speaks of an island within the archdiocese of Trondhjem, twelve days distant from all other countries, in which, because of the smallness of the population, the people cannot marry except within the prohibited degrees laid down by canon law. The Pope is willing to grant the bishops the right to allow marriages down to the fourth degree but not beyond that. It has been argued that this island was Greenland, but it is much more likely that it was Iceland, where in the twelfth century the aristocracy was time and again in difficulty with the church authorities for marriages within the prohibited degrees. Moreover, Greenland was not regarded as an island by Icelanders or Norwegians in the Middle Ages but as an extension of Asia. In any case, consanguineous marriages do not necessarily diminish the vitality of a race.

It has also been urged that epidemics and plagues killed off the people. The only evidence that epidemics or plagues reached Greenland is that one or two mass burials have been found in the churchyards of the country. Christen Leif Vebaek discovered such a grave at the nunnery right opposite the island of Unartok in the Western Settlement.[8] This cannot be regarded as proof of an epidemic, for the adults and children buried in this grave may well have been killed in an avalanche or drowned at sea. Had epidemics or plagues of any importance afflicted Greenland, they would almost certainly be revealed through archæological remains or written sources. It may be confidently asserted that the Black Death, for example, never reached Greenland. Moreover, we know that the Western Settlement had disappeared before the advent of the Black Death in Europe and that the Eastern Settlement was in a flourishing condition long after the disease struck Iceland more than fifty years after its main ravages in Europe.

It has been alleged that the worms of a butterfly (*Agrotis occulta*) destroyed vegetation.[9] This theory belongs in the realms of fantasy. It is possible that in certain years such devastation may have occurred but the ruins of the farmsteads in the Eastern Settlement show that husbandry flourished to the end of the fifteenth century at least. In any case, such ravages are always temporary.

It has been asserted, too, that a disequilibrium of the sexes – the females outnumbering the males – brought about the extinction of the colonies. Of this, there is absolutely no evidence, for the amount of skeletal material from Greenland is both so small and so haphazardly located that no conclusions of this nature can be drawn from it.[10]

What, then, happened to the Icelanders in the Eastern and Western Settlements? We know from Bishop Gisli Oddsson of Skalholt that in 1342 the inhabitants of the Western Settlement "fell voluntarily from the true faith and Christian religion, and abandoning all good *mores* and true virtues, turned to the people of America."[11] In that summer, Ivar Bardarson, the administrator of the see of Gardar in Greenland, was sent to the Western Settlement to investigate the condition of the inhabitants thereof. When he reached it, he found no man, neither Christian nor heathen, in the settlement, only some wild sheep and cattle.

Both these accounts contradict the opinion so often advanced that warfare existed between the Skraelings and the Icelanders. On the other hand, they attest that racial intermixture took place. Indeed, the analysis of skeletons found in the churchyards of the Western Settlement show that this began early. Fischer-Moller's account of this is eminently reasonable but for the fact that he thinks that the Icelanders were attacked by Eskimos who, as we have seen, did not exist at this time, except in so far as intermixture between the Skraelings and Icelanders had taken place to produce the hybrid race which we now know as the Eskimos. Fischer-Moller comes to the conclusion that by 1300 a mixture of the Nordic and Eskimo races had already begun in the Western Settlement, but, while there were hybrids, no mixed race had arisen at that time.[12] He finds untenable the widely held theory that climatic deterioration reduced the livestock of the settlements, resulting in malnutrition among the inhabitants and a consequent inhibitive effect on reproductivity. Under such circumstances, it has been maintained, the Icelanders were reduced by poverty, chronic disease, and isolation to a state in which they were unable to offer resistance to Eskimo aggression. On the basis of skeletal evidence, Fischer-Moller is forced to reject this theory. He thinks it improbable that chronic disease or degeneration had any bearing on the question of the disappearance of the Icelandic settlements in Greenland. He finds no sign of them in the skeletons, no symptoms of undernutrition, bad teeth, or a particularly short life. He argues that the inhabitants of the Western Settlement fled before a vigorous Skraeling attack, a view for which, as we have seen, there is no evidence.

We can only conjecture why the people of the Western Settlement chose to migrate to Baffin Island, Labrador, or some other part of America in the year 1342. It may well be that the pruning-knife and the constant encroachment by the sheep and cattle on the foliage of the district may have resulted in a dearth of fodder, which made husbandry more and more difficult. Again, the fact that the Church had by now come to possess all the farms in the settlement and was possibly making exhorbitant demands in tithes and rents, may have prompted the inhabitants to seek relief by moving beyond the limits of the church's effective authority. Whether the impending visit of Ivar Bardarson, the administrator of the see of Gardar, may have had as its object the collection of tithes and rents which were in default, and whether knowledge of this mission existed in the Western Settlement, are matters on which we cannot pronounce. Most important, possibly, was the heavy intermarriage in the preceding century between the Icelanders and the Skraelings, leading to an increased emphasis on hunting at the expense of husbandry.

Indeed, it is important to realize just what the racial intermixture between the Icelanders and the Skraelings implies. We may be sure that as soon as the boothsitters or Tunnit had established themselves in northern Greenland and in various regions of the Canadian Arctic, where the Skraelings were to be met, intermixture of the races took place naturally. The offspring of these unions would be brought up by the mother, who in most cases would be a Skraeling, for it cannot be presumed that Icelandic women in any numbers accompanied the hunters to Nordrseta. This would mean a loss both of the Icelandic language and the Christian religion. The process must have begun in Nordrseta almost as early as the founding of the Icelandic farming settlements in Greenland, although the settlements themselves would not have been affected by it for another two or three centuries.

As we have seen, the settlers met with no Skraelings on the southern part of the west coast of Greenland when Eric the Red led his colonizers thither. By 1266, however, there were indications that the aborigines were pushing southward, as some men coming from Nordrseta found evidence of the presence of Skraelings on Kroksfjardarheidi.[13] Some priests then boarded a ship and set sail from Kroksfjardarheidi to ascertain the status of things in the north. They sailed until they lost sight of land and, meeting with south winds accompanied by darkness, had to let themselves be driven before the wind. When they were able to take bearings, they saw many islands and all kinds of game – seal, whale, and polar bears in great numbers. At the bottom of a bay they saw a glacier to the south and some old Skraeling abodes, but were unable to go ashore because of the numerous polar bears. They sailed south again for four days and found some more abodes of the Skraelings on islands south of Snaefell. They then made their way back to Kroksfjardarheidi and from thence to Gardar.

We see from this account that, by 1266, the Skraelings were advancing to the Holsteinsborg-Sukkertoppen region and no doubt soon reached the Western Settlement, as indeed the skeletal remains mentioned above testify. Intermixture must then have proceeded apace in the Western Settlement, leading to the "Eskimoization" of the Icelanders there and their abandonment of husbandry in favour of the life of hunting in the game-rich regions of America. Starting as Tunnit, they became, through intermixture with the Skraelings, the Eskimo of the Thule Culture.

But what about the Eastern Settlement? Through archæological excavations, we know that it lived on into the sixteenth and seventeenth centuries. Unfortunately, the churchyards here have yielded little evidence for the fourteenth and fifteenth centuries, which are the earliest dates when we might expect to find evidence for intermixture between the two peoples. The excavations, however, have provided ample evidence for a flourishing economy as late as the beginning of the sixteenth century. They have also provided evidence for a mass emigration about that time. This must again have been prompted by some or all of the reasons which were set forth above for the abandonment of the Western Settlement. It cannot be definitely stated when this took place, for the Eskimos did not move into the bottoms of the fjords until the seventeenth or eighteenth century.

That the intermixture between the Skraelings and Icelanders took place with the consequent loss of the European culture by the latter is amply attested by the descriptions given of the people by the earliest European explorers in the sixteenth and seventeenth centuries. In 1519, on his way from Iceland to Copenhagen to be consecrated bishop of Skalholt, Reverend Ogmundur Palsson was driven by bad weather south and west of Greenland. When the ship passed Herjolfsnes, he was able to observe some people and saw sheep in folds. Thus husbandry must still have been practised at this time.[14] That this was so, also, as late as 1542 is evident from the account of the accidental visit of Jon Graenlendingur to Greenland. This is described as follows:

> In the memory of living men, Jon Graenlendingur, who was for a long time associated with German merchants from Hamburg, testified that on one occasion, when they were driven to Greenland, the ship was carried near crags and high cliffs and they thought it would strike the rocks. But a single passage opened there; when they entered this, they saw the bay was so wide and large that they could not see where it would end; and in this bay or fjord were several islands. This bay was sheltered from storms and rough seas. They cast anchor at a small, uninhabited, outlying island, but avoided

those that were inhabited. They saw, however, that the land was inhabited, and also many of the islands. They put out a boat and stepped onto the little island at which they lay. There were ship shelters and some fishing booths, and many drying sheds made of stone, like those here. They found there a dead man, lying face down. He had on his head a well sewn hood and his clothing was both of wadmal and seal-skin. Beside him lay a crooked carving knife, very much ground and wasted; they took this knife with them to show. This Jon was called Graenlendingur because he was thrice driven to Greenland with sailors and had much to report thence.[15]

We cannot, of course, tell whether the inhabitants of the islands mentioned were still Icelanders or the hybrid race of Eskimos, but it is evident that until the early part of the sixteenth century, at least, Icelanders had been utilizing the characteristic structures of their civilization. This is further confirmed by the fact that the corpse was clad in clothes made of wadmal.

In 1578 the English explorer, Martin Frobisher, and his men landed in Greenland. On their approach, the natives fled. Edward Sellman, who was a member of this expedition, says in his account of the voyage: "Some of our men that were with the Generall aland did see in their tente nayles like scupper nayles, and a tryvet of yron."[16] Dionyse Settle, a gentleman who accompanied Frobisher on his second voyage and who wrote an account of it, comments on the natives they had met: "They have some yron, whereof they make arrowe heades, knives, and other little instrumentes to woorke their boates, bowes, arrowes, and dartes withal. . . ."[17] George Best, a captain of one of the ships on Frobisher's third voyage, wrote the following about the inhabitants of Meta Incognita (Frobisher's name for Baffin Island): "For their weapons they have . . . arrows headed with sharp stones, bones, and some with yron."[18] These are all relics of the Icelandic culture of Greenland and really attest to trading relations with European fishermen in the waters off Greenland, Newfoundland, or Labrador. John Davis, who made three voyages to the Arctic in the 1580's, reports on his encounter with the Eskimos: "I shooke hands with one of them, hee kissed my hand and we were very familier."[19] This type of salutation is European and reveals contact with or recollection of Europeans. Davis also found crosses in a grave. On his third voyage, he saw evidence of salt production in latitude 64° N on the west coast of Greenland – another vestige of Icelandic culture.[20]

In 1606 James Hall, a native of Hull, and John Cunningham, a Scot, both of whom served the Danish king, captured five natives in Greenland and brought them to Denmark. Two of these are described as being small, stout black men, having almost round feet and hands. They seem to have been unacquainted with iron – in other words, almost pure Skraelings. The other three are described as follows:

> Both the other ships came later to Greenland and had been 60 weeks of sea farther north off the country than the first ship; and they captured three Greenlanders, at great risk to their lives, and killed many of them before these were captured; they got a good wind and flew home. The Captain gave them blue clothes and had them take off their own, and he taught them to leap about the ship when he nodded to them; and when they came to Copenhagen, the 10th August, and made for the town, the Greenlanders ran upon the mast platform and furled the top sail as quickly as any of the king's men. They were more intelligent and human than the other two, for the latter bit people like dogs, and every louse they found on themselves they ate. But the other three, when they came to the palace courtyard, ran about, placed their hands on their waists, held their heads in their characteristic manner, and were pleased withal. It is believed that they are more likely to learn the language than the others.[21]

Isaac de la Peyrère, a Frenchman who visited Denmark at this time, saw the five captives. He makes a sharp distinction between the two small and dirty ones and the other three who, he says, were much cleaner and better physical specimens.[22] We are obviously dealing here with almost pure Skraelings and Icelanders only slightly, if at all, intermixed. These captives made some attempt to escape to Greenland in kayaks which had been seized at the time of the capture of the natives, and explained that they would follow the coast thither and not attempt to cross the open sea – a piece of Icelandic geographical lore.

In the National Museum in Copenhagen there is a painting of four Eskimos brought to Scandinavia from the Godthaab region in 1654 – three women and one man. The latter is a European type, tall and with a full beard; the features of the women are more Eskimo in appearance, but not noticeably so. In fact, Adam Olearius describes one of the women as follows:

> The one in the center, Kabelau, was not as black as the others, had larger eyes, showed also more intelligence, skill and gaiety. It was supposed that she must be a descendant of the Christians who lived in that country some hundreds of years ago, or that she must belong to some peculiar sect, for she did not eat everything that the others did, such as impure animals and birds, (horses, beasts with claws, birds with talons, the eating of which the church forbade) nor the internal organs of animals such as the lungs, liver, heart and intestines.[23]

To this evidence of the intermingling of the races, one might add statements from the eighteenth century when the Danes began their missionary work in Greenland. For example, Hans Egede, who came to Greenland in 1721 on a missionary venture, describes the people he met as follows:

> The Greenlanders are well proportioned men, stout, with large and full limbs; some of them are of great and tall stature, some short and fat, but all strong, yielding nothing to the strongest and largest among us, neither in lifting nor carrying. Among the women one finds some so delightfully beautiful creatures that if they were washed and adorned according to the style of our land they would stand comparison with the most beautiful ladies of Europe.[24]

In his *History of Greenland*, David Cranz wrote in 1765:

> One finds also a few who have a moderate white skin and ruddy cheeks, and still more have a long face, and who would easily pass undistinguished among Europeans, especially among the inhabitants of certain mountains in Switzerland. I have also seen Greenlanders, who were Europeans on their father's side, but who have been brought up in the Greenlandic way; and they do not differ from the others in complexion, but only in a few facial features. On the other hand I have seen children of another European by a half-Greenlandic girl, and they were as beautiful as any one may see in Europe.[25]

Numerous other such statements on the physiognomy of the Greenlander might be quoted.

The most significant passage, however, describing the Skraelings, Icelanders, and their intermixed descendants, is possibly that of Nicolas Tunes, who in 1656 made a voyage from Flushing to Davis Strait. Late in June, he landed in latitude 64° 10′ N and thence sailed as far north as latitude 72° N. Most historians are agreed that his landings were made on the west coast of Greenland rather than on the east coast of Baffin Island. Some of the wares he brought home with him, such as elk hides, suggest that he may also have visited Labrador or, if not, attest to communications between it and Greenland at this time. Be that as it may, Nicolas describes the inhabitants of Davis Strait as follows:

> As to the people who inhabit this land, our travellers saw two kinds, who live together in good accord and perfect amity. The one kind are of tall stature, well built physically, of a rather fair complexion and very swift of foot. The others are very much smaller, of olive complexion, their members fairly well proportioned except that their legs are short and thick. The first take delight in hunting, to which they are inclined by reason of their agility and their fine natural aptness; the others occupy themselves with fishing. Both of them have very white and close set teeth, black hair, bright eyes, and features so regular that no deformity is to be remarked. They are also so vigorous and of so strong a constitution that many were seen who, having passed the hundredth year of their life, were still very alert and robust.[26]

We have here a perfect description of Tunnit Icelanders and the offspring which resulted from the intermixture of the Tunnit and the Dorset people. It is the same as the description we possess from Frobisher's voyages of the inhabitants of Baffin Island. The Skraeling is described as follows:

> He was a very . . . good shape . . . and strongly pight . . . made . . . his head, his nek, his brest . . . a very brode face and very fat and fu[ll] his body. But his legs shorter and smaller [than the pro]portion of his body required, and his hands . . . [h]is heare cole blak and long hanging and "tyer" tyed [in a knot] above his forehead. His eyes little and a little (cole) blak beard. His cullor of skyn all over his bo[dy and fa]ce of a dark sallow, much like to the tawny Mores, [or ra]ther to the Tartar nation, whereof I think he was. [His] countenance sullen or churlish and sharp withall.[27]

The Icelanders are described thus:

> They are men of a large corporature and good proportion: their colour is not much unlike the Sunne burnt [English] Country man, who laboureth daily in the Sunne for his living.[28]

Both Stefansson[29] and Duason[30] have pointed out that the ease with which the persons whom Frobisher met were able to make themselves understood by signs, and their acquaintance with writing, indicate previous contact with Europeans, who could hardly be other than the Icelanders in Greenland.

From Gaspar Corte-Real's voyage of 1500, we possess the following information concerning the inhabitants of Labrador at this time. It must refer to the intermixed Tunnit.

> This folk is very barbarous and wild, almost like the people of Santa Cruz,[31] except that they are white, but so tanned by the cold that their whiteness disappears with age, and they become brownish in colour. They are of average stature, and good bowmen. They use burnt poles as javelins and make as good use of them as if they were made of iron. They dress in hides of animals, of which there is a plenteous supply in the country. They believe in supernatural things. They practise matrimony, and are very jealous of their women.[32]

Similar to this, is the description of three men taken captive in Labrador in 1501 and brought to England:

> This yeere also were brought unto the King three men, taken in the newe founde Island, that before I spake of in William Purchas time being Maior. These were clothed in beastes skinnes and ate raw flesh, and spake such speeche that no man coulde understand them, and in their demeanour like to bruite beastes, whom the King kept a time after. Of the which upon two years past I saw apparelled after the manner of Englishmen in Westminster

Pallace, which at that time I could not distinguish from Englishmen, till I was learned what they were. But as for speeche, I heard none of them utter one word.[33]

From the eighteenth century, we have further descriptions of the natives of Labrador which force us to conclude that racial intermixture has taken place, either between Icelanders and Skraelings or between Eskimos and early European mariners or fishermen. The former is the more likely. Pierre François Xavier Charlevoix, in his history of New France which was published in Paris in 1744, writes of these people as follows:

> It is almost the only nation [in America] where the men have beards, and they are so thick and reach to the eyes that the face is hardly distinguishable. For that matter they have something terrifying about them, small eyes with a wild look, large and very dirty teeth; the hair is usually black, sometimes blond, and in great disorder, and all their exterior is of a very brutish appearance. Their manners and character correspond to their evil outward appearance. . . . They have skins which are almost as white as ours, which is no doubt the result of their not going about naked no matter how warm it is. Their blond hair, their beards, their white skin, and the fact that they do not resemble and have very little intercourse with their nearest neighbours, make it impossible to doubt that their origin is other than that of the rest of the inhabitants of America; but the opinion that they are the descendants of the Basques seems to me to have little foundation, especially if it be true, as I am informed, that the languages are unrelated. . . . As far as I am concerned, I am convinced, that they originated in Greenland.[34]

Joseph François Lafitau, in his description of the American "savages," writes in 1724:

> They are people of great stature, well formed, and whiter than other savages; they let their beards grow; they have curly hair and cut it below the ears; on almost all of them it is black, but sometimes blond and in other cases red as on the peoples of northern Europe.[35]

About 1704 Augustin Legardeur, Seigneur de Courtemanche, attempted to establish the first French-Canadian colony in Labrador. He remained there until 1717. In that year he took captive four Eskimos: a woman, two girls, and a boy. The woman related that there were three types of people in Labrador: one with blond hair, a second consisting of dirty black dwarfs, some three feet in height, and a third which possessed only one hand and one foot.[36] All these reports confirm the thesis that the Icelanders intermixed with the Skraelings and emigrated to Baffin Island and Labrador.

It is not, however, only in these lands but farther west in the regions and islands north and west of Hudson Bay that we find evidence of the intermingling of the Icelanders and the Skraelings. General A. W. Greely, an intrepid Arctic explorer, collected most of the evidence found in the reports of earlier explorers in those regions in an article he wrote in 1912.[37] It would be superfluous to quote this at length here, but let it suffice to say that this material deals with the following regions: Lyon Inlet, Southampton Island, Back River, the mouth of the Coppermine River, the Mackenzie River, Cape Bathurst, Peel River, Wallaston Land, and Prince Albert Sound.

We must not, however, pass over the "blond" Eskimos whom Vilhjalmur Stefansson claimed to have discovered on Victoria Island in 1910. Stefansson, whose career ended with his death in 1962 at the age of eighty-two, was undoubtedly the greatest Arctic explorer of this century and possessed a knowledge of the Eskimo second only (if indeed second) to that of Knud Rasmussen. Stefansson was not only a trained anthropologist but was also very well acquainted with the history of the mediæval colonies in Greenland. Like Nansen, he did not believe in the formerly prevalent theory of the extermination of the Icelanders by the Eskimos in warfare but was convinced that racial intermixture accounted for the disappearance of Icelandic culture and Christianity in Greenland. It was therefore no surprise to him when, in the course of his travels in the Arctic, he encountered Eskimos who seemed to possess European features and characteristics, which he could account for only by a hypothesis of considerable infusion of European blood in past centuries. He has vividly described his first encounter with these people who had never before met a white man and who mistook him for an Eskimo. He made detailed observations of them and found some who had blue eyes, light brown beards, light brown, dark brown, or rusty red hair, which was in some cases curly. According to Stefansson, the head measurement revealed that many of these people were of mixed white descent. He did not assert categorically that they were descendants of a mixture of the aborigines of America and the Icelandic colonists but he did very strongly suggest that the most reasonable explanation for the presence of European traits and features in the Victoria Islanders was intermixture between the ancestors of these people and the Icelandic colonists in Greenland. He points out, too, that intermixture between Eskimos, Russians, and Americans in the last two centuries has produced in northern Alaska no such type of Eskimo as those he met on Victoria Island.[38]

Many others have noticed the Icelandic or European physiognomy of the Eskimos of northern Canada. Commenting on the diary of Hans Egede in 1860, the historian and sociologist, Eilert Sundt, says that it is not at all certain that the Norwegian (that is, Icelandic) population of Greenland was completely destroyed by the Eskimos. Although European contacts had been lost, it was possible to live in the Eskimo manner. "Then it could have happened," he writes, "although it is very embarrassing for us to think about it – that one and another of the Norwegian families had to make friends with the Eskimos, take up their manner of living and begin to travel with them along the coast where there is most food." He also mentions that "Rink found so much European appearance among the Greenlanders that he assumes that there had been a considerable mixing of the Norwegians."[39]

Both Roald Amundsen[40] and L. T. Burwash[41] also stress the European aspect of many of the Eskimos whom they met. More weight should probably have been given, however, to the testimony of the only man who in this century has rivalled Stefansson's knowledge of the Eskimos. This was Knud Rasmussen, who was himself part Eskimo, and who has written the best descriptions of the Eskimo in this century. One or two extracts from his writings will not be out of place here. Of the Eskimo west of the Melville Peninsula, whom Rasmussen met in 1922-1923, he writes:

> They were unusually imposing and handsome people, of a type which in many ways differed from that of the common Eskimos; they were tall, well formed people with facial features reminding one more of Indians than Eskimos. Only their big, broad smile and their open, sympathetic disposition were in all ways the same as what is characteristic of all Eskimos; and it was not long until we had become good friends.[42]

Again, he describes two young women from Bathurst Inlet in the following words:

> I went visiting with two young girls as escorts. They were inseparable and seemed to have determined that I become acquainted with everyone in one afternoon. They were taller than the other women, and with their long, braided hair, which at the front fell down in big waves below the temples and cheeks, they resembled Indian more than Eskimo women. Their skin was light and fine, and their faces had the blondness which seems to characterize so many Eskimos in these regions.

He describes an Eskimo who invited him to a séance[43] in the same district as decidedly blond, bald, with a red beard, and a little dash of blue in the eyes. Rasmussen sums up his remarks on the Eskimos in these words:

> In fact these blond types are not peculiar to Victoria Island, but both on King William Island and at the Great Fish River and among the Musk-ox people I met with types which had the same physical features, the same light complexion, the reddish or brownish hair, the gray, often almost blue eyes, a surprisingly luxurious growth of beard – things which otherwise are unusual among Eskimos. All these features I met with among other tribes that have no traditions of blood admixture at any time, and lived so far from the said Copper Eskimos (i.e. the "Blond Eskimo") that influences from these regions may be said to be inconceivable.

It should be pointed out that the remarks quoted above are the studied conclusions of the two men who were best acquainted with the present-day

Eskimos in this century, the latter, a native Greenlander, and the former, a trained anthropologist.[44]

Diamond Jenness attempted to refute Stefansson's contention that the "blond" Eskimos of Victoria Island were the product of an intermixture between the aborigines of America and the mediæval Icelandic inhabitants of Greenland[45] by pointing out that other Eskimos in various parts of the Canadian Arctic displayed similar traits or characteristics which Stefansson called European. The weakness of Jenness's argument is that he failed to realize that all the Eskimos of the Canadian Arctic and Greenland must needs display such European features because they are all to a greater or less extent the product of an intermixture between the Icelanders of Greenland and the Dorset people. Thus it is no refutation of Stefansson's theory to say that the same characteristics as those of the Victoria Islanders can be matched in other parts of the Arctic. We have here another example of the fallacy of a "pure" Eskimo race, a fallacy that results from studying the Eskimo in a historical vacuum without taking into account the groupings of peoples and their intercourse one with another in the Canadian Arctic between the years 1000 and 1500.

Scholars are sometimes surprised to find affinities between the Thule Eskimos, whose eighteenth- and nineteenth-century remains have been excavated by archæologists in Alaska, and those of some Greenland and Labrador Eskimos.[46] This again is a result of the failure to take cognizance of the movements and intermixture of peoples in Greenland and the eastern Canadian Arctic in the later Middle Ages. In all these cases there is nothing which is difficult to explain when viewed in the historical context of the five centuries between 1000 and 1500.

It is beyond the competence of the author of this work to assess the relevance and validity of studies which have been made of the physiognomy of the present-day Eskimo, compared with that of other races. Yet it must be said that, to a layman, some of these studies seem to indicate that the Eskimo is the product of an intermixture between an aboriginal people of America, Mongoloid in origin, and a European people. Dr Bruce Chown's studies[47] of blood groups in anthropology, with special reference to Canadian Indians and Eskimos, have not gone far enough to allow us to assert that the Eskimos are a mixed race but they do suggest that the Eskimo is certainly not a pure Mongoloid. As to the evidence supplied by the cephalic index and height and bone structure, reference may be made to Duason's summary[48] of the investigations carried out on both the Eskimo skeletons and living Eskimos, where all these studies are summarized and statistics given. One should also mention Jorgen Balslev Jorgensen's study of the Eskimo skeleton, in which he minimizes the racial intermixture between the Icelanders and the Skraelings whom he regards as Eskimos.[49] Furthermore,

Dr Lawrence Oschinsky's studies of the dentology of the Eskimo suggests that certain features of this indicate racial intermixture of long standing with Europeans.[50] All these matters, however, must be left to the experts, but it may be said that none of these studies contradicts the thesis advanced in this work.

It may be worth while to mention that this thesis, which explains the disappearance of the Icelandic colonies in Greenland, is one whose antiquity is both hoary and respectable. It is implied in the annals of Bishop Oddsson (1632-1638), which we have already quoted, that in 1342 the inhabitants of Greenland turned toward the people of America.[51] It is again implied by Rector Sigurdur Stefansson of Skalholt.[52] And it is more explicitly stated by Visa-Gisli when in 1647 he wrote to the king as follows:

> . . . and finally complete anarchy reigns – the worst evil of society – or tyranny, and in the end our course is set for the goal of barbarism – from which God preserve us – as our neighbours, the Greenlanders, sorrowful to relate, experienced in former times.[53]

In 1776 the Icelander, Egill Thorhallason, who had spent some time in Greenland, published a book in which, after a discussion of archæology in Greenland, he advanced the same theory.[54]

Thus, before the nineteenth century, there seems to have been virtually complete agreement that the Eskimos were the lineal descendants of the Icelandic boothsitters (the Tunnit) and the Skraelings, the two people – and at this time the only two people – who were to be found in Nordrseta.

There is another and striking confirmation of the intermingling of the two races. This is furnished by certain carvings in reindeer horn and wood, which have been found in cultural sites at Igloolik or near Alarnerk, and wrongly ascribed to the Dorset Culture. The faces shown on these carvings are of two types, one of the Skraeling or Dorset people and one of the Icelanders in Greenland. To suggest, as has been done, that these carvings are the work of the Dorset Eskimos, is most unconvincing for it seems clear that these carvings cannot have been made without iron cutting tools, so sharp are the incisions, so Nordic too, are many of the faces. We need only compare some of the faces on the so-called Dorset carvings with the faces on the crucifix from Sandnes in the Western Settlement, to see that we are dealing with carvings made by the Icelanders in Greenland.[55]

We are actually confronted here with the same kind of error which Jorgen Meldgaard made in his assessment of the settlement which he found south of Igloolik near the hunting-station of Alarnerk.[56] Here he found 208 rectangular depressions, spread over an area of 3 square kms., on raised terraces from 8 to 22 m. above sea-level – the largest pre-historic settlement known in Arctic Canada or Greenland. But this is not a pure Dorset settlement. It

D

is rather an intermixed settlement of Skraelings and Icelanders, with the rectangular houses and the art found in them stemming, not from the Dorset people, but from the Tunnit. No primitive people such as the Dorset could have carved the faces from Igloolik, and this opinion is buttressed by the fact that we possess from Upernavik in Greenland similar carvings showing both Nordic and Skraeling faces.[57]

The Igloolik settlement with its rectangular houses is another proof of the intermingling of the Dorset and Icelandic peoples to form the Thule Culture. Nor can I see anything except Icelandic features in much of the art which Meldgaard classifies as Dorset.[58]

All the above material tends to show that the Thule Culture is the result of an intermingling of the Dorset people with Icelandic boothsitters, who are known in Eskimo legends as the Tunnit and who gradually, in the course of two or three centuries, through the extinction of their language and religion, lost not only these but much of their technical skills and their identity. What was left went to form the modern Eskimo culture of the Canadian Arctic.

CHAPTER 12

Other Aspects of the Eskimo Culture

It has been suggested that the word *karalit*, which the Eskimos in parts of Greenland and in Labrador use to designate themselves, is derived from the Icelandic word *karlar*.[1] The contention is that this is a class name and is based on the division of the classes among the primitive Germans as expounded in Rigsthula, one of the poems in the elder *Edda*. Whether this is so or not is debatable, but there can be no doubt that the Icelanders never called the Eskimos Skraelings (a term reserved for the bearers of the Dorset Culture and, possibly, Indians encountered at the time of the Vinland voyages on the east coast of America), and the modern Eskimos never refer to themselves as such. The word used over one of the boothsitters' regions, Karlbudir, indicates that the word *karl* was used of the Icelandic boothsitters from the farming settlements. In any case, I am not competent to deal with the necessarily philological aspects of this subject.

There are, of course, many other facets in the Eskimo culture and spiritual life. There is the typical square or rectangular house which has been mentioned before. Cranz found this type of house in common use among the Eskimos when he was in Greenland, and there can be little doubt that the platform (*set*) is an Icelandic innovation. It cannot have originated with the Skraelings nor can the window which is a prominent feature of the rectangular house have done so. It must have come from the Icelanders.[2]

The same is true of the Eskimo lamp which is still known by its Icelandic name, *kollek* – the Eskimo pronunciation of the Icelandic word, *kola*. Whether the other peoples of America possessed lamps at this time is doubtful.[3]

E. B. Tylor pointed out long ago that the dress of the Eskimo,

> . . . their coats with hoods, skirts, breeches, stockings, shoes, and boots, form, taken together, a mediæval European costume. The inference is here considered to be that the Greenlanders, early in the eighteenth century, were

wearing the costumes of the old Scandinavians, in which, however, for want of woolen and linen, the material throughout had come to be skin, fur, etc., and the fashion had been in some measure adopted to suit the peculiar conditions of Polar life.[4]

It has also been contended that the sea clothing of the Eskimos is of Icelandic origin; that the treatment of hides and skins among the Eskimos has been learnt from the Icelanders; that the method of sewing is similarly Icelandic; that the coiffure of the Eskimos is Icelandic, going back to Germanic times; in fact, that the whole dress of the Eskimos, both male and female, is modelled on Icelandic mediæval fashions.[5]

It would seem, judging from descriptions of those who first met the Eskimos in the seventeenth and eighteenth centuries, that many of the games and dances of the Eskimos are of Icelandic origin. There is, for instance, the game known in Icelandic as Hel-bridges (heljarbru), in which a number of stones are laid out in a straight line and one has to hop on one foot from stone to stone. The Eskimos agree that the Tunnit played this game.[6] Certain games involving physical prowess, such as the finger-hook and arm-hook, were tests of strength in mediæval Iceland. Forms of Eskimo wrestling are also similar to Icelandic mediæval wrestling. There is considerable evidence that many of the Eskimo dances and songs are based on Icelandic mediæval songs and dances.[7] To kiss a hand in greeting, as was done by one of the people whom John Davis met in 1585, is a European and not an Eskimo custom, as is the manufacture of salt for which he found evidence in Greenland.[8]

There is some evidence to show that the burial customs of the Eskimos stem from the customs of the early Christian Tunnit. As the Tunnit, however, lost their Christian religion in their gradual intermixture with the Skraelings, a combination of heathen and Christian burial customs took place, and evidence of this is to be seen in several graves which have been excavated in various parts of Greenland. This same intermixture of pagan and Christian rites is to be seen in the cairn burial chambers which occur frequently in the Thule Culture.[9]

One might expect to find Icelandic words in the Eskimo language. This, however, is not the case except in a very few instances but is easily explained by the fundamental differences in the two languages. That the Skraelings found it difficult to pronounce Icelandic is to be inferred from the fact that the Skraelings said that the Tunnit barked like dogs, as well as from the fact that several of the consonants in the Icelandic language cannot be employed at the beginning of a word in the Eskimo language because of the difficulties of pronunciation.[10] Egill Thorhallason, in 1776, suggested a few Eskimo words which he thought were derived from the Icelandic. The Icelandic words are shown in parentheses.

Words and names which resemble the Old Norse, as for instance: Hvann (Hvonn), *Angelica*; Kollek (Kola), a lamp; Nisa (Hnisa), a porpoise; Nouk (Hnukur), a high point or ness. Terkelin, Olak, Uttuk, Sunnilik, I think, mean Thorkell, Oli, Otto, Gunnhildur.[11]

Experts are not in agreement on the soundness of some of these derivations.

It is much easier to find mediæval Icelandic geographic concepts. The Eskimos whom Paul Egede met in southern Greenland told him many things about the northern regions, including information about an Icelandic bear trap which they denied that the Eskimos had constructed. The southern Eskimos also knew of the numerous islands north and west of Baffin Bay and of the strong currents in these regions.[12]

There are also vestiges of Eddic cosmology in the legends of the Eskimos, such as the idea that the heavens revolve on a sacred peg or pillar. An Eskimo asked Paul Egede in 1736 whether the heavens were not supported by a pillar and in the next year, another Eskimo referred to the pillar. Several other references are made to this belief. The Norse belief in Bifrost as a bridge leading to heaven is echoed in several Eskimo legends. Some have found traces of the Norse belief in the Midgard Serpent in the legends of the Eskimos, which is there described as a tremendous worm. Similarly, echoes of the tale of Gefjun and the moving of Selund have been detected in the legends of the sorcerer, who towed Disko Island from the vicinity of Godthaab to its present location, some four hundred miles north. Ideas of heaven and hell may reflect either Eddic or Christian beliefs. The Eddic concept of the end of all things, *ragnarok*, has been thought to have been adumbrated in the description that a Greenlander gave Paul Egede of the end of the world. All these Norse or Eddic echoes are confused, if, indeed, they stem thence, but men well acquainted with both the Eskimo legends and Norse mythology have seen a connection.[13]

As to Christianity, David Cranz wrote:

> Yet the Greenlanders may have heard and learned something from the old Norwegian [Icelandic] Christians and then later forgotten this, or changed it through their coarse mentality, provided that the remnants of the Norwegians [Icelanders], as one supposes, united with them and resulted in one people.[14]

He further writes on the past acquaintance of the Eskimo with Christianity:

> Yet one becomes aware, when one has learned their language better, not only from their ideas about the soul and spirits, although their views are very divergent, and their anxiety, which is mixed with dread, about the state of the soul after death, but also from easy conversation with completely uncivilized Greenlanders (if one only does not turn the talk to themselves and try to make them see their duty, for which they have no inclination) that the

opposite is true and that their ancestors worshipped a being on high and served it, but that later generations gradually abandoned this worship, the more they were separated from intelligent, civilized peoples, until finally they lost all clear knowledge of a divine being. That a dim conception of a divine being is still retained by them can be seen by the fact that they accept completely and without protest the teaching about God and his nature (even though they do not wish to follow this belief and thus have not faith). Only their natural idleness, their dumbness and carelessness prevent them adopting right rules of behaviour through an orderly speculation about the work of creation and the dread filled anxiety about the future life.[15]

Hans Egede similarly believed that the Eskimos or their fathers in the past had had some knowledge of Christianity. In 1723, he wrote:

One thing I remarked among them, which leads me to think that they may have had some knowledge of God: viz. that when we have a book and paper in front of us and ask them what these are, they point and look up to heaven and say: Ajune. Yesterday I took Muller's Evangel. Slutz-Kette from my chest in the entrenchment, whereupon the Greenlanders gathered round and wished to see this big book. When I opened the book and showed them a picture of the Lord Jesus and also a picture of the deceased Muller, asking them at the same time what this was, they pointed to heaven and beat their breasts as if they would say: God, their creator.[16]

The early missionaries to Greenland were convinced that the Eskimos knew the stories of the fall, the flood, and the resurrection of Christ. David Cranz believed they also knew something of the Christian teaching of the end of the world.[17]

The being or force called *sila* by the Eskimos may be reminiscent of the Christian God or of the Holy Ghost.[18] Other examples might be cited, but it seems clear from the above that in the process of intermixture with the Tunnit, the Skraelings learned something of both the old Norse mythology and the Christian faith of the mediæval Icelanders. Vague recollections of this survived the extinction of the Icelandic language and the Christian religion.

Much has been written of Icelandic or Norse motifs in the Eskimo legends. This is an obscure and complicated subject which cannot be dealt with here. Let it suffice therefore to refer the reader to what Nansen and Duason have to say on this matter.[19]

Vestiges of political organization have been detected by some in reports given by sixteenth- and seventeenth-century European explorers who visited Greenland and the Canadian Arctic. These are, however, so vague that very little can with certainty be concluded from them. They do, however, indicate that the Skraelings came into contact with a people who were acquainted with and practised organization on both the political and social levels. These can only have been the Tunnit.[20]

CHAPTER 13

The Canadian Arctic in
Mediæval Europe

We have seen that, in the centuries following the tenth, the Icelanders became acquainted with Greenland, Labrador, Hudson Bay, and the islands of the Canadian Arctic archipelago as far west at least as Victoria Island. They also made voyages, although possibly for only a limited number of years, to the eastern shores of the United States. Of this contact we know little beyond the frustrating accounts of the Vinland voyages in the *Eiriks saga rauda* and the *Graenlendinga saga*. In contrast to what it has revealed in the regions of Greenland and the Canadian Arctic, archæology has been able to supply no supplementary information about Vinland.

Yet is seems that some communication with the parts of America south of the Gulf of St Lawrence must have been maintained for at least a century or two. During his excavations at the farmstead of Sandnes in the Western Settlement, Norlund found a piece of anthracite coal. Such coal is not found in Greenland, but only in the New England region of America. He also found a flint arrow-tip of a type not found in Greenland Eskimo finds, but which occurs in northern Canada. Johannes Iversen also found in the Western Settlement a specimen of the plant *Iridace Sisyrhynchium angusti-folium* which grows in the temperate zone in America and not in Greenland. All these point to sailings to the east coast of Canada and the United States, and, of course, it cannot be said that these pieces do not stem from the Vinland voyages of the sagas.[1] It is also to be noticed that references to Vinland are few and far between in the literature and geographical writings of mediæval Europe. It is true that Adam of Bremen, writing about 1076, was acquainted with Vinland and its geographical position.[2] It is again true that Ari Thorgilsson, writing in the first half of the twelfth century, refers incidentally to Vinland in a way that suggests he regarded it as a well-known country.[3] Against this is to be set the fact that Icelandic annals report *sub anno* 1121 that Bishop Eirikr Gnupsson went in search of Vinland, implying, it would seem, that its location was no longer known.[4] Yet

91

in the fourteenth century, as noted above, Icelandic geographical treatises show knowledge of the fact that Vinland lay south of Markland. The maps of Sigurdur Stefansson, from *circa* 1590, and Bishop Hans Poulsen Resen, from 1605, show that the memory if not the location of Vinland was still known at that time.[5]

How much knowledge of Vinland became imbedded in the literature of western and southern Europe in the Middle Ages? There are some who think that the promised land of the saints in the *Navigatio Brendani* is a reflection of the Vinland of the sagas. This seems rather doubtful, although it must be admitted that much of the material of the *Navigatio* stems from the Icelander's knowledge of the North Atlantic.[6] There is a passage in the tenth book of the *Ecclesiastical History* of Ordericus Vitalis which reads:

> The Orkneys and Finlanda, together with Iceland and Greenland – but to the north of the last, there is no land – are subject to the King of Norway, along with several other lands and islands, all the way to Gotland, and treasures from every part of the earth are brought in ships thither.[7]

This work was completed in 1141. It has been contended, because of the mention of islands, and especially Iceland and Greenland, that Finland is a clerical error and that Vinland is the land meant. This may well be so, for the passage clearly shows that Ordericus had knowledge of the geographical location of Iceland and Greenland and thus may well have known of the existence of Vinland.

Certainly, Giraldus Cambrensis (1147-1223) did know the approximate location of Iceland and something of its social structure. He also says that "the land produces and exports gerfalcons and big and noble hawks."[8] One might be tempted to read into this some knowledge of Greenland and Baffin Island, whence came the noblest hawks, but this would probably be too bold an assumption. In any case, one cannot presume knowledge of Vinland on his part. Indeed, it does not seem to be mentioned in later literature in Europe. It is true that there is a reference to "a fair level land where many beautiful [lacuna] in the east there stretches out an arm of land which is nearly all wooded" in the *Inventio fortunata* (1364).[9] Again, in the *Description of Greenland* of Ivar Bardarson, written sometime in the years between 1360 and 1380, a concluding paragraph reads:

> Item much snow falls in Greenland. It is not as cold there as in Iceland or Norway. There grow on the high mountains and below them, all kinds of fruit as big as some apples which are good to eat; there grows the best wheat that can be found.[10]

It might be argued that both these references are to Vinland. Certainly, the one to the wheat, but it would be dangerous to argue from this that either of the authors knew the geographical location of Vinland or had more than a legendary knowledge of it.

It is a different matter in the case of the other lands of the Icelanders in America: Greenland, Labrador, the lands around Hudson Bay, and the islands of the eastern Canadian Arctic. It would be tedious to list all the references to Greenland in mediæval literature and mediæval maps.

In the thirteenth century, Greenland was so well known that the Emperor Frederick II (ob. 1250), in his marvellous book, *The Art of Falconry*, was able to write: "in a certain island, which lies between Norway and Greenland (Gallandium) and which is called in the Teutonic tongue Iceland. . . ."[11] This shows that at least in the circles where falconry was practised, Greenland was better known than Iceland, nor is this strange when we remember that it was through Greenland and Norway that that peerless hunting-bird, the white falcon, reached southern Europe from Baffin Island, where it was captured by the Icelanders.

It is worth noting that such was the fame of the falcons of the Canadian Arctic, Greenland, and Iceland, that the islands of the Canadian Arctic were known often as the Falcon Islands, or the islands whence the falcons came. Thus the Arab writer, Abu'l-Hasan 'Ali Ibn Sa'id, describes Baffin Island as follows:

> The island Harmûsa, which lies in the northernmost part of the inhabited world is almost 12 days' journeys in length and at the centre, ca. 4 days' journeys in breadth. From it, men get the good falcons. Its centre is: longitude 28° and latitude 58°. Around it lie small islands, which have falcons, and to the west of it is the white falcon island, which is almost 7 days' journeys in length from west to east, and almost 4 days' journeys in breadth. To it, and to the little northern island, men go to obtain the white falcons which are brought thence to the Sultan of Egypt, and the price of them, which is usually entered among the expenditures in his treasury, is a thousand denarii, but if they bring dead falcons, they get 500 denarii.
>
> There is also found the polar bear. He walks out into the sea, swims, and catches fish, and what he cannot eat, or what he has no appetite for, these falcons take, and this is their food, for no birds are found there on account of the great cold. The pelts of these bears are soft, and it frequently happens that such pelts are brought to the royal residence in Egypt (or: to the Egyptian lands).[12]

We need not be surprised at this. We know that there were very close relations between the Emperor Frederick II and the Sultan El-Kamil in Damascus and we know that there was great friendship between the King of Norway, Hakon Hakonarson, and Frederick II, who often exchanged gifts – among which will have been hawks and polar bears.[13] Knowledge of the home lands of the rare birds and beasts would accompany the gift, and it is not surprising that the best-informed geographers of Europe in the twelfth and thirteenth centuries, the Moslems, would record some of this information in their writings. It is not an obstacle to the identification of Harmûsa that its geographical position, according to our source, approximates that of Denmark, for it was through Norway or Denmark that these darlings of mediæval rulers reached southern Europe, Africa, and Asia. Moreover, the description of Harmûsa can fit no other island except Baffin Island.

Indeed, the fame of the white falcon carried with it knowledge of its home lands as far east as the realm of the great Khan in the thirteenth century, if not earlier. Marco Polo writes:

> It is also on islands in that sea (north of Bargu at Lake Baikal) that the Gerfalcons are bred. You must know that the place is so far to the north that you leave the North Star somewhat behind you towards the south! The Gerfalcons are so abundant there that the Emperor of China can have as many as he likes to send for. And you must not suppose that those Gerfalcons which the Christians carry into the Tartar dominions go to the Great Khan; they are carried only to the Prince of the Levant.[14]

Here again, only the Canadian archipelago can be meant, and this identification is greatly strengthened if Bargu is rightly believed to lie south of Lake Baikal, for the meridian through the lake would strike Ellesmere Island in the Canadian Arctic. The identification is further strengthened, although indirectly, by a second passage in Marco Polo:

> The country [Russia] is so great that it reaches even to the shores of the Ocean sea, and 'tis in that sea that there are certain islands in which are produced numbers of Gerfalcons and peregrine falcons which are carried in many directions. From Russia also to Oroech [Norway] it is not very far, and the journey could be soon made were it not for the tremendous cold.[15]

Here the reference to Norway can make sense only if its meaning is that the falcons were to be obtained there, having been sent from Iceland or the Canadian Arctic.

In fact, it would be possible to cite many mediæval maps which have transferred to Norway inscriptions belonging to the Arctic lands of Canada and especially Baffin Island. On the two maps of Angelino Dalorto, the one from 1325 has inscribed on Norway: "Here are white bears, and many animals" – "The desert of Norway; thence are brought birds called gerfalcons." And on the one from 1339 is written: "Here are white bears, and they eat raw fish" – "Here are gerfalcons."[16] The Bianco map of 1346 has on Norway: "Very many white bears and gerfalcons and other animals."[17] For other maps containing similar inscriptions from the fourteenth and fifteenth centuries, the reader may be referred to Bjornbo, *Anecdota Cartographica*.

In the same way, the anonymous letter to Pope Nicholas V (1447-1455), giving information about the kingdom of Norway, refers to white falcons, white foxes, white bears, as indigenous to that country.[18] This is, of course, erroneous, just as the descriptions on the maps are, for no white foxes, no white falcons, no polar bears are to be found in Norway. These are to be found only in the Arctic lands of Canada which were part of the realm of the king of Norway. It is not surprising that this confusion should exist in the minds of southern Europeans, especially when many Norwegians, Icelanders, and southern Europeans considered Greenland to be contiguous or connected by a land bridge to Norway, and that these islands lay west and south of it. Some writers call them the African Islands, reflecting the belief which was prevalent in some circles that Vinland was an extension of Africa.[19] Even as early a work as the *Historia Norwegiae* calls the Canadian Arctic archipelago, the Islands of Africa.[20] They are sometimes called the Islands of Iceland and also the Icelands. Even Greenland is sometimes called Iceland.[21]

The thirteenth-century *Geographia Universalis* contains the following passage which cannot refer to Iceland but only to Greenland:

> Yselandia is the outermost part of Europe, on the other side of Norway to the north . . . the more distant parts of it are always buried under enduring ice at the coast of the Outer Sea to the north, where the ocean is frozen, and turns into ice because of the dreadful frost. To the east of it, is Eastern Scythia; to the south, Norway; to the west, the Irish Sea . . . it is called Yselandia, as the land of ice, for there the mountains are said to be frozen together, in the severity of the icy cold. There is crystal. In that region are to be found many very large and wild polar bears, who break the ice assunder with their claws, and make large openings in it. Through these, they dive into the sea, and catch fish beneath the ice. They pull them up through the said openings and carry them to the coast and live on them. The earth is barren of vegetation in a few places. . . . For this reason, the people live, for the most part on fish and game and meat. Sheep cannot live there because of the cold, and therefore the inhabitants protect themselves against the cold and dress in the skins of wild animals which they kill. . . . The people are very fleshy, doughty and white (alba).[22]

Greenland was well known in the fifteenth century, as is seen from the maps of Claudius Clavus Swart and Nicolaus Germanus.[23] No less well known were the islands of the Canadian Arctic. In the Vienna text of the later map of Clavus, we find this inscription: "Norway possesses 18 islands, which are joined to the mainland, because of ice, and are seldom separated from it, unless the summer be very warm."[24]

Johann Schöner similarly reports that Norway possesses eighteen islands which are joined to the mainland because of ice, except in a very hot summer. He then goes on to say that one of them is Tile, which is a part of Norway but not reckoned as an island, although separated by a channel from the mainland, for the ice joins it to the mainland for eight or nine months of the year and therefore it is reckoned a part of it. These are again the Arctic Islands of Canada and Tile is very likely Ellesmere Island.[25]

One might go on to mention other references to the Canadian Arctic in mediæval writings. The Hyperborei and Arumpei, which are mentioned in the works of Roger Bacon and appear in the polar regions on a circular map in the *Imago mundi* of Cardinal Pierre d'Ailly (1350-1420), are probably references to the Icelanders or their lands in the Canadian Arctic.[26] The *Inventio fortunata* (*circa* 1364) seems to have contained detailed descriptions of the eastern part of the Canadian Arctic.[27] Cardinal Guillaume Fillastre (*ob.* 1428) made an annotation on the earlier map of Clavus to this effect:

> However, he says nothing about the two bays, the one at Norway and the one at Greenland. In these northerly regions, various nations live, including Unipeds and pygmies (pimei); item giants (griffones) as in the Orient, as is shown on the sheet.[28]

We might also mention the information concerning the Arctic lands possessed by the Portuguese court in the fifteenth century, but this will be dealt with later.

But what do mediæval maps show us as to the transmission of the geographical lore of the Icelanders and Scandinavians to western and southern Europe from the time of the settlement of Greenland to the sixteenth century? One of the earliest depictions of Greenland and the neighbouring regions is on the map of Heinrich of Mainz, which is dated from 1100 or 1110. This is a wheel map (a circular map with Jerusalem as the centre of the world), which depicts the Scandinavian Peninsula as jutting out to the west of the Baltic. Iceland is situated in a bay of the peninsula. To the west of this bay another peninsula veers to the west which bears the inscription Rozeya, and southwest of this peninsula, is an island marked Ganzmir. Part of another island is shown at the edge of the map separated by a narrow sea from Ganzmir. West of Rozeya is another bay and a peninsula.[29] What have we here? Rozeya is unquestionably Greenland, the name being derived from *ros* or *ross*, part of *rostungur* or *rosshvalur*, that is, the walrus, and Ganzmir is probably the region around Greipar which was the nearest hunting-station for walrus north of the farming settlements. The bay west of Greenland is the tract of sea separating Greenland from the islands of the eastern Canadian Arctic, and the farther bay may be Hudson Bay, although these regions are understandably treated as parts of eastern Asia.

A similar depiction is to be found on the Hereford map which dates from 1280. Greenland is again shown as a peninsula and called Rozeya, but in this case, Ganzmir appears on its west coast. The two bays are again shown as on the earlier map.[30]

The name Albania, or White Men's Land, occurs, it seems, as a description of Greenland and possibly adjacent regions. On the somewhat earlier Beatus-type map from Osma, dated 1203, a peninsula juts out which is called *aluania*, that is, Albania, on which is inscribed *mons aquilonis* (the mountain of the north, or Himinrodafjall). West of *aluania* there is a bay called *mare caspium*, that is, the Caspian Sea. This Albania, which can only be Greenland, has thus been confused with the Albania in southern Europe.[31]

The Psalter map from London, dating from the thirteenth century, contains in the place of Rozeya and *aluania*, the words *ipboria* and *arumphe*. On the mainland are shown two Albanias, Albania Inferior and Albania Superior. The latter is no doubt the White Men's Land of the sagas (*hvitramannaland*) which was a term employed over all the American territories through which the Icelanders roamed in the Middle Ages. The Psalter map also shows, just off Albania Superior, an island called *abatia in* (Albania insula), and the following inscription: "abatia insula is very large; it is three days' sailing to it from the coast of Scythia," that is, from the shores of east Asia.[32]

On later maps, we come across the concept of white people under the title of *quij populi*, that is, *quit populi*, which is a translation of the Icelandic *hvitir menn* (white men). An example of this is the globe of Gemma Frisius and Gerhard Mercator from 1537 and the Nancy globe from 1545 which contains the word "QII" opposite Greenland.[33] Again on the Nancy map of Clavus, from about 1427, we find the words *quiteum mare*, which is no doubt a mistake for *quitum mare*.[34]

The islands of the Canadian Arctic are shown on other maps such as the Catalan world map in the Biblioteca Estens in Modena from 1350, which contains the inscription, "on these islands are many beautiful gerfalcons and falcons and the inhabitants of the island do not dare to capture them without the permission of the great Khan, the ruler of all the Tartars."[35] A similar inscription is found on the Mallorca map in the National Archives in Paris, which dates from 1375.[36] On the Borgia map, which dates from the early fifteenth century, there is shown at the Bay of Albania in Asia, a European type of boat, and on the coast, animals. Between the sea and Montes Hyperborei there occurs the inscription, "Albania the Great, dogs stronger than lions."[37] The Catalan world map also shows the islands of the Canadian Arctic under the title of "islandes."

Even Arabic writers were acquainted with Greenland and the Arctic archipelago. Sjams Ad-Din Abu 'Abdallah Muhammed Ad-Dimasjof (1256-1327) writes of an island thus:

In the sea on the far side of the deserts of Qipdjakanna [south Russia, Turkestan, and Siberia] on the 63° latitude, it is 8 days' journeys long, but its breadth varies to 3 days' journeys. In this sea is a large island, inhabited by men who are tall, of light complexion, have blond hair and blue eyes, and who can hardly understand the speech of humans. It is called the Ice Sea, because it all freezes in the winter, and because it is surrounded by icebergs. They are formed when in the winter, the waves impelled by the wind break against the beach. The moment they freeze, they are thrown against the ice-covered edges, which grow bit by bit and layer by layer, until they form the peaked heights, and walls which surround it.[38]

This can only be Greenland.

This Albania, which is identified as a portion of Scythia, can only have been the lands of the Icelanders in America or what was believed to be Asia at that time. Bjorn Jonsson, writing in the eighteenth century, says: "The late Rev. Erlendur Thordarson had acquired abroad a map of the Albania, or Hvitramannaland, which lies opposite Vinland the Good."[39]

Two maps, one from the fourteenth century and one from the fifteenth, amply testify to the knowledge of the lands of America which were peopled by the Icelanders at this time. The first is the Medici marine chart from 1351. This shows Greenland as an extension of Norway but nothing beyond it.[40] On the other hand the second map, the Genoa world map from 1447 or 1457, shows the whole of the eastern Canadian Arctic. This shows Norway, and west of it a peninsula which can only be Greenland. Lelewel thought he could read the name Grinland but this is not now possible because the inscription has faded so much. This, however, is of little consequence as there is pictured on it a polar bear which can only refer to Greenland. Next to it is a bay filled with many islands and then a large land mass on which is depicted a fox. This must be Baffin Island, which is recorded in the sagas as being the land of foxes. West of it, with two or three islands, is Hudson Bay.[41]

In the fifteenth century the Dane, Claudius Clavus Swart, drew at least two maps of Greenland. The first of these was made during the years 1413-1427. The second is after 1450. On it is the inscription: "Norway possesses eighteen islands which in the winter are because of ice contiguous to the mainland and are seldom separated from it unless the summer is very hot."[42] Again, Nicolaus Germanus, after the year 1466, drew a world map on which he shows Greenland. He must have obtained his information from the Greenlanders, for on the map is shown an *insula glaciei* which can only be Newfoundland and points to knowledge derived from Greenland of the ice in the Labrador current.[43]

In 1492 Martin Behaim constructed his famous globe on which the Arctic regions of Canada are depicted. Here two Greenlands are shown: one, with the name Groenland, connected by a land bridge with Norway, and the other an island, which is nameless, but has the shape of Greenland, on which is shown a hunter in a very full dress, firing an arrow at a polar bear. Opposite this is shown another large island with the inscription, "here one catches white falcons," which must obviously be Baffin Island. Sixteen other islands are shown off these two large islands.[44] We have here two types of information recorded on the same map, one a traditional or classical depiction of the north and the other stemming from knowledge of these lands furnished by the Icelanders in Greenland or possibly from information supplied by the Portuguese contacts with Denmark.

Many other maps might be discussed, but what has been said here is sufficient to show that knowledge of the Arctic regions of Canada had penetrated the literature and cartography of the pre-Columbian period of European history. It is significant, too, that the Papal Bull of 1493, dividing the world between Spain and Portugal, makes no mention of the north-western quarter of the globe, that is, the lands belonging to the King of Denmark which were known by some such name as Albania Superior or White Men's Land. This argues that it was well known that these lands had long been inhabited by Christians and had long been under the jurisdiction of a Christian state.

CHAPTER 14

The Mythical Voyages to America

So far we have dealt with the voyages to the New World that have their source in historical fact. Much has also been written, however, of other pre-Columbian voyages and, fabulous as most of them may be, they deserve mention. The voyage of Bishop Eirikr Gnupsson, who sailed from Greenland in 1121 in search of Vinland, has already been mentioned. We know nothing of this voyage beyond the bald entry in the Icelandic annals. Yet this has not prevented the spinning of fantastic tales. A flourishing Norse Christian colony has been postulated and Eirikr has been credited with the building of a round church at Newport, Rhode Island – the famous Newport Tower which recent archæological work has shown to be unquestionably built in the seventeenth century colonial period of American history.[1]

In the twelfth century, a Welsh prince by the name of Madoc is also supposed to have visited America and established colonies there. The location of these ranges from the Maritimes and Newfoundland to Mexico. Madoc is supposed to have gone to America and found the country so attractive that he returned to Wales and took out a large band of Welshmen to some place in America. Both the Yarmouth Stone and the Newport Tower have been ascribed to Madoc and he has also been identified as Quetzalcoatl, the legendary white man or god who came to Mexico in the Middle Ages. Madoc and his colonists are said to have taught the Indians the Welsh language and, in the colonial period of America, Welsh-speaking Indians were often reported; when anyone wished to track them down, however, they were never to be found. The truth of the matter is that Madoc's voyage to America is a wholly legendary concoction of the Tudor Englishmen who wished to establish a claim for the English possession of America.[2]

One of the most persistent myths is that the Irish discovered America even before the Norse. This takes several forms. Sometimes the discovery is attributed to St Brendan (ob. 584). This view is based on the fable-filled *Navigatio Brendani*, which dates from the tenth or eleventh century. What facts it has stem from relations of Irish monks who, in the seventh, eighth, and ninth centuries, visited the islands of the north Atlantic, and the accounts given by Norsemen who settled Iceland and Greenland.[3] There is no question that the Irish in their curraghs made their way to Iceland as early as, if not earlier than, the eighth century. When the Norse came to Iceland *circa* 870, they found Irish monks (*papar*) there. These fled from the heathen Norse and, according to another version of the Irish discovery of America, made their way to America where they established a flourishing colony, although some would have it that they went to Greenland where they "went native" and "fathered a tribe of nominally Christian half-castes on Eskimo women."[4]

Most writers, however, locate the Irish colony in or around the Gulf of St Lawrence, basing their arguments for the existence of this colony on three passages in the Icelandic sagas which refer to a White Men's Land or Ireland the Great. It may be stated categorically that all these passages are the result of a confusion in the minds of the saga writers between a region in Ireland known as Tir na-Fer Finn (White Men's Land) and the Icelandic lands in America which were then known as White Men's Land or Albania.[5]

The absurdity of the thesis of an Irish colony in America which has left no archæological traces whatsoever should not require discussion, but reputable historians still give credence to these fancies, not to mention those who believe that Patee's Caves at North Salem, New Hampshire, are the work of Irish monks. Recent writings tend to identify them equally absurdly as a megalithic-type sanctuary of the pre-Christian era.[6] The passages on which the belief in Hvitramannaland is based occur in the *Landnamabok*, the *Eyrbyggja saga*, and the *Eiriks saga rauda*. The passage in the oldest of these, *Eiriks saga*, as referred to in Chapter 3, tells of the capture of two Skraeling youths in Labrador:

> They said that a land lay there opposite their land, which was inhabited by men who wore white clothes and carried poles before them, to which poles cloths were attached, and that they yelled loudly, and men deem that this was White Men's Land or Ireland the Great.[7]

No reliance can be placed on this passage. The names given by the youths, according to Thalbitzer, are not names, and to think, as some do, that the boys are here describing either a religious procession or a Germanic military procession, is to strain one's credulity.[8]

The passage in *Landnamabok* is even more far-fetched:

> Ari . . . was driven across the sea by heavy storms to Hvitramannaland which some call Ireland the Great. It lies west in the sea near Vinland the Good. It is said that one can sail to it (from Ireland) in six days. Ari was unable to escape and was baptized there. This tale was first told by Hrafn Limerick-farer who had spent much time in Limerick in Ireland. Thorkell

Gellisson said also that Icelanders had related on the basis of what they had heard from Thorfinn, Earl of the Orkneys, that Ari had been both seen and recognized in Hvitramannaland from which he was not permitted to depart, but where he was nevertheless held in great esteem.[9]

There is no land six days west of Ireland, and one may wonder that an inhabitant or a visitor to Limerick and an Earl of the Orkneys were so cognizant of events in America.

The third reference, from the *Eyrbyggja saga*, tells of a certain Gudleifr Gunnlaugsson, an Icelandic merchant who set out from Dublin for Iceland. Strangely enough, he sailed along the west coast of Ireland. He encountered storms and northeast winds and was driven far west and southwest over the sea. Finally he came to a land which neither he nor his crew recognized. They landed there and were met by men whose language they could not understand but which they thought was probably Irish. (Having spent some time in Ireland, it might be thought that they would have recognized Irish, but then they may have spent all their time among the Norse settlers there.) Several hundred men surrounded them and they were taken captive and brought inland. Their fate was then debated, some wishing to kill them and some to enslave them. While their fate was still in suspense, a band of men came riding to the spot, led by an elderly white-haired man, whom all the natives saluted as if their leader. He spoke to Gudleifr and his men in the Norse language and, after enquiring about people in Iceland, the chieftain set them free and gave them presents to take to Iceland.[10]

The saga does not identify this country as Ireland the Great, but many have assumed that the reference is to it. The whole tale cannot, of course, refer to America, for men did not ride horses in America in the eleventh or twelfth centuries. On these three flimsy narratives, we are asked to believe in a flourishing Irish colony, of which no trace has ever been found except in the confused imagination of the saga writers.

Equally preposterous and based on even flimsier evidence, is the tale of a royal Norwegian expedition which is supposed to have been sent out from Norway in the year 1355. It has even been called a Holy Crusade and "one of the world's greatest exploration expeditions." The tale is as follows, according to Hjalmar R. Holand, the greatest champion of the theory that this expedition ever took place. In 1342, we have learned from the annals of Bishop Oddsson, which he completed writing in 1637 and which are undoubtedly based on earlier annals which existed in the archives of Skalholt, that the inhabitants of the Western Settlement apostasized from the Christian faith and turned themselves to the people of America. News of this event did not reach Norway until 1354, because of infrequent sailings and the complete interruption of sailings to Greenland when the Black Death struck Norway in 1349. The news of this wholesale falling away from the faith so affected King Magnus Eiriksson that on October 28, 1354, he issued a letter to Poul Knutsson, a former local legal officer, instructing him "to take all the men who shall go in the knorr [the king's ship in the possession of the crown of Norway, which was regularly used for sailing between Bergen and Greenland] whether they be named or not named, from my bodyguard or other men's attendants." He was to proceed with these men to Greenland and, the letter continues, "we ask that you accept this our command with a right good will for the cause, as we do it for the honor of God and for the sake of our soul and our predecessors, who have introduced Christianity in Greenland and maintained it to this day, and we will not let it perish (*nederfalle*) in our days." This letter is genuine, but it is also the sole document surviving from the Middle Ages concerning this matter and furnishes no proof that the expedition ever sailed.[11]

We are, however, asked to believe that this expedition took place and that its timetable can be "hypothecated as follows." In spite of the urgency expressed in the king's letter, the expedition did not sail in 1355, "which was so stormy in the north that, according to Icelandic annals for that year, no ships ventured out."[12] In what Icelandic annal this is stated we do not know, but Icelandic annals do state that Bishop Gyrdr went abroad from Iceland in that year.[13]

Holand has also stated that Bishop Arne of Greenland had died in 1348 or 1349, and that the fact that his successor, Bishop Alfr, was not consecrated until 1365 implies that "no vessel had returned from Greenland in the intervening years until shortly before 1365.[14] Holand forgets to mention in this connection that Bishop Jon Skalli had been consecrated Bishop of Greenland in 1343 when a false report of Bishop Arne's death reached Norway and that he retained the title of Bishop of Greenland until he was consecrated Bishop of Holar in 1357.[15] If no vessel returned from Greenland from 1349 until shortly before 1365, several other implications arise. We know that a ship arrived in Iceland from Greenland in 1347.[16] Was this the ship that brought news of the apostasy? If so, or if the news were brought in 1348 or 1349 before Bishop Alfr's death, which occurred in 1376, how is it to be explained that King Magnus delayed five to seven years before issuing the letter in which he says, "We will not let it [Christianity in Greenland] perish in our day"? Why did he, on October 28, suddenly issue a frantic order to equip an expedition to Greenland at a time of the year when such an expedition could not possibly sail for several months? It is true that Icelandic annals state that no ship came to Iceland in 1355 but they do not say that that year was so stormy in the north that no ships ventured out. In fact, they record the voyage abroad from Iceland of both Bishop Gyrdr and an Andreas Gislasson. There are no grounds for thinking that the weather was such that a ship could not reach Greenland from Norway. But

Holand now holds that the expedition departed in 1356, although, of course, there is no evidence that it ever departed. He then states that the expedition probably stayed some days in the Eastern Settlement, made a trip to the Western Settlement to see if the apostates had returned, then sailed back to the Eastern Settlement. Desiring to establish a "headquarters in a good harbor where a fortified base of operations could be built and food grown," Knutsson and his men sailed for Vinland where they established a fortified base, likely at Rhode Island. Here they erected the Newport Tower. This view is maintained in spite of overwhelming evidence for the construction of this tower by seventeenth-century colonists. It is somewhat strange, too, to find Knutsson establishing his headquarters as far south as Rhode Island, when we are told that the lost Greenlanders "were accustomed to a cool climate" and the search would therefore have to be "mainly northward."[17] We are told that in 1358, thirty men in two light ships, which were pre-sumably carried on the *knorr* for such an emergency, searched the shore from Rhode Island to the north of Nova Scotia. "In 1359 the islands to north and Newfoundland could perhaps be covered; and in 1360 the St. Lawrence basin and part of the coast of Labrador, probably as far north as Hamilton Inlet."[18] Let us remember that all this is sheer conjecture.

Having failed to find the apostates on the east coast, the party sailed north around Labrador, west to Hudson Bay, hopefully looking for "green meadows." Late in the season, their hopes, it may be presumed, now utterly dashed, they reached the mouth of the Nelson River "perhaps in the fall of 1361." Dissension now arose as to the route to be taken for the return journey to the base in Vinland. Twenty men of the thirty wished to sail up the Nelson and thus make their way to Vinland, although it meant going into the unknown, but perhaps they would find themselves in the fabulous lands which Marco Polo had so enticingly described. The rest of the party was left to guard the two light ships. We are not told where the twenty adventuresome souls got the boat large enough to carry them up the Nelson, across the length of Lake Winnipeg, and up the Red into the interior of what is now Minnesota, for that is the locality which these twenty men, we are told, eventually reached. While there, they camped by two skerries. Ten of them went fishing one day and when they came home they found ten men red with blood and dead. The remaining ten then presumably travelled for three or four days, covering seventy-five miles, until they found a stone on which they could carve a runic inscription. The inscription reads:

8 Goths [Swedes] and 22 Norwegians on exploration journey from Vinland westward. We had camp by two skerries, one day's journey north from this stone. We were and fish[ed] one day. After we came home [we] found 10

[of our] men red with blood and dead. AVM [Ave Virgo Maria] save [us] from evil.

[We] have ten men by the sea to look after our ship[s] fourteen days' journey from this island. Year 1362.[19]

We are given to understand that, after carving this inscription, the surviving ten fell in with the Mandan Indians, taught them the arts of European civilization and the Christian religion, and made them "the greatest enigma in the study of North American Indians."[20] The survivors may even have carved another rune stone for, in 1738, Pierre de la Verendrye, visiting the Mandans in North Dakota, discovered a pillar of stone "in which was fixed a small stone inscribed on both sides with unknown characters." Unable to decipher the inscription, although he kept it with him for five years, he showed it to some Jesuit scholars in Quebec in 1743. They found the inscribed characters "perfectly like Tatarian inscriptions" but could not translate it, so the stone with its "mystic inscription" was sent to Count Maurepas, the Minister of Colonies in Paris. Since Tatarian inscription and runic inscription look almost the same, the Jesuits may have been mistaken. Unfortunately, the stone disappeared shortly after its arrival in Paris and has not been seen since.[21]

Fortunately, however, the earlier runic stone was discovered five hundred and thirty-six years later, clasped, it is said, in the roots of a tree on a farm near Kensington in Minnesota. Olaf Ohman, the owner of the farm, found it, he said, while grubbing. Brought to the attention of runologists, it was immediately pronounced a forgery and lay neglected until it was rediscovered in 1907 by Holand, who has from then to this day been the indefatigable defender of the authenticity of this inscription, which may be confidently pronounced a nineteenth-century concoction and whose authenticity not one runologist has ventured to defend.[22]

But what happened to the ten men left at the mouth of the Nelson? In answering this question, Holand has produced an equally fascinating story.[23] One of the ten men was none other than a friar from Oxford named Nicholas of Lynn, a mathematician, maker of an astrolabe, intrepid Arctic explorer, and author of a famous geographical treatise entitled *Inventio fortunata*. The stay at the mouth of the Nelson enabled Nicholas to use his astrolabe to good advantage and also discover the location of the magnetic pole. He and seven others of the party of ten returned to Norway in 1363 or 1364, after having evidently abandoned all hope for the survival and return of their twenty companions who had gone to Minnesota. There they told of the wonders they had seen and Nicholas wrote the *Inventio fortunata*. Other scholars have recently taken a slightly different view of Nicholas, while still assigning him an exalted role in the history of scientific exploration. Helge Ingstad has made him the leader of the earliest English expedition to the Arctic.[24] Asgaut Steinnes, state archivist of Norway, asserts that Nicholas sailed from Hull in 1360 on a ship with an English crew.[25] Professor E. G. R. Taylor of the University of London has called him the "outstanding figure of the fourteenth century in geographical research."[26] Samuel Varshavsky has recently credited Nicholas with the discovery of America, one hundred and thirty years before Columbus.[27]

For all these claims there is hardly a shred of evidence, except possibly that of Professor Taylor, and even this is slim indeed. The only reason for ascribing the *Inventio fortunata* to Nicholas is that Richard Hakluyt has entitled a legend on Mercator's map which he printed in his *Navigations*, "The voyage of Nicholas de Lynna, a Franciscan Frier, and an excellent Mathematician of Oxford." In a second title, Hakluyt also claims for Nicholas the honour of writing the *Inventio*: "A Testimonie of the learned Mathematician master John Dee, touching the foresaid voyage of Nicholas De Linna."[28] Neither extract, however, mentions the "explorer" and author of the *Inventio* by name. In fact, Dee's account reads as follows:

> Anno 1360 (that is to wit, in the 34 yeere of the reigne of the triumphant king Edward the third) a frier of Oxford, being a good Astronomer, went in companie with others to the most Northren Islands of the world, and there leaving his company together, hee travailed alone, and purposely described all the Northerne Islands, with the indrawing seas: and the record thereof at his returne he delivered to the king of England. The name of which booke is Inventio Fortunata (aliter fortunae) qui liber incipit a gradu 54. usque ad polum. Which frier for sundry purposes after that did five times passe from England thither, and home againe.[29]

It may be stated conclusively that Nicholas of Lynn was not the author of the *Inventio fortunata*. The author is always described as a Franciscan or a Minorite, and Nicholas was a Carmelite. We know little about him, not even that he ever wrote a book on his travels such as the contemporary Franciscan, Hugh of Ireland, did, and whose name has been suggested as the author.[30] This, however, is most unlikely, for the author is always called English, and Hugh is always identified with Ireland. We are faced with the fact that the author of the *Inventio* is unknown and we know nothing about him except that he was a mathematician and acquainted with the astrolabe.

The anonymity of the author of the *Inventio* does not, of course, answer the question, "Did he visit America?" It may be said at once, nevertheless, that he certainly did not visit the Canadian Arctic as a member of a mythical Norwegian expedition which is supposed to have been in American and Canadian waters and in the interior of Minnesota in the years 1355-1364. Had such an expedition taken place, it would certainly be mentioned in some surviving sources and particularly the so-called *Description of Greenland* which stems from the priest Ivar Bardarson. Ivar was administrator of the see of Gardar in the years *circa* 1340-1362, the very years in which the Knutsson expedition is supposed to have come to Greenland and then spent eight or nine years reconnoitring the east coast of America, the shores of Labrador and Hudson Bay, and the interior of Manitoba and Minnesota in their search for the Icelanders who had in 1342 renounced the Christian faith and turned to the peoples of America. Ivar was actually the man who was sent to the Western Settlement in 1342 and found no inhabitants there, Christian or heathen, and only wild sheep and cattle. As administrator of the see of Gardar, he would be the first man to whom a royal expedition sent to seek out the apostate inhabitants of the Western Settlement would turn. Ivar returned to Norway in 1363 or 1364, when the *Inventio fortunata* is said to have been written.[31]

Unfortunately the *Inventio* is no longer extant, but it is mentioned and some of its contents summarized in the fifteenth and sixteenth centuries. The earliest mention of it occurs in 1497. This is in a letter from an English merchant, John Day, addressed to the Lord Grand Admiral of Spain, probably Columbus himself. It begins:

> Your Lordship's servant brought me your letter. I have seen its contents and would be most desirous and most happy to serve you. I do not find the book *Inventio Fortunata* and I thought that I (or he) was bringing it with my things, and I am very sorry not to find it because I wanted very much to serve you. I am sending the other book of Marco Polo . . .[32]

Again, on his world maps dating from 1507 and 1508, Johannes Ruysch has four legends stemming from the *Inventio fortunata*. Both Fernando, the son of Columbus, and Bartolomé de Las Casas refer to it in their writings.[33]

The most detailed information as to the contents of the *Inventio*, however, is supplied by Mercator, who has six or seven legends based on it on his chart of the polar regions from 1569. In addition he supplied John Dee, in a letter dated April 20, 1577, with a summary of its contents based on a fourteenth-century book written by a certain Jacobus Cnoyen of Herzogenbusch, of whom nothing is known. I have elsewhere tried to analyse this material and have come to the conclusion that it reveals only the knowledge which the Icelanders in Greenland and adjacent lands had acquired in the course of their almost four-hundred-year-old occupancy of these lands.[34] The *Inventio* contains some fantastic material, such as the expedition of King Arthur to Greenland about 530 and, in garbled form, much information about the Canadian Arctic. It shows acquaintance with Hudson Strait and Hudson Bay, Fox Basin, possibly Fury and Hecla Straits, Baffin and Ellesmere Islands, Lancaster Sound, Jones Sound, as well as the Thule district of Greenland, the mountains south of Thule, the high-pressure region in the north, and the deviation of the compass. It may also, though this is doubtful, reveal a knowledge of Vinland. All this had long been known to the Icelanders. What is new is only the mention of the astrolabe and possibly the employment of degrees of latitude.[35]

It is difficult to believe, however, that the Minorite who is said to have travelled alone through the Arctic by his magical arts, not once but six times, ever visited these regions. The garbled form in which the information is found in the extracts we possess from the *Inventio* argues against personal knowledge of the regions described and, indeed, neither Ruysch nor Mercator could depict from it anything like a true picture of the Canadian Arctic and polar regions. There is only one source which suggests itself for the information contained in the *Inventio* and that is Ivar Bardarson, but in transcribing the information which Ivar gave, the author – through lack of understanding or simply confusion – presented a most muddled picture of the regions which must have been well known to Ivar and through which he may well have made five or six tours of duty. One cannot help agreeing with Thomas Blundeville, who had this to say about the author of the *Inventio fortunata*:

> Neither doe I beleeve that the Fryer of Oxford, by virtue of his Art Magicke, ever came so nigh the Pole to measure with his Astrolabe those cold parts together with the foure floods, which Mercator and Bernardus do describe both in the front, and also in the nether end of their mapes, and unlesse hee had some colde devil out of the middle Region of the aire to be his guide, and therefore I take them in mine opinion to be meer fables.[36]

The reader may now well ask what became of the main part of the expedition that remained on the fortified base on Rhode Island and there constructed the Newport Tower. What became of the *knorr*? What was the number of the men who originally sailed in the *knorr* and the number who, we are told, dwelt for many years in Newport and left behind no artifacts of other signs of their occupation of this site? Silence shrouds their fate, and their ghosts are seen no longer, not even that of the old Indian chief, a woman bearing the name of Magnus – the name of the king who, three centuries earlier, had ordered the Knutsson expedition – and who was captured and put to death by the English in 1676. Only the tower remains, devoid of any artifact which might attest to the presence of Norsemen.[37]

But we are not done with myths. In 1398, we are told, Henry Sinclair discovered Nova Scotia. This again is a fascinating tale.

In 1558, there was published in Venice a book purporting to record that two native sons, Antonio and Nicolo Zeno, sailed into the north Atlantic in the last two decades of the fourteenth century. Here they entered the service of a prince named Zichmni and made many voyages among the islands of the north Atlantic, sometimes accompanied by the prince.

On these voyages, as was to be expected, they discovered many marvellous things. They were, for instance, looking for a land encountered some time after 1370 by some fishermen from the realms of Zichmni. These fishermen were driven by a storm to an island called Estotiland and there spent some five years on the island and learned the language of the inhabitants. The latter were very intelligent and possessed all the arts known to Europeans. In the king's library were to be found Latin books but unfortunately the inhabitants, not knowing Latin, could not read them. All kinds of metals existed on the island and especially an abundance of gold. The residents traded with Greenland, importing thence furs, brimstone, and pitch. One of the fishermen then spent thirteen years in other parts of the country which were very different from the parts first encountered. Here, the people were rude and uncultivated and ran around naked, suffering cruelly from the cold. Fortune favoured the fisherman and he was able to return home, where his recital of the riches of Estotiland, which some commentators on the Zeno narrative confidently identify as Newfoundland, prompted one of Zichmni's expeditions.[38]

On an earlier voyage, Nicolo Zeno visited Greenland (Engroneland) where, on the east coast somewhere around latitude 75° N, he encountered a Dominican monastery and a church dedicated to St Thomas, situated near a hill which spat fire like Vesuvius and Etna. The monastery was also situated near hot springs which the ingenious monks used to heat the buildings. No less ingenious were the monks in constructing their buildings. Here, they used only the cinders which the fiery hill spewed out on the surrounding countryside. These cinders are said to be indestructible, very light, and of great beauty and consistency. The friars possessed vessels of brass, tin, and stone. They had beautiful gardens. They were also able to offer employment in various handicrafts to workmen and masters who flocked to the spot, attracted by the high pay and pleasant life.[39]

One would presume that such absurdities as these would be enough to discredit the Zeno narrative, but such has not proved to be the case. Speculation continues as to the identity of Prince Zichmni. The most popular nominee for this honour seems to be Henry Sinclair, Earl of the Orkneys, who died in 1404. He was a capable prince but there is no record of his ever having made trans-Atlantic voyages. However, identified as Zichmni, he is credited with the discovery or rediscovery of Nova Scotia in 1398 and only recently his travels and explorations there have been traced in great detail. It has also emerged from these investigations that the legendary hero of the Micmac Indians, Glooscap, is none other than Henry Sinclair, Earl of the Orkneys. The Micmacs had difficulty in pronouncing Norse names and "Jarl Sinclair" became, in their mouths, "Glooscap," just as "Sinclair" had become, in the inept mouths of the Venetians, "Zichmni."[40]

The protagonists of the identity of Sinclair with Zichmni and Glooscap find corroboration for their views in some obscure markings on a rocky ledge at Westford, Massachusetts, which they believe to depict a helmeted knight, holding a sword, a shield, and clad in armour. Even heraldic emblems are present which have enabled the figure to be identified as that of a late fourteenth-century knight "a kin to the first Sinclair, Earl of Orkney." Some, however, see the figure as that of an Indian and others fail to see any identifiable figure at all.[41]

As long ago as 1898, Lucas showed that the Zeno narrative is a sixteenth-century fabrication, concocted possibly to add glory and lustre to the Venetians by giving them a share in the discovery of lands west of the Atlantic.[42] One can only marvel that such a fantastic tale ever received, and even more surprising, still continues to receive, credence.

Included with the Zeno narrative was a map of the northern regions. This map, far from dating from the fourteenth century, is, like the narrative, a sixteenth-century product based, however, on the fifteenth-century maps of Swart and the sixteenth-century map of the northern regions of Olaus Magnus. It shows some imaginary islands and because it was accepted by many as a true depiction of the north, continued to lead mariners astray for a century or more after its appearance.

Before leaving this subject of legendary contacts with Greenland and Canada in the Middle Ages, mention may be made of one or two minor things. Icelandic annals *sub anno* 1285 mention that land was found in the west opposite Iceland, that Duneyjar (Down Islands) were found, that two Helgasons found a new land, and in another version, that the Helgasons sailed to the wastes of Greenland. We do not know what lands these were. In the Atlantic there were no undiscovered lands. If the Arctic north of Iceland is meant, the land could only be Jan Mayen. The thesis that the Helgasons must have spent some time in Labrador is untenable. That country was too well known to be called a new land.[43]

Equally untenable is the belief that the presence of the Vikings in the vicinity of Lake Superior is proven by the discovery, near Lake Nipigon at Beardmore in Ontario, of a genuine Viking sword, an axe, a bent strip of metal, and a shallow iron bowl which is said to have broken into fragments when touched. The discovery was supposed to have been made by a James Edward Dodd, a railroader. He claimed to have unearthed these objects while working a mining claim on May 24, 1930. It was not until 1936, however, that the weapons came to the attention of the public when they were bought by the Royal Ontario Museum. The news of the find aroused considerable public interest and, while no one doubted the authenticity of the weapons, there was some questioning of the circumstances of the find. It was known that a young Norwegian had lived in the house which Dodd now rented. Recent disclosures would seem to indicate that the articles were brought to Canada from Norway in the 1920's.[44]

Finally, mention may be made of the Yarmouth Stone. This was discovered on the shore of the Bay of Fundy, opposite Yarmouth in Nova Scotia, sometime in the third quarter of the nineteenth century. It contains what looks like an inscription which has defied all attempts to decipher it. Henry Phillips thought it a runic inscription and deciphered it as "Harkussen Men Varu," which he said was to be translated into English as "Harko's son addressed the men." Somewhere in the Icelandic sagas he found that one of the men on Thorfinnr Karlsefni's expedition was named Harko. Of course, the reading is an impossible one. But hope springs eternal and in 1939, Olaf Strandwold succeeded in reading the so-called runes on the Yarmouth Rock as "Leivur Eriku Resr," which he translated into English as "Leif to Erik raises," presumably raising the rock as a monument. Again, this is an impossible interpretation even if the symbols on the stone were runes, but then one must remember that, according to Erik Moltke, Strandwold was "able to find runes in any crevice or groove and decipher them." So the Yarmouth Stone still rests in the Yarmouth library, awaiting a scholar to explain its message.[45]

There is no end to these myths, and no doubt in the future both passionate cranks and sober scholars will continue to propagate them. It is possible that these myths, absurd as they are in detail, may rest on the fact of established and continued contact between Greenland and the Arctic lands of Canada on the one hand, and Scandinavia on the other. Greenland was the focal point for any penetration into the Canadian Arctic. The knowledge of lands beyond the Atlantic worked on the minds of men and some gave their imagination a free rein. Thus, we may presume, many of the myths concerning the pre-Columbian discovery of America were born.

CHAPTER 15

Voyages to Greenland and
the Canadian Arctic

While the imaginary expeditions discussed in the last chapter were not being made, voyages continued to be made between Greenland, Iceland, and Norway. There was, it is true, a diminution of sailings between Iceland and Greenland, as the Crown throughout the fourteenth century made trade with both Iceland and Greenland more and more a state monopoly. In 1294, Bergen was made a staple for wares between Norway and these two islands. It is not, however, until the middle of the fourteenth century that sailings between the various realms of the king of Norway were placed under severe restrictions. There were many reasons for these new restrictions: for example, the desire of the Norwegian kings in the first half of the fourteenth century to increase commerce and encourage the growth of towns, and the rise of a merchant class. Most important of all was probably the social dislocation caused by the Black Death, which struck Norway in 1349 and enfeebled her in numerous ways for decades thereafter.

During the thirteenth century the Germans and especially the Hansa merchants increased their commerce with Norway and other lands of the Norwegian king. When Bergen was made a staple in 1294, Germans trading with the various cities of Norway were forbidden to sail north of Bergen and all foreign merchants were similarly restricted in 1306. They were also forbidden to sail to Iceland, Greenland, and other tributary lands of the Norwegian king. This ban was reiterated in 1348 and, at this time, Bergen merchants took the first step toward the monopoly which was to be fully confirmed to them by King Hakon Magnusson in 1361, that is, the sole right to trade with Iceland, Greenland, and the other tributary lands of the Crown. It would seem from Ivar Bardarson's *Description of Greenland* that some time between 1294 and 1364, Sandr, the harbour of Herjolfsnes, was made a staple in Greenland, for he calls it a public harbour for Norwegians and merchants.[1]

There can be no doubt that up to the Black Death, communications between Norway and Greenland were frequent, and many wares from that country and the Canadian Arctic made their way to Norway. Church tithes and taxes were, for example, paid in walrus tusks and ropes made from the hide of the walrus. We do not know, of course, whether the Crown lived up to its old obligation to send at least two ships a year to Greenland, but we do know that Icelandic annals do not mention any lack of sailings to Greenland as they do at times to Iceland. It is, however, likely that, especially after the extinction of the Western Settlement in 1342 and the possible establishment of a staple at Sandr, only one *knorr* – a large one – was sent out every year or every other year. As we shall see, Icelandic annals in the latter half of the fourteenth century speak of the Greenland *knorr* and not *knarrar*.

In the fourteenth century it is stated that in five years, no ship came from Norway to Iceland (1326, 1350, 1355, 1374, and 1390) and there were six years in which only one ship made its way to the country (1324, 1333, 1357, 1362, 1367, and 1392). Icelandic annals do not as a matter of fact usually mention sailings to and from Greenland except on some special occasions and then usually indirectly, such as the arrival and departure of the bishops of that country (1289, 1309, 1315). In 1346 it is, however, directly stated that the *knorr* (the merchant ship the Crown sent to Greenland) came thence with a very valuable cargo. In 1347, the annals record the arrival of a ship from Greenland lacking an anchor, which had made for Markland and then been driven to Iceland. There were eighteen men aboard it, and it made its way to Norway the next year. This indicates that the Greenlanders kept up their contacts with Labrador on their own ships, likely to obtain timber, the importation of which from Norway would be prohibitively expensive. It shows also that although the Greenlanders do not seem to have sailed on their own ships to Norway, yet their ships were seaworthy enough to make such voyages.

The export of stockfish from Iceland, which began in the second quarter of the thirteenth century and was to increase greatly from then on, seems to have stimulated sailings to that country (for example, eleven ships came to Iceland in 1345 and thirteen in 1347) but we do not know whether Greenland shared in this new trade, although fish is mentioned among the exports of Greenland.

The Black Death which, as we have said, struck Norway in 1349, completely disrupted the country and its commerce. No ship sailed to Iceland or Greenland in 1350, and the two countries were consequently spared the ravages of the Black Death, although it did reach Iceland and devastated it later in 1402. It is likely, however, that sailings were resumed to Greenland not later than 1353. Unless a ship returned from Greenland in 1354, it is difficult to explain why King Magnus Eiriksson issued his frantic letter

to Poul Knutsson in October 1354, ordering him to take the *knorr* to Greenland for the purpose of preventing Christianity from perishing in that land.
We know again that the *knorr* must have been sent to Greenland in 1362
or 1363, for Ivar Bardarson reached Norway from Greenland in either 1363
or early in 1364. We may presume that sailings to Greenland continued in
a fairly normal state from then on. In 1365, Bishop Alfr was consecrated to
the see of Gardar, although he did not reach Greenland until 1368. We know
that in 1366, a *knorr* was sent to the island and it seems to have been
wrecked on its return voyage in 1367, as was the *knorr* which had carried
Bishop Alfr to Greenland in 1369.

There is a curious incident in the Icelandic annals *sub anno* 1379 which
relates that the Skraelings attacked the Greenlanders, killed eighteen of
them, and carried off two boys and enslaved them. This sounds much more
like an attack by European freebooters than by the harmless and unwarlike
Skraelings, who were the most unlikely people in the world to carry off
people to enslave them. If this is so, it might indicate a visit by German freebooters, but nothing definite can be asserted in this matter.[2]

In 1382 a ship belonging to the see of Skalholt was wrecked but its crew
and passengers escaped death and reached Greenland in a boat. They returned to Norway the next year in a ship which had been in Greenland for
two years. It brought news of the death of Bishop Alfr, which had occurred
six years previously. This would seem to indicate that sailings to Greenland
did not take place regularly every year, or even every alternate year. In
1385, four ships bound for Iceland were driven to Greenland. They spent
two winters in that country and did not reach Iceland until 1387. When
they returned to Norway, the crews were accused of trading illegally with
the Greenlanders, thereby infringing the monopoly which the merchants of
Bergen enjoyed in the matter of trade with Greenland. They were, however,
able to clear themselves. In 1406 a number of Icelanders who had sailed
from Norway for Iceland reached Greenland instead and remained there for
four years until they returned to Norway in 1410. This has long been popu-
larly regarded as the last contact of the outside world with Greenland until
the Age of the Great Discoveries. Research in written sources and archæology has shown this to be a complete fallacy.

It is important, however, to realize the conditions which followed upon
the establishment of the Bergen monopoly in 1361 or earlier. The Norwegian Bergen merchants who had been granted this monopoly of trade
with the tributary lands found it increasingly difficult to maintain themselves in a competitive position with, first, the Hansa merchants, and a little
later, the English merchants. Gradually, in the latter half of the fourteenth
century, the Norwegian merchants lost control of trade with Iceland, Greenland, and other tributary lands of the Norwegian Crown, to the Hanseatic

counter in Bergen, which by 1400 had attained a virtual monopoly of the extra-territorial trade of Norway.[3]

It was not only the Hanseatics but also the English who came to be a threat to the Norwegian merchants. In the fourteenth century the merchants of Bristol, Hull, and King's Lynn were gradually increasing the sphere of their activities and by 1412, if not earlier, they had included Iceland within the sphere of their operations and it was not long before they had a virtual monopoly of trade with Iceland, much to the disgust of both the king of Norway and the Hanseatic merchants of Bergen. In fact, this new competition forced the Hanseatics to begin equipping and dispatching vessels to Iceland in order to counteract the severe inroads made by the English on the trade with Iceland, which they had been able to handle from Bergen and which, up to 1412, had been carried largely in Icelandic or Norwegian bottoms.[4]

We do not know whether the Bristol and other English merchants sailed to Greenland as well as to Iceland, but there can be little doubt that they obtained information about Greenland and the Canadian Arctic, both from the inhabitants of Iceland and by being driven off course to Greenland and other parts of America. We have, however, no reports of this although we do know, as will be discussed later, that by 1480, and no doubt earlier, the Bristol merchants were turning their eyes to the lands across the Atlantic.

Unfortunately, Icelandic sources, from which most of the information about the Arctic lands of Canada in the Middle Ages is derived, virtually disappear in the fifteenth century. Throughout the century, after 1430, the writing of annals in Iceland almost ceased, and the increasing trade with English merchants, who offered high prices for Icelandic wares and supplied foreign goods at a reasonable price, brought to an end the sailings abroad of the Icelanders in their own bottoms. This hiatus in Icelandic sources is no indication that communications with Greenland ceased. An added reason for the silence of Icelandic sources on intercourse with Greenland is the fact that the old sailing course to Greenland was abandoned. Up to 1350, or even later, it had been customary to sail from Norway to Iceland, thence west to the east coast of Greenland, south along it to Cape Farewell and then up the west coast to Sandr or some other harbour in the Eastern Settlement. However, with the development of more seaworthy vessels and better navigational instruments, such as the compass, a great circle route directly across the Atlantic, south of Iceland, became both more feasible and less dangerous than the old course. To explain this change of course, it is entirely gratuitous to assume that a climatic deterioration made the old route more difficult than in former centuries. Ships proceeding to Greenland and using the new route would therefore not have come to the attention of the Icelanders nearly as much as in previous centuries when they touched at or coasted

Iceland. Nor is there any reason to think that trade with Greenland became less profitable, as the price for iron and other wares exported to Greenland rose greatly. The monopolists would have things their own way and while they charged more for the wares they carried to that country, they could pay even less for the valuable exports of Greenland and the Canadian Arctic.

Even if the Norwegians had ceased to sail to Greenland after 1410, there is every reason to think that the Germans and the English would have sailed to that country. And indeed, there is reason to think that they may have done so, although not nearly to the same extent as they did to Iceland. The Danish kings who, since the Union of Kalmar in 1397, ruled the three Scandinavian countries in the fifteenth century, repeatedly renewed the decree forbidding foreigners and especially Englishmen to sail to Iceland, Greenland, and other tributary lands of the Crown. Thus, in a treaty signed between the English and the Danes in December 1432, the English promised to respect the ban.[5] And it is significant that, while there are numerous complaints about violations by foreigners of the trading restrictions with Iceland, there are none with respect to Greenland. This silence suggests that the monopolists enjoyed uninterrupted commerce with that country throughout most of the fifteenth century.

It is significant, too, that the best maps of Greenland date from the middle of the fifteenth century. Claudius Clavus Swart, on his map from *circa* 1440-1450, writes that he has seen the little pigmies who are only a cubit in height, after they were taken prisoners on the sea in a small skin boat, which in his day hung in the cathedral at Nidaros. He also says that a long skin boat was to be found there which had formerly been taken with such pigmies aboard. Again, he says that he has seen the heathen Karelians (Skraelings) who came to Greenland from the north.[6] We need not believe that Clavus, who was a most unreliable scholar, actually visited Greenland, but it can hardly be denied that he received information thence and that his depiction of Greenland is based on contemporary testimony and not derived from earlier written sources. (The anonymous letter to Pope Nicholas v, dated 1448, is almost certainly based on fourteenth-century information.) The maps of Nicolaus Germanus and the globe of Martin Behaim also testify to continued intercourse with Greenland.

A strong case has been made out for the presence of Bjorn Thorleifsson and his wife in Greenland in the years 1445-1446. They spent a winter in the country and then returned to Iceland. This is a controversial matter, for some maintain that the sources refer to Bjorn Einarsson, who was driven to Greenland in one of four ships making for Iceland in 1385. However, the weight of evidence would seem to favour Bjorn Thorleifsson and the dates, *circa* 1445-1446, when everything would seem to have been normal in the

Eastern Settlement. Certainty in this matter is not possible.[7] It should be mentioned that the supposed return of Bjorn Thorleifsson from Greenland in 1446 has been connected with a letter of Pope Nicholas V, dated 1448, to two purported bishops of Iceland. In this, the Pope states that certain barbarians, coming to Greenland with a fleet, attacked the people living there and laid waste with fire and sword many of the churches in the country. They carried off the inhabitants into slavery, although these later managed to return and effect the repair of their dwellings.[8] No reliance can be placed on this letter, which is addressed, not to genuine bishops of Iceland, but to two notorious imposters, Marcellus, a German, and his confederate, Mathæus, who had wormed their way into the confidence of Nicholas V and obtained the appointment to the bishoprics of Iceland. Neither was in any position to obtain information from Bjorn Thorleifsson about the condition of the Greenlanders which he might then pass on to the Pope. The contents of the letter must be considered a concoction of the two, designed to gain them some advantage. In fact, the story of the barbarian attack, the destruction of all except nine parish churches in remote areas of Greenland (there were none so situated), the enslavement and removal of the inhabitants to the barbarians' country and their return to their homes, is too preposterous for one to believe that it contains even a vestige of truth.

Admittedly, we know little of the history of Greenland and the Canadian Arctic in the sixty years following 1410, except that knowledge of it and communications with it must have been maintained, as is evidenced by the cartographical material bearing on it and dating from the years before and after the middle of the century. Fortunately, our sources from the last thirty years of the century, although still scanty, are fuller and enable us to assert that contact was never broken.

In the fifteenth century, Portugal, under Prince Henry the Navigator 1394-1460), became the foremost nation in maritime enterprise. Prince Henry's concern was to discover a sea route to Asia. It is not therefore surprising that, since Greenland was regarded as an extension of Asia or as a land lying off the east coast of Asia, the Portuguese should be interested in learning something of the "Asiatic" lands belonging to the king of Denmark.

Indeed, friendly relations between the Danish court and the Portuguese were established at the beginning of the fifteenth century. In 1406 the Danish king, Eirikr of Pommern, married Philippa, the daughter of King Henry IV of England. Her aunt, Philippa, was married to King Joao I of Portugal. Their sons were Prince Henry the Navigator and Dom Pedro. Dom Pedro travelled widely over Europe and, in 1423, he and young King Eirikr of Pommern accompanied Emperor Sigismund to Hungary at the

E

time of the Turkish menace. Both Pedro and Eirikr took part in the siege of Prague during the Hussite Wars, and it is likely that the two talked of the lands in the realm of King Eirikr. Pedro visited Denmark in 1426 at a time when King Eirikr was the sole and absolute ruler of Norway, Sweden, and Denmark. The king was keenly interested in maritime ventures (his motto was Mit Haab staar til Havet – my hope is on the sea). There can be no doubt that he and Dom Pedro exchanged information about their home-lands, the Danish and Portuguese realms. This was the time when Claudius Clavus was drawing his first maps containing the most accurate depiction of Greenland up to this time. Dom Pedro will have carried back to Portugal information about the Arctic lands of the king of Denmark.[9]

Then, about 1448, when Christoffer of Bavaria was king of Denmark, we find one Vallert, the Dane, present at Prince Henry's court in Sagres, and here he became, as far as is known, the only foreigner to be made captain of a caravel in the attacks launched by the Portuguese on the Moors of Africa. He disappeared on this expedition.[10]

Relations continued to be cordial in the years following Vallert's death. King Christian I sent to Alfonso V of Spain his pursuivant,[11] Laalland, who took part in a crusade against the Moors in 1458. Laalland returned to Denmark in 1461, and King Alfonso sent to King Christian a letter in which, among other things, he said of Laalland:

> We have often inquired of him about the state of your kingdom and about various other matters abundant within your dominion which serve to render it famous. About all of which he has given us such full and detailed informa-tion that it seemed to us almost as if we saw it with our own eyes.

The king ends the letter with a strong recommendation for the promotion of Laalland.[12]

Around 1470 we find in Denmark two Portuguese noblemen, Joao Vaz Corte Real, a brother of Gaspar, and another whose identity is not known. At the request of Alfonso V, Christian I undertook to convey these Portu-guese emissaries to his lands west of the Atlantic. To head this expedition which, if it be true that communications with Greenland lasted until the end of the fifteenth century, would be only routine, the king chose two of his most trusted admirals, the Germans, Didrik Pining and Hans Pothorst. The pilot was an Icelander or Greenlander, Jon Skulason, referred to in the sources as Joh. Scolvus, or in like terms. This expedition sailed in 1470, reached Greenland late in that year, and wintered there. In 1471 the two Portuguese may have set out from Greenland on the Icelanders' boats, which still made annual voyages to Baffin Island, Labrador, and possibly New-foundland. Returning to Greenland in 1471, they again wintered there and in 1472 either made another expedition to the lands of the Canadian

Arctic or returned to Norway, reaching home in Portugal either early in 1473 or 1474.[13]

The evidence for this contact with Greenland and the lands of the Canadian Arctic, twenty or so years before Columbus, have been so well documented by both Sofus Larsen and Jon Duason that it would be superfluous to cite here the source material their conclusions are based on. Let it suffice to mention the letter of the burgomaster of Kiel, Carsten Grypp, to Christian III, March 3, 1551. In it he writes:

> This year has also been published in Paris, France, maps of your Majesty's land, Iceland, which depicts the marvels there to be seen; there it is openly written that Iceland is twice as large as Sicily and Italy, and that both the admirals, Pining and Pothorst, were supplied with a few ships and sent by your Majesty's grandfather, Christian I, at the request of the king of Portugal, to sail to and find new islands in the lands of the north. . . .[14]

One might also cite the inscriptions in Portuguese which are to be found on the representation of Baffin Island on the globe of Frisius and Mercator, dating from 1537, and the inscription west of Baffin Island and north of Hudson Strait, which reads: *Quij populi ad quos Ioes scoluus danus pervenit circa annum 1476* (White people whom Ioes Scoluus, a Dane, reached about the year 1476). On Hudson Bay itself we find: "The northerly strait or the Three Brethren Strait, which the Portuguese tried to sail through to the Eastern lands and India and the Malucca Islands."

Finally, the Spanish historian, Francesco Lopez de Gomara, wrote *circa* 1552-1553: "Thither [to Labrador] have also gone men from Norway under the guidance of Juan Scolvus and the English under Sebastian Cabot."[15] All in all, there can be little doubt that the two Portuguese visited Greenland, Labrador, and Hudson Bay.

It would seem that in the 1480's Didrik Pining was granted by the Crown the right to trade with Greenland. We are told:

> Item Punnus [Pining] and Pothorse have inhabited Island certayne yeeres, and some times have gone to sea and have had their trade in Groneland. Also Punnus did give the Islanders their Lawes and caused them to be written, which lawes do continue to this day in Island and are called by the name Punnus Lawes.[16]

The reference is to the well-known *Piningsdomur* concerning commerce and trade, adopted by the Althing in 1490, with the acquiescence and possibly at the instigation of Pining, who was governor of Iceland at that time.

We do not know when Didrik Pining died, although it is often stated that his death occurred about 1490. It is very likely, however, that he lived longer. Olaus Magnus writes:

In the preceding chapter a little has been said about the cliff Hvitserkr, which is midway between Iceland and Greenland, and we wish now to repeat this here and say nothing more about it.

On it lived around 1494 two notorious pirates, Pining and Pothorst, and they who shared their guilt, such a refractory behaviour and contempt for the flotillas and armies of all states, since they had been excluded through the strict orders of the Norse kings from all human society and outlawed because of their terrible robberies and cruel attacks on all ships, which they were able to seize, far and near. . . . On the peak of the very high cliff, the above-mentioned Pining and Pothorst made a compass of lead in a large circle with rings and lines; this makes it easier for those who wish to perpetrate robberies, since they obtain thereby information as to what direction they shall sail out on the sea in order to get much booty.[17]

It is most unlikely that the Danish king would deprive himself of the services of Pining for no other reason than the complaints of the Hanseatics. The latter may well have regarded Pining's interference with their trade and his attacks on their shipping in the North Atlantic as piratical, whether Pining was acting on his own as a freebooter or carrying out orders of the Danish king to prevent illegal trading with his tributary lands. Pining and Pothorst lived in an age when the distinction between naval heroes and pirates was very fine. In order to preserve friendly relations with the Hansa, the Danish king may well have spread or allowed to be spread, the rumour that Pining was dead. That Pining, who had been governor of Iceland, was now entrusted with the care of Greenland and trade with that country is not surprising.

Portuguese interest had not completely ended with the visit or Joao Vaz Corte Real in the 1470's, but it had been relegated to a secondary role in the years 1474-1487, when the efforts of the Portuguese were directed to the circumnavigation of Africa, which was partially achieved by Bartholomeu Diaz on his voyage of 1486-1487, when he rounded the Cape of Good Hope. But with the mutiny of his crew it was realized how long and arduous this course to India would be. There was thus a slackening for some years of Portuguese efforts to make contact with India by way of the Cape of Good Hope and a renewed interest in reaching India by way of the Canadian Arctic.

There was in Denmark in the 1490's a continuing but intensified interest in Greenland and the Greenlanders, who were scattered about the Canadian Arctic. It would seem that Pining and Pothorst sailed to Greenland in 1490, that on their return in 1491, they brought news of a new and major apostasy from the faith. It was in the following year that a document in the Papal Archives, dated July 9, 1492, informs us that Pope Innocent VIII had accepted the resignation of Jacob Blaa as bishop of Gardar, who had done nothing for his see, and had appointed Mathias Knudsson to succeed him.[18] This likely came about because of the news of the apostasy.

It was at this time that the King of Portugal sent two emissaries to the Danish king asking, it would seem, that they might make an exploratory journey to the Asiatic (American) lands of the Danish king. These two men were Pedro de Barcellos and Joao Fernandez. All the evidence points to their having sailed to Greenland on a Danish ship in 1492, remaining there during the winter and summer of 1492-1493 and returning to Denmark in the fall of 1493. The Portuguese then returned home in 1494, or possibly not until the summer of 1495.[19] The reports which these two explorers gave of the Arctic lands of Canada may have prompted the King of Portugal to renew his efforts to reach India by way of the Cape of Good Hope – a feat performed by Vasco da Gama in 1497-1498.

The information obtained by Fernandez was, as we shall see later, to be passed to the English and assisted them in their early ventures into Canadian waters. Admittedly, the evidence for the voyages of the Portuguese, both in the 1470's and 1490's, is circumstantial, but there is no reason to doubt that they were made and that the northern sea route to "Asia" was well known when Columbus set out on his epoch-making voyage in 1492. What was in doubt was how to get from the rather inhospitable lands of Asia (Greenland, Labrador, and the Canadian Arctic archipelago) to the fabulously rich lands of the Great Khan, wherein Marco Polo had dwelt. Certainly, it was the answer to this problem which the Portuguese were seeking, both in the 'seventies and 'nineties of the fifteenth century.

In the past few pages an attempt, based largely on written sources, has been made to show that contact was maintained between Scandinavia and Greenland throughout the fifteenth century. It might be added that there is a report that in 1484, the Hanseatics massacred forty sailors who were accustomed to sail each year to Greenland and transport thence precious articles. The occasion of the massacre is said to have been their refusal to sell these wares to German merchants, who thereupon invited them to dinner and killed them all. The veracity of this story is highly dubious but it at least indicates an awareness of contact with Greenland in the late fifteenth century.[20]

Fortunately, however, we are not dependent on such tales for proof of intercourse between Europe and Greenland and the Canadian Arctic throughout the fifteenth century. As has been mentioned, Poul Norlund's excavations at Herjolfsnes in 1921 have provided indisputable evidence of contact with Europe in the latter half of the fifteenth century. Norlund found well preserved in the permafrost the only clothing of the common people of Europe which has been preserved from the Middle Ages. The style of some of the clothes he found is that fashionable in Europe about the middle or latter half of the fifteenth century. This proves conclusively that there was contact between Greenland and Europe in the decades preceding 1500.

Norlund writes in this connection:

> We may further assert that the dresses from Herjolfsnes on the whole belong to a higher social level than the ordinary dresses of the common people which we know from European representations. . . . On the whole neither dresses nor other objects bear the stamp of a culture that is degenerating into barbarism. If we subject the dresses to a close examination, we are astonished at the amount of careful labour bestowed on them, and the experience embodied in the cut of such an article of clothing. . . . Also the wooden objects may be designated as "tidy work" which amply attests that the inhabitants have been in possession of first class tools, so sharp and exact are the incisions. This is not without significance, for it would be exactly in the domain of tools that a less frequent connection with Europe would first be apt to show itself.

He goes on to say:

> So much, however, we may venture to assert without hesitation, that the find gives us the impression of a community which, throughout the 14th century, in spite of the hard conditions of life which must always have prevailed, and which set their mark on the race, was to a certain extent prosperous and in good contact with Europe. . . .[21]

Norlund might well have said fifteenth instead of fourteenth century, for the best building at the farm, a banquet hall 11 by 5.6 metres, constructed with great care, dates from the fifteenth century. A fragment of a Rhenish stone jug, found at the foundation of the banquet hall at Herjolfsnes, is also said to date from the fifteenth century. It is significant, too, that achæological research has not shown that there is any greater lack of metal in the implements of the Eskimos in the fifteenth century than in any other. Thus, all the evidence points to continuing contact between the Canadian Arctic and Europe in the fifteenth century. Although the contact with Iceland and the Scandinavian countries seems to have come to an end about 1500, it was replaced by contact with the Portuguese, French, and especially the English, in the sixteenth century.

CHAPTER 16

The Beginnings of
the English Explorations

We have seen that the English, and especially the merchants of Bristol, began in the fifteenth century to drive a flourishing trade with the tributary lands of the king of Norway and especially with Iceland. Although trade was also undertaken from Lynn and Hull, Bristol was by far the most important centre for this commerce. Trade between Bristol and Iceland dates from 1411-1412.[1] From this beginning, it increases steadily throughout the century, and indeed the English merchants became paradoxically both welcome and unwelcome visitors to Iceland. They were welcome because of the high prices they offered for the exports of Iceland, chiefly hardfish, and the much lower prices they charged for imported wares than the Bergen merchants were wont to demand. They were unwelcome because they frequently plundered, robbed, and even carried off the inhabitants of the country, to be sold into slavery.[2] Despite this, however, we suspect they were more welcome than unwelcome.

Up to the beginning of the fifteenth century, for a period of at least fifty to seventy-five years, trade with Iceland had been a monopoly of the merchants of Bergen and these merchants had been able more or less to set the price of the stockfish which in the fourteenth century became the main export of Iceland. When the English began to trade with Iceland, they offered such high prices that the Icelanders received as much as six times more for their fish than they had been receiving from the Bergen merchants. From 1411, the visits of the English increased very greatly. In 1413, for instance, one merchant ship and thirty or more English fishing-ships were to be found in Icelandic waters. Twenty-five English ships were lost in a storm off Iceland in 1419. The king of Denmark, throughout the fifteenth century, issued decree after decree forbidding foreign vessels to sail to Iceland but all in vain, as far as English bottoms were concerned. The men of Bristol took the most prominent part in this fishing and trading with the Icelanders and many of them wintered in Iceland. Small boys were even placed in Icelandic homes, in order to gain a mastery of the language. There can be little doubt that these boys and indeed the sailors who, owing to storms, were driven to the vicinity of Greenland, must have been curious about the lands of the Icelanders in the western sea, and would enquire and receive accounts of these lands from the Icelanders, both in Iceland and in Greenland.[3]

Unfortunately, this cannot be confirmed from written sources, nor can we say that the beginnings of sailings into the western Atlantic, which the English undertook after 1480, were the result of reports which they had received in Iceland of the lands of the Danish king west of the Atlantic. This is, however, very likely.

What we do know is that, as early as July 15, 1480, a ship belonging to John Jay and commanded by a man called Thloyde (to be identified as John Lloyd, an expert mariner) sailed from Bristol into the western Atlantic in search of the island of Brasil. This was one of the legendary islands of the Atlantic and has neither been successfully identified nor has the meaning of the word been satisfactorily explained. They wandered fruitlessly about the sea for some two months and finally, by September 18, had taken refuge in an Irish port. Others who may have had a share in this voyage were Thomas Croft, collector of customs, William Spencer, Robert Straunge, and William de la Fount, all merchants of Bristol, if indeed the licence granted to these men to trade for three years to any regions with two or three ships of sixty tons or under, refers to this expedition.[4]

In the next year, 1481, two ships, the *George* and *Trinite*, set out from Bristol on July 6 to search for Brasil. Thomas Croft had an interest in both ships and sent out forty bushels of salt in each of the vessels. This would indicate that the object of the voyage was to discover fishing-grounds. Nothing further is known of this expedition to Canada, but the *Trinite*, at least, returned, for it is known to have been trading with Portugal in 1483.[5] Be that as it may, we know from a report made by Pedro de Ayala to Ferdinand and Isabella in 1498, that the merchants of Bristol did not give up their search for the island of Brasil. In his communication, Pedro de Ayala writes:

> For the last seven years the people of Bristol have equipped two, three [and] four caravels to go in search of the Island of Brasil and the Seven Cities according to the fancy of this Genoese [John Cabot].[6]

We do not know whether these expeditions succeeded in finding any land west of the Atlantic, although there is one recently discovered document – a letter of John Day to the Lord Grand Admiral (very likely Columbus himself) which may be dated 1497, and which may throw some light on this matter. After describing Cabot's voyage, Day says:

It is considered certain that the cape of the said land (discovered by Cabot) was found and discovered in the past by the men from Bristol who found "Brasil" as your Lordship well knows. It was called the Island of Brasil, and it is assumed and believed to be the mainland that the men from Bristol found.[7]

This would seem an unequivocal statement attesting to the discovery of a portion of the eastern coast of America some time before the first voyage of Cabot. It is impossible, however, to determine when the men of Bristol are supposed to have found this land or whether communications were maintained with it after the discovery. It is true that John Dee wrote in 1578 and inserted on a map of the North Atlantic, which he drew in 1580, that "Circa An. 1494. Mr. Robert Thorn his father, and Mr. Eliot of Bristow, discovered Newfound Land." But as this discovery is introduced along with the mythical expeditions of Lord Madoc and St Brendan, it is doubtful how much reliance can be placed on it. That such a voyage actually took place is somewhat strengthened by a statement made by Robert Thorn, the younger, in 1527, to the effect that his father, with a Bristol merchant named Hugh Eliot, "were the discoverers of the Newfound Landes." Certainty, however, is precluded by the fact that Thorn gives no date, and the original of his statement no longer exists. Does Day's statement of a discovery of Brasil "in the past" by the men of Bristol refer to a 1494 discovery of the American mainland by Thorn and Eliot? We do not know.[8] In fact, we are so much in the dark concerning fifteenth-century contact with America, even contacts of the Greenlanders with Markland and Newfoundland, that we can only make plausible guesses. It is, however, strange that on the map of Andreas de Bianco, dated 1436, there occurs the name y *Rouercha* and near it the word *stocfis*. It is difficult to determine what land is adjacent to *stocfis* – although there can be no doubt that Greenland is meant by y *Rouercha*.[9] If the land off which *stocfis* appears is Labrador, then this would indicate either a much earlier discovery than is usually postulated, or organized fishing and export of hardfish to Europe on the part of the Greenlanders. The latter would seem more likely.

However, in spite of their daring attempts to sail directly west across the Atlantic, it was not the Bristol merchants who were to bring the new world within the ken of Englishmen. This achievement fell to a foreigner, John Cabot (Giovanni Cabato). It seems that Cabot was born in Genoa about the middle of the fifteenth century and obtained citizenship in Venice on March 28, 1476. He seems to have engaged in trade and commerce and travelled widely while in Venice to cities in the eastern Mediterranean and even to Mecca. When he moved to England is not known. It may have been about 1484 and almost certainly not later than 1490, although it has recently been argued that he may not have come to England until 1495. The arguments for this last view seem rather weak.[10] There is no doubt that he did live in Bristol, and if so, he was probably employed in some position by the Venetians trading with England, at least to begin with. This, however, is not known. If he lived in Bristol, he probably became acquainted early with the attempts of the merchants there to discover lands beyond the sea. At this time, stockfish from Iceland and trade with that country loomed large in the economy of Bristol. Whether Cabot himself made voyages to Iceland is not known, but there can be no doubt that he was aware of the existence of Iceland and also of Greenland as lands lying off the east coast of Asia, north of the fabulous realms of the Great Khan. Indeed, this information was a commonplace among those at all interested in geography, exploration, and the lands revealed through the enterprise of Columbus.

What is certain is that Cabot grew increasingly interested in finding a passage to Asia by way of the north. It would seem that he was in Portugal in 1495 and that he may there have obtained information about Greenland and Canadian lands from either Joao Fernandez or Pedro de Barcellos. On March 5, 1496, John Cabot and his three sons, Lewis, Sebastian, and Sancio, petitioned Henry VII to grant them letters patent under the great seal. On the very same day, Henry issued the letters patent to Cabot and his sons, granting them

> . . . full and free authority, faculty and power to sail to all parts, regions and coasts of the eastern, western and northern sea under our banners, flags and ensigns, with five ships . . . and with such mariners and men as they wish to take with them, at their own proper costs and charges, to find, discover and investigate whatsoever islands, countries, regions or provinces of heathens and infidels, in whatsoever part of the world placed, which before this time were unknown to all Christians.[11]

The king also grants them the right to all profits accruing to them from this venture, saving a fifth part for the Crown. The fact that the petition and the letters patent are issued on the same day shows that negotiations must have been going on for some time before March 1496. On March 28, the Spanish ambassador was instructed to protest the granting of these letters patent, although any mention of sailing to southern regions was omitted in them.[12]

It has been suggested, and the recently discovered letter of John Day supports this, that Cabot made a preliminary and unsuccessful voyage in 1496. Day writes that Cabot went with one ship, "his crew confused him, he was short of food and ran into bad weather, and he decided to turn back." There is some slight evidence, also, that John Cabot may have gone as far as Iceland in 1496. Duason has drawn attention to an old Icelandic folk tale called "The Guest at Ingjaldsholl." This relates that there came to Rif at Snaefellsnes (one of the chief trading-centres of the men from Bristol) on a large merchant vessel from Bristol, a Latin man (*latneskur madur*). His gentlemanly bearing, his great learning, and his novel geographical ideas greatly and favourably impressed the Icelanders who met him. He desired to obtain information about the lands which the Icelanders had discovered, settled, and explored, west of the Atlantic. All possible information was given him and he then departed on the ship which had brought him. The following summer, he returned on a small ship with a small crew. In the district of Snaefellsnes, he enlisted the services of a native to pilot him to Labrador. Neither the pilot nor the distinguished gentleman ever returned to Iceland from this voyage.[13] If there be any truth in this tale, one must conclude that it refers to a visit to Iceland by Cabot in 1496 and his return to pick up the pilot on his first voyage in 1497. It is absurd to think that it can refer to the much disputed visit of Columbus to Iceland in 1477, for Columbus, even if he visited Iceland in 1477, never returned to the island. It is, however, entirely in character for Cabot, who visited Portugal in 1495 in order to obtain information from the Greenland-farers who had just returned from Denmark, to have gone to Iceland. Through his connections with Bristol, he knew that there he could obtain information about the lands west of the Atlantic and the sea route thither.

CHAPTER 17

The Voyages of John Cabot

No topic in the annals of the Age of the Great Discoveries has led to greater controversy than the voyages of John Cabot and the supposed voyages of his son, Sebastian. There can, however, be no doubt that John Cabot believed that by sailing the old Vinland course of the Icelanders, he would reach the northeast corner of Asia and that by sailing southeast from there, he would eventually reach Cipango (Japan), and from there make his way to India. We do not know in which degree of latitude he expected to find Cipango, but certainly he expected it to be in a degree of longitude far west of the lands which Columbus had discovered. Cabot knew well enough from his reading of Marco Polo and possibly other mediæval writings that the lands which Columbus is said to have believed to be Asia could not be the rich domains of the Great Khan, so vividly depicted by Marco Polo in the book describing his travels and sojourn in east Asia.

Unfortunately, the accounts of the two voyages of John Cabot, those of 1497 and 1498, are in the same category as the accounts of the Vinland voyages in the *Eiriks saga rauda* and the *Graenlendinga saga*, although the former are even skimpier than the latter. Moreover, the accounts given by John Cabot's son, Sebastian, do little but confuse the matter. As we shall see, there is really no shred of reliable evidence for believing that Sebastian Cabot ever made an independent voyage into the Arctic in search of a northwest passage to Asia or for any other purpose. Therefore, all that he relates of such a voyage is either pure fiction or refers to the voyages of his father. This has caused great confusion.

Although John Cabot made both a map and a globe illustrating his discoveries, neither has survived. We are therefore dependent on accounts by others of his first voyage, and of his second in 1498, at which time he is believed to have perished, we have virtually no information at all.

The figure of Cabot is, however, at once so commanding and so attractive in the history of the first contacts of others than Scandinavians with the eastern and northern parts of Canada, that at least a few pages must be devoted to his two voyages. At the same time, it must be clearly understood that the inadequate information we possess on these voyages makes it impossible to pin-point, except in the most general terms, the localities he visited on his first expedition in 1497. Much less can one determine whither he sailed and where he landed on the voyage in 1498, from which he did not return.

What, then, are the sources that bear on these two voyages? First and foremost are the letters patent granted to John Cabot and his sons, giving them "full and free authority . . . to sail to all parts . . . of the eastern, western and northern sea."[1] This does not tell us much, but it may be stated that "eastern" does not refer to a northeast passage to Asia but to the eastern parts of Asia by way of the west, as has been explained above in discussing Cabot's aims. The letters patent show clearly that Cabot intended to sail north and west to the Asiatic lands of the Danish king and from them to the "regions or provinces of heathens and infidels . . . which before this time were unknown to all Christians." For this purpose, Cabot sailed from England, perhaps early in May of 1497, in a small ship (possibly fifty tons) called the *Mathew*, with a crew of eighteen. He returned from his voyage about August 6, for he was present at the court of Henry VII on August 10 to give to the King his report on the "newe founde launde," as Cabot's discovery is called in a later document.[2]

A second important source is a letter dated August 23, 1497, from Lorenzo Pasqualigo to his brother at Venice. He wrote:

That Venetian of ours who went with a small ship from Bristol to find new islands has come back and says he has discovered mainland 700 leagues away, which is the country of the Grand Khan, and that he coasted it for 300 leagues and landed and did not see any person; but he has brought here to the king certain snares which were spread to take game and a needle for making nets, and he found certain notched (or felled) trees so that by this he judges that there are inhabitants. Being in doubt he returned to his ship; and he has been three months on the voyage; and this is certain. And on the way back he saw two islands, but was unwilling to land, in order not to lose time, as he was in want of provisions.

The letter goes on to say that King Henry VII has promised Cabot ten armed ships for an expedition the next year. It then describes the honours paid Cabot in England for his discoveries.[3]

A third communication concerning Cabot's return was written the following day, likely by Raimondo de Soncino to the Duke of Milan, and reports that a Venetian who has "good skill in discovering new islands . . . has found two very large and fertile new islands. He has also discovered the

Seven Cities, 400 leagues from England, on the western passage." Soncino wrote again in greater detail on December 18.

> Perhaps amid the numerous occupations of your Excellency, it may not weary you to hear how his Majesty here has gained a part of Asia, without a stroke of the sword. There is in this Kingdom a man of the people, Messer Zoane Caboto by name, of kindly wit and a most expert mariner. Having observed that the sovereigns first of Portugal and then of Spain had occupied unknown islands, he decided to make a similar acquisition for his Majesty. After obtaining patents that the effective ownership of what he might find should be his, though reserving the rights of the Crown, he committed himself to fortune in a little ship, with eighteen persons. He started from Bristol, a port on the west of this kingdom, passed Ireland, which is still further west, and then bore towards the north, in order to sail to the east, leaving the north on his right hand after some days. After having wandered for some time he at length arrived at the mainland, where he hoisted the royal standard, and took possession for the king here; and after taking certain tokens he returned.
>
> This Messer Zoane, as a foreigner and a poor man, would not have obtained credence, had it not been that his companions, who are practically all English and from Bristol, testified that he spoke the truth. This Messer Zoane has the description of the world in a map, and also in a solid sphere, which he has made, and shows where he has been. In going towards the east he passed far beyond the country of the Tanais. They say that the land is excellent and temperate, and they believe that Brazil wood and silk are native there. They assert that the sea there is swarming with fish, which can be taken not only with the net, but in baskets let down with a stone, so that it sinks in the water. I have heard this Messer Zoane state so much.
>
> These same English, his companions, say that they could bring so many fish that this kingdom would have no further need of Iceland, from which place there comes a very great quantity of the fish called stockfish. But Messer Zoane has his mind set upon even greater things, because he proposes to keep along the coast from the place at which he touched, more and more towards the east, until he reaches an island which he calls Cipango, situated in the equinoctial region, where he believes that all the spices of the world have their origin, as well as the jewels. He says that on previous occasions he has been to Mecca, whither spices are borne by caravans from distant countries. When he asked those who brought them what was the place of origin of these spices, they answered that they did not know, but that other caravans came with this merchandise to their homes from distant countries, and these again said that the goods had been brought to them from other remote regions. He therefore reasons that these things come from places far away from them, and so on from one to the other, always assuming that the earth is round, it follows as a matter of course that the last of all must take them in the north towards the west.[4]

Soncino here gives a very good account not only of how people reacted to Cabot's discovery but also of the geographical notions of the time, and especially those of Cabot himself and what he was trying to accomplish.

A Bristol chronicle, written by one Maurice Toby about 1565, records that in 1497 the merchants of Bristol, in a ship called the *Mathew* which left Bristol May 2, found on June 24 the land of America and returned home August 6. The Paris World Map of 1544 has as its eighth legend a report that the land adjacent was discovered by John Cabot and his son Sebastian on June 24, 1494.

> . . . they gave the name First Land Seen (*Prima Terra Vista*), and to a large island which is near the said land they gave the name Saint John, because it had been discovered on the same day. The people of it are dressed in the skins of animals; they use in their wars bows and arrows, lances and darts, and certain clubs of wood, and slings. It is a very sterile land. There are in it many white bears, and very large stags like horses, and many other animals; and likewise there is infinite fish, sturgeons, salmon, very large soles a yard long, and many other kinds of fish, and the greater number of them are called baccallaos (codfish); and likewise there are in the same land hawks black like crows, eagles, partridges, linnets, and many other birds of different kinds.[5]

Admittedly, these passages which have been quoted above do not give us much information about the course sailed by Cabot on the voyage of 1497. Raimondo de Soncino says, however, that after passing Ireland Cabot turned north and then began to sail to the Orient, having the pole star on the right. This can only mean that Cabot was threading islands, that is, sailing the old Vinland course of the Norsemen. He sailed from Ireland to Iceland, then west to the east coast of Greenland, south along it to Cape Farewell. Whether he sailed up the west coast to latitude 67° 30', or whether he then continued south to the coast of Labrador, is difficult to determine. Soncino says that he got as far as the land of the Tanais in the Orient. This would likely be the Scythia of mediæval maps, to be identified almost certainly with Labrador, which was regarded as lying in the northern part of Asia. Soncino's statement that the explorers reported the land to be fine and the climate temperate and believed that they would there find Brasil wood and silk, is no doubt to be interpreted simply as propaganda to induce the King of England and merchants to support further expeditions. The categorical assertion that the sea is full of fish is, however, no doubt a statement of fact concerning either the sea off Labrador or Newfoundland. If Cabot followed the Vinland course, then there is every reason to believe that Labrador was the first land sighted. Greenland was too well known to cause any interest on the part of Cabot. He had no doubt heard of its existence and location either from Bristol sailors who ventured each year to Iceland or from the Icelanders themselves, if Cabot had made a voyage to that country in 1496. Again, Cabot may have heard of the land of the labrador, as Greenland was

to be known for many years during the sixteenth century, from Joao
Fernandez, when the former visited Seville and Lisbon "seeking to obtain
persons to aid him in this discovery" (that is, his voyage to Asia). It is
certain that he can only have made this trip to the Iberian peninsula before
March 1496, for there would be no reason for seeking aid in Spain or
Portugal after he obtained his letters patent from Henry VII. The obvious
inference then is that Cabot, having heard of the return of Joao Fernandez
and Pedro de Barcellos, went to Portugal in 1495 to seek information from
them and there learned of the land of the labrador.

Much of this is admittedly conjectural but it is by no means impossible.
The whole question of the course Cabot took to the New Found Land and
his landfall there is bedevilled by the intriguing but exasperating question
of the character of Sebastian Cabot and the veracity of his reports on his
voyages and exploits. Sebastian Cabot is one of the most controversial and
enigmatical characters in history. We possess many accounts that he is
supposed to have given to various people about his voyages to the north.
In a work written in 1515, Petrus Martyr reports as follows:

A certain Sebastian Cabot has examined those [frozen coasts], a Venetian
by birth but carried by his parents whilst yet a child into the island of
Britain, they going thither as the habit is of Venetians, who in the pursuit
of trade are the guests of all lands. He equipped two ships at his own cost in
Britain, and with three hundred men steered first for the north, until even in
the month of July he found great icebergs floating in the sea and almost
continuous daylight, yet with the land free by the melting of the ice. Where-
fore he was obliged, as he says, to turn and make for the west. And he extended his course furthermore to the southward owing to the curve of the
coastline, so that his latitude was almost that of the Straits of Gibraltar and
he penetrated so far to the west that he had the island of Cuba on his left
hand almost in the same longitude with himself. He, as he traversed those
coasts, which he called the Bacallaos, says that he found the same flow of
the waters to the west, although mild in force, as the Spaniards find in their
passage to their southern possessions. Therefore it is not only probable but
necessary to conclude that between these two lands hitherto unknown lie
great straits which provide a passage for the waters flowing from east to west,
which I judge to be drawn round by the attraction of the heavens in their
rotation round the earth, but not to be blown out and sucked in again by
the breathing of Demogorgon, as some have supposed because perhaps they
have been led to connect it with the flow and the ebb [of the tides]. Cabot
himself called those lands the Bacallaos because in the adjacent sea he found
so great a quantity of a certain kind of great fish like tunnies, called bacallaos
by the inhabitants, that at times they even stayed the passage of his ships.
He found also the men of those lands clothed in skins and not anywhere
devoid of intelligence. He says there are great numbers of bears there, which
eat fish. For the bears plunge into the midst of a shoal of those fish, and

MAPS OF THE NEW WORLD

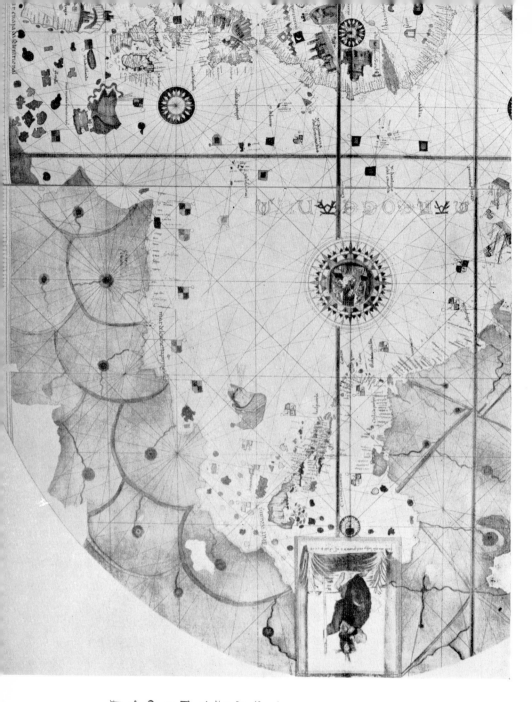

*World map of
Juan de la Cosa,
1500
overleaf:
The Arctic and
the Antarctic.
from the map of
the earth by
Nicolaus Joannis
Visscherius, 1639.*

2

From
the Contino Chart,
anonymous undated
manuscript chart
of the world,
circa 1500.

3

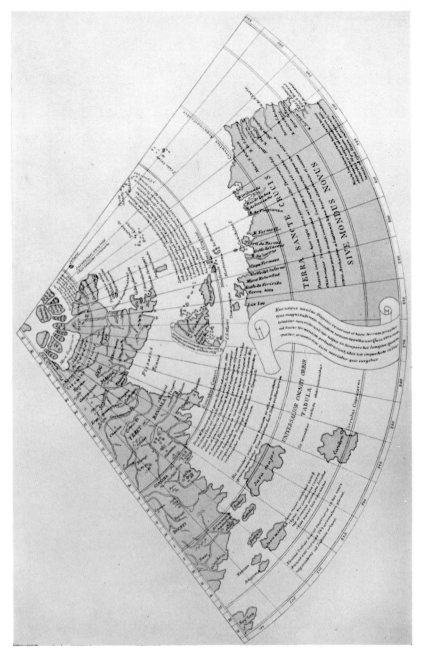

Map of
Johannes Ruysch,
1508.

4

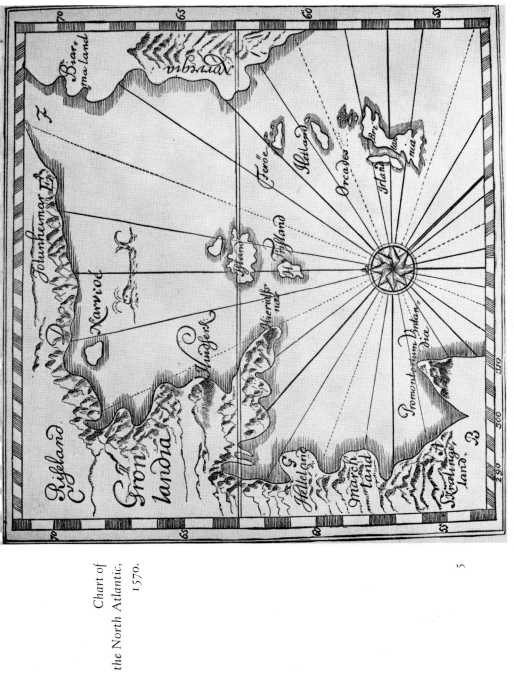

Chart of
the North Atlantic,
1570.

5

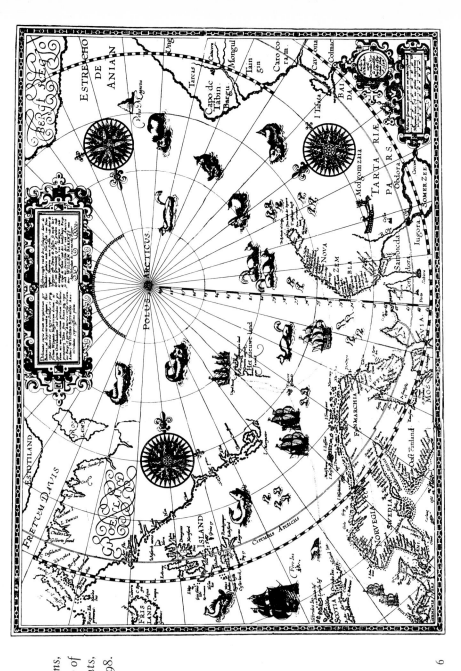

The Arctic Regions,
from the map of
Willem Barents,
1598.

6

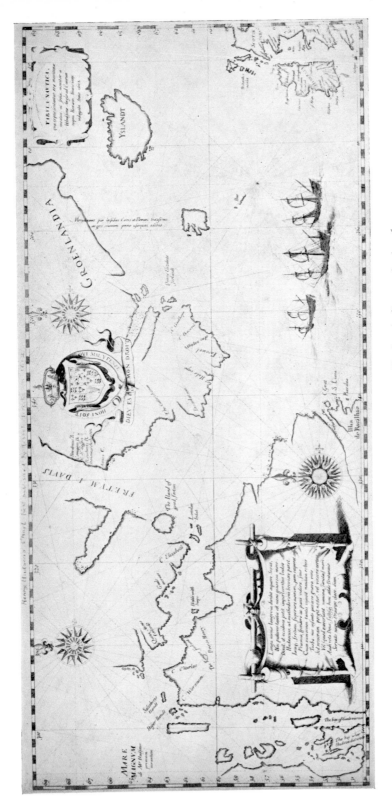

7   The 1612 chart by Hessel Gerritz of Henry Hudson's discoveries in 1610-11.

Jens Munk's representation
of his wintering at Hudson Bay,
1619-20.

falling upon them with their claws grasping the scales draw them to shore and eat them; on which account, he says, the bears are less dangerous to men. Many say that they have seen copper ore in places in the hands of the inhabitants. I know Cabot as a familiar friend and sometimes as a guest in my house. . . . Spaniards are not lacking who deny that Cabot was the first finder of the Bacallaos and do not allow that he went so far westwards.[6]

Giovanni Battista Ramusio, in his work on navigation and voyages published in Venice, 1550, gives the gist of the account which Sebastian Cabot gave to a certain Mantuan gentleman (Galeatus Butrigarious, papal envoy in Spain?) sometime during the years 1533-1547. According to this, Sebastian told the gentleman that

his father having left Venice many years ago and having gone to England to trade, he took him with him to the city of London when he (Sebastian) was rather young, but not before he had learnt his humanities and the sphere. His father died at the time when news came that Signor Don Christophoro Colombo the Genoese had discovered the coast of the Indies, and it was much spoken of in the court of King Henry VII, who then reigned, where they said it was a thing rather divine than human to have found that way never before known to go to the East where the spices are produced. "Whence there was born in me (said Sebastian Cabot) a great desire and an eagerness of heart that I should do some signal deed also, and knowing by reason of the sphere that if I sailed by way of the north west I should have a shorter road to find the Indies, I at once communicated my thought to his majesty, who was very pleased and equipped for me two caravels with all things needful, and it was, I believe, in 1496 at the beginning of summer. And I began to sail towards the north-west, thinking not to find land until I came to Cathay, and from thence to turn towards the Indies. But at the end of some days I discovered land, which ran to the north, which greatly displeased me; and then going along the coast to see if I could find some gulf which turned, it fell out that having gone as far as 56 degrees under our pole, seeing that there the coast turned eastwards, and despairing of finding a gulf, I turned back to examine again the same coast from that region towards the equinoctial, always with the purpose of finding a passage to the Indies, and came as far as that part now called Florida. And, my victuals being short, I decided to return to England, where, on my arrival, I found great disturbances, of the people in rebellion and of a war with Scotland. There was no further thought of sailing to those parts, for which reason I came to Spain, to the Catholic King and to Queen Isabella, who having heard what I had done received me and made good provision for me, arranging for me to sail along the coast of Brazil, in order to explore it, on which voyage I found a very great and wide river, now called La Plata. I wished to navigate it and ascended it more than 600 leagues, finding it always most beautiful and inhabited by multitudes of people, who in wonderment ran to see me, and into which an incredible [sic] number of tributaries run. I made afterwards many other voyages, which I pretermit, and at last finding myself old I wished to rest, so many experienced and valiant young sailors having come to the fore; and now here I am with this charge that you know of, enjoying the fruits of my labours." This is what I learned from Signor Sebastian Cabot.[7]

As can be seen from the above accounts, if the authors are quoting him correctly, Sebastian is attributing to himself the voyages made by his father and to ensure that he should have the credit for these, he even dates the death of his father prior to the return of Columbus from his voyage of 1492. The question then arises, of course, whether all of Sebastian's accounts of his supposed voyages to northern Canada do not refer to the voyage made in 1497 by John Cabot, in which Sebastian may have participated. The vivid description of the Arctic regions seem to point to an eye witness. Another reason for discounting any voyage by Sebastian is the statement that the king had given him two ships, and the contradictory statement that he himself fitted out two ships with a crew of three hundred, entirely at his own cost. The crew of three hundred is also too absurd to merit consideration.

It is true, however, that Petrus Martyr says that the Bacchalaos were discovered by Cabot sixteen years before 1524. This would date Sebastian's voyage to 1508-1509 – the date indeed usually assigned to it by those who believe that Sebastian Cabot made a voyage to the north in search of a north-west passage. This statement of Petrus Martyr's is patently absurd, for the Bacchalaos were discovered long before this by John Cabot or others. Marc Antonio Contarini's report of 1536 to the senate of Venice, stating that Sebastian had two ships from Henry VII in which he sailed with three hundred men so far that he found the sea frozen and had to turn back and found the king dead on his return, might seem an argument in favour of a voyage in 1508 or 1509, but we know nothing of Contarini's authority for this statement.

Francesco Lopez de Gomara, in his history published in 1552, says:

> There is a great tract of land and coast which is called Bacallaos, and its greatest latitude is forty-eight and a half degrees. The people there call a species of large fish bacallaos, of which there are so many that they impede ships in sailing. And he who brought news of that land was Sebastian Cabot the Venetian, who equipped two ships in England, where he had lived since he was a child, at the cost of King Henry VII, who desired to trade in the spice region as did the King of Portugal; others say at his own cost. And he promised King Henry to go by the north to Cathay, and to bring thence spices in a shorter time than the Portuguese did by the south. He went also to learn what sort of land the Indies were to inhabit. He took three hundred men and went by way of Iceland to the cape of Labrador (Greenland) until

he reached fifty-eight degrees, although he himself says much more, relating that there were in the month of July such cold and so many pieces of ice that he dared not go farther; and that the days were very long and almost without night, and the nights very clear. It is a fact that at sixty degrees the days are eighteen hours long. Cabot then seeing the cold and strangeness of the land set his course towardes the west, and refreshing himself at the Bacallaos he followed the coast as far as thirty-eight degrees and returned thence to England.[8]

This is obviously simply another version of Sebastian's claim to the credit for the 1497 voyage on which he may have gone with his father. It cannot refer to a voyage made in 1508 or 1509, when the regions called Bacchalaos were already well known. So one might continue.

Similar accounts occur in various other writings of the sixteenth century, all of which have this in common, that they do not mention John Cabot but only Sebastian. This is true of André Thevet's account of 1558, of Antonio Galvão's of 1563 (he dates the voyage 1496), of Urbain Chauveton's of 1579 (the voyage here is dated 1507), of Richard Eden's of 1555, who calls Sebastian "a woorthy owlde man yet lyving," and of Jean Ribault's of 1563 (the year here is 1498).[9] Sir Humphrey Gilbert, writing before 1566, says that Sebastian's charts are still to be seen "in the Queenes Majesties privie Gallerie at White hall" and that June 11 (no year) Sebastian sailed as far north as latitude 67° 30'.[10]

To resolve the problem of whether Sebastian Cabot ever sailed at his own or the king's expense to the region of the Bacchalaos, one may finally mention the plans for an expedition in 1521. Here the king approached the Drapers' Company of London, soliciting support for the venture. They replied respectfully but in no uncertain terms, as may be seen from the following:

And we thynk it were to sore aventour to joperd v shipps w^t men & goodes unto the said Iland uppon the singuler trust of one man, callyd as we understond, Sebastyan, whiche Sebastyan, as we here say, was never in that land hym self, all if he makes reporte of many thinges as he hath hard his ffather and other men speke in tymes past.[11]

In spite of all that has been said, this is pretty strong evidence that Sabastian Cabot never undertook any voyage to the northwest, unless he accompanied his father in 1497 or 1498, and indeed not in 1508 or 1509. What we have in the writings which attribute various voyages to Sebastian Cabot is to be referred to the voyages made by his father in 1497 and 1498.

We may then sum up by saying that in 1497, John Cabot, after carefully collecting all the evidence he could, sailed early in that year to the New World. He sailed by way of Iceland and Greenland, and this explains to some extent why it took him fifty-two days to reach America from Ireland.

On his way, he might stop for three or four days in Iceland and probably spend some time in Greenland when he arrived there. We do not know, although there is a strong presumption based on Sebastian's account of his purported voyage in 1496 or 1497, that John Cabot took a course which led him either in 1497 or 1498 to Iceland, Greenland, and possibly up the west coast of Greenland to the 67° latitude and that he then turned about, sailed west past Baffin Island to Labrador and that on his second voyage in 1498 he sailed further south, off the east coast of what was to become the United States of America. On this voyage he was lost, or so we must presume, and his son Sebastian, who may have accompanied him on both voyages, succeeded in returning to England. Then and in later years Sebastian ascribed to himself the achievements of his illustrious father and possibly used maps illustrating the achievements of other early sixteenth-century explorers in describing some of his purported travels.

If Sebastian did make a real and not just a fictitious voyage in 1508-1509, it is a strange thing that no letters patent are extant concerning it. It is scarcely within the realm of credibility to argue that the letters patent of 1496 would suffice to cover an expedition in 1508. Indeed, John Cabot himself secured a second letters patent on February 3, 1498, for his voyage of that year and in this there is no mention of Sebastian or of his other sons. When Sebastian returned to England in 1548, he asked for a copy of the letters patent of 1496. If letters patent, now lost, dealing with the 1508 expedition, had been issued, why did he not ask for copies of them? Why, too, if Sebastian led an expedition in 1508, did he not publicize it on the continent after he left England, instead of ascribing to himself, to the exclusion of any mention of his father, the latter's expeditions of 1497 and 1498? Some of our sources say that Sebastian undertook his expedition at his own expense and others say that the king fitted out the ships. If the first had been the case, one may well ask where Sebastian obtained the money to outfit such a large expedition and if the second had been the case, why there is no record of any expenditure by the king on such an expedition. Those who believe that Sebastian did actually make a voyage in 1508 or 1509, a voyage which was an attempt to discover a northwest passage to Asia, and that in the course of this voyage, Sebastian sailed through Hudson Strait and into Hudson Bay, are confronted with some embarrassing questions. Why, while in the service of the King of England, or even on a venture financed by English merchants, was this remarkable discovery of a sea route to Asia not followed up? It is hard to believe that Henry VIII would not have been as interested as his father in the discovery of a new sea route to the fabulously wealthy lands of the east.[12] Why, too, in the years 1509-1512, while Sebastian was still in England, did he not publicize his discovery of the northwest passage, for he was never a man to hide his light under a bushel? Is it not rather fanciful to suggest that one of the reasons prompting King Ferdinand to employ Cabot in 1512 may have been to "disarm a dangerous man by taking him into his pay"?[13] One may well ask how dangerous Sebastian could have been if, in three years, he had been able to interest no one in following up what one would think to have been one of the most epoch-making discoveries in an age which was interested in little else than the discovery of new routes to Asia. Let us not forget, however, that the Icelanders in Greenland had known of the existence of Hudson Strait and Hudson Bay for centuries and had even erected a polar-bear trap on the Melville Peninsula, and Thule Culture settlements were to be found on Southampton Island and other regions adjoining Hudson Bay. If we accept the view that Joao Fernandez and Pedro de Barcellos were in Greenland from 1492 to 1494, then it becomes easy to account for the appearance of the opening of Hudson Strait on Portuguese maps of the pre-1508 period and for the appearance of the strait on the globe of Gemma Frisius, *circa* 1537. It is contended[14] that not only is Hudson Strait shown on the globe, but also Hudson Bay, as a large body of water, and that this information stems from the supposed voyage of Sebastian Cabot in 1508-1509. It is, however, difficult to see why the strait should be called the *Fretum articum sive trium fratrum* if indeed the information concerning it is based on a voyage in which "Sebastian Cabot did discover Hudson strait and part of Hudson Bay in 1508-1509."[15] Indeed, we know nothing of the three brethren, unless they be, as has been conjectured, the Corte Real brothers.[16] It may, however, be noticed that there are those who contend that Hudson Bay appears on fifteenth-century maps such as the Genoese World Map of 1447 or 1457. It is also difficult to see why one should reject the inscription on it north of the strait, *Quij populi ad quos Ioes Scolvuus danus pervenit circa annum 1476*, as attesting the presence of a Danish expedition in Hudson Strait and Hudson Bay, about the year 1476, for which there is indeed other evidence, as we have seen. It seems gratuitous to assume that it reached Greenland only.[17]

It has been noted that, with the exception of a mention on the Paris map of 1544, the name of John Cabot does not occur in any of the sixteenth-century writers previous to Hakluyt. "For them, John Cabot was an unknown name, and Sebastian stood for the sum of English discovery."[18] We may finally observe that John Cabot's son, Sebastian, is believed by many to have made a voyage into Hudson Strait and Hudson Bay in 1508-1509. He believed that he had discovered the North-West Passage. This, if true, was or would have been accounted a great achievement and sufficient to establish the reputation and fame of any man. Why, then, secure in the hall of fame, did he when describing the expeditions of 1497 and 1498 led by John Cabot – and most sixteenth-century reports of the voyages of his father would seem to stem from Sebastian – begrudge his father the credit for these ventures and claim them for himself? He could so easily have seen to it that his father's name would not pass into oblivion.

John Cabot's achievement may be called a remarkable and even an epoch-making one. This remains true even if it be conceded that the merchants of Bristol had already come upon the shores of America. They do not seem, however, to have been searching for the realms of Asia but for legendary islands in the Atlantic. John Cabot was actuated solely by the desire to reach Asia, which Columbus claimed to have found in 1492 but which, it soon became apparent, must lie beyond the lands which Columbus had reached and which could only, at the best, be outposts of Cipango and the rich domains of the Khan. Cabot, knowing of the northerly Asiatic lands of the King of Denmark, conceived the idea of sailing thither and then south and west until he reached his goal. For this purpose he gathered, as we have seen, all the information he could obtain on these northern lands. In 1497, Cabot followed the old Vinland course to Iceland and Greenland. He sailed north along its west coast to the vicinity of latitude 67°, which was the route Thorfinnr Karlsefni had used some five hundred years earlier. Here Cabot turned west and south and, sailing off Baffin Island, reached Hudson Strait. Prevented by ice from sailing through, he turned around and made his way south along the east coast of Labrador. How far he went we do not know but he may have reached the Strait of Belle Isle, and the northern tip of Newfoundland may have been the *prima terra vista* after passing the lands familiar to the Icelanders in Greenland or to his Icelandic pilot. We can only conjecture, as indeed is evident from the failure to identify definitely Cabot's landfall after the years and years of effort which have gone into the study of the early maps of Newfoundland and the Maritimes and the countless words these efforts have produced.

Having reached the Strait of Belle Isle and noticing the westward and southern trend of the coast, Cabot may then have sailed south off the east coast of Newfoundland until he came to Cape Breton Island, or – and this is more likely – the season growing short, he may have turned east and sailed for home. As has often been emphasized, there can be no doubt that Cabot returned to England jubilant and firmly convinced that he had reached the northern parts of Asia, that he had found indications that by following the coast of America farther south and west, he would anticipate Columbus in reaching the realms of the Khan. He was received in England as one who had accomplished the impossible and both king and merchants promised to support him next year with ships and men which would enable him to carry out completely what he had so auspiciously begun. The king issued a new letters patent, authorizing Cabot to "take at his pleasure vi englisshe shippes in any porte . . . within our realme of

Englond . . . and them convey and lede to the londe and Iles of late founde by the seid John in oure name. . . ."[19]

Cabot sailed on his second voyage with one ship provided by the king and four by the merchants of London and Bristol. The date of departure from Bristol was in late April or more probably in early May. A storm forced one ship to make for an Irish port as the fleet was passing that island. Whether it was Cabot's own ship or not is a much debated question but in any case, Cabot made his way to America, possibly this time directly across the Atlantic and not by way of Iceland, although this is not known. From here on we know nothing certain, but it has been well argued that although Cabot himself likely perished on this expedition, some ships and some members of the expedition did succeed in carrying out exploration of a part of the eastern coast of Canada and the United States. The territory covered, however, would not include any parts of northern Canada. It seems to be generally agreed that place names on the eastern coast of America, as depicted on the world map of Juan de la Cosa of 1502, are derived from information supplied by survivors of the second voyage of John Cabot.[20] In any case, the expedition failed to bring back the sought-after information on an easy route to the fabulous lands of the east.

Instead, it would seem that it now gradually dawned on Englishmen, as well as others, that the lands to which Cabot sailed in 1497 and 1498 could not conceivably be those of the Asia of the Marco Polos. But here was a new land, inhabited by rough savages, devoid of treasures and important only for its fisheries and game. Beyond it somewhere Asia must lie, and the task which now confronted men was to find a way around it. One such way, and the only one open to Englishmen, was a northwest passage, and here the already known strait, which was to receive Hudson's name, opened up the possibilities. It was the discovery of this which Sebastian Cabot was to claim to have made. Assuming, as has been shown we have every right to do, that neither in 1508-1509 nor at any other time did he sail through it or even come near it after his father's death, how is this extraordinary claim to be explained? One answer might be suggested. Sebastian may, as a young lad, have sailed with his father on the voyage of 1497 when his father, as has been conjectured, sailed as far north as the 67° of latitude and on his southward course passed Baffin Island and entered Hudson Strait; or, he may have heard his father describe this strait. Later, when it had become increasingly clear that the new found land was indeed a new land, not a stepping stone to Asia but a barrier on the way thither, the young man may have begun to reflect. The strait he had seen or heard of was the northwest passage to the real Asia. Thenceforth, he had no hesitation in using all means to persuade others to allow him to prove the veracity of his claims and reach Asia by a northwest passage which he, from his own experience, already knew existed. This was really the life work of Sebastian Cabot – although he allowed himself at times to be diverted from his real purpose, as when he led the expedition in 1526-1530 to the River Plate in an attempt to find a passage through the great land mass which prevented direct contact with the east. Or was he only seeking his own fame?

As we conclude this discussion of John Cabot and his son Sebastian, let us recall what the dean of Cabot studies, J. A. Williamson, has written in his most recent book of "hym that founde the new Isle." It is a masterly summary of the achievements of one who will always occupy a leading place in the post-mediæval history of Canada. At the same time, it un-wittingly places John Cabot's son, Sebastian, in his proper niche.

> At this stage we leave John Cabot, and may essay some estimate of him. In his Venetian period he was a merchant of enterprise sufficient to take him to Mecca and to think of new ways of working the Far Eastern trade. He had read Marco Polo and mastered the information on China and Japan which enabled him to expose the falsity of the Spanish claim to have reached Asia. . . . He had studied also cartography and could express his ideas not only by maps but on a globe, a considerable professional achievement. . . .
>
> That he was an able advocate and spoke with authority is clear from his acceptance by Henry VII and the grant of the letters patent. Soncino testifies to his eloquence and conviction, and both Soncino and Pasqualigo suggest a certain magnificence and magnetism which fired the ignorant public no less than it drew support from the wary circle round the King. We may discern that John Cabot was a veritable leader of men, deprived of rounded historical greatness by premature death and lack of record. There he was unfortunate, for his son Sebastian did not play the part of Las Casas and Ferdinand Columbus, without whose devotion Christopher Columbus would not today be the great figure that he is. Sebastian did nothing for his father's repu-tation. . . .
>
> John Cabot's position in the enterprise may be seen more clearly since the publication of the John Day letter. The Bristol men had already found their Brasil and knew the way to it. There is no hint that they based any plan of Asiatic trade on their discovery, which was of so small promise that London, for all we can tell, had not heard of it. Cabot, seeking aid in Lisbon and Seville, where there were Bristol men to talk with, learned of it and decided that England must be his base. That would appear to have been his entry into the affair, although we lack the dates to prove it. There was land in the west, well clear of the Spanish activities. This land could be a stepping-stone on the way to Cipango. He came in therefore not only as a navigator but as a geographer and a specialist in the spice trade and, it is clear, as the commander in full control. He would extend a fishing voyage into a new trade-route that would divert the richest of all trades to an English port. It was sound enough had the world-map been true as he and Columbus viewed it. But the unsuspected presence of America defeated them both.[21]

CHAPTER 18

The Followers of John Cabot

The 1498 voyage of Cabot revealed that the new found lands were not Asia but a barrier to it. This did not altogether dampen the spirits of the Bristol merchants and others. They could in any case recoup the expenses of voyages to the east coast of America through the rich fisheries which were to be found off its coasts, whose exploitation probably began even before the voyages of John Cabot.

Joao Fernandez seems to have arrived in England about 1500. This controversial figure now joins with the merchants of Bristol in transatlantic voyages. In October 1499 he had been given letters patent by King Dom Manuel of Portugal, in which Fernandez is said to be "desirous to make an effort to seek out and discover at his own expense some islands lying in our sphere of influence." Because of this laudable enterprise on the part of Fernandez, the king granted him the governorship of any island or islands, either inhabited or uninhabited, which he may "discover and find anew" (*descobrill e achar novamente*).[1] This implies that Fernandez had already undertaken some exploration and no doubt refers to the voyage he made to Greenland in a Danish ship in the years 1492-1495, as discussed above. It is very likely that it was the information about Greenland which Fernandez brought from this voyage that led to the designation of Greenland for some decades during the early sixteenth century as the land of the labrador (*Terra laboratoris*). Fernandez was an Azorean llabrador (landowner, farmer, or husbandman) who had property on the island of Terceira. We know that sometime in the 1490's, Cabot was in Seville and Portugal – probably in 1495 – the year in which Fernandez returned from Denmark. Here he may have obtained information about Greenland from Fernandez, and when on his 1497 voyage he sighted Greenland, he called it the labrador's land. Indeed, Santa Cruz, in his *Islario* of 1541, tells us:

> It was called the Labrador's land because a husbandman from the Acores islands gave tidings and information about it to the king of England when

he sent Antonio Gabato, the English Pilot and father of Sebastian Gabato, who was Your Majesty's Pilot-major, to explore it.[2]

T. E. Layng, head of the Map Division of the Public Archives of Canada, has shown that the name "labrador" first makes its appearance on one of the prototypes used in compiling the Oliveriana map. This is an anonymous and undated map preserved in the Biblioteca e Musei Oliveriana at Pessaro. It may, however, be confidently dated to 1503 or shortly thereafter. Layng has made out a convincing case for the view that the northwest quarter of the Oliveriana map was based on the result of discoveries made before 1500. If this is so, then this information must derive either from Joao Fernandez or from the voyages of John Cabot. But Layng has attempted to show that the Oliveriana map is a record of John Cabot's pursuit of a course previously set by Joao Fernandez. Probably what happened is that Cabot relied on the information which he received from Joao Fernandez in 1495, and also possibly on the experience he gained on an abortive voyage in 1496 or on the information given him by a merchantman from Bristol on his visit to Iceland in that year. Layng has argued that Joao Fernandez headed an exploratory expedition to the north in 1496, and that it was the information derived from this voyage which Santa Cruz says was passed on to the English king. This, however, is impossible. All our sources say that Joao Fernandez spent three years on his voyage. Layng thinks the years are 1496, 1497, and 1498, but if this were so, the information Santa Cruz speaks about could not possibly be that which was passed on to the king of England when he sent Cabot to explore the labrador's land.[3] Everything points to the conclusion that the expedition referred to is that of 1492-1495, when the two emissaries of the Portuguese king sailed to and beyond Greenland on a Danish ship. This explains also why no letters patent authorizing the expedition are extant. That it is said to have been made in the reign of King Manuel, who came to the throne in 1495, may be explained by the fact that he was on the throne when the explorers returned.

As we have seen, Fernandez received letters patent from King Manuel on October 28, 1499, but in 1501, if not earlier, he was certainly in England where, in company with Richard Warde, Thomas Asshehurst, and John Thomas, merchants of Bristol, and his compatriots, Francisco Fernandez and Joao Gonsalves, he petitioned King Henry VII for letters patent on March 19, 1501. On the same day, the king issued letters patent, authorizing these men to "find, recover, discover and search out whatsoever islands, countries, regions or provinces of heathens and infidels, in whatever part of the world they may lie, which before this time were and at present are unknown to all Christians. . . ."[4] We know nothing further of this voyage or whether it achieved any results.

In the meantime, the Portuguese were continuing their voyages to America. Gaspar, the son of Joao Vaz Corte-Real, who had sailed to Labrador with Ioes Scolvus in 1472-1476, obtained on May 12, 1500, a patent from the king of Portugal in which it was stated that he had in times past "exerted much effort in searching out and finding several islands on the mainland at his own expense in ships and men," and as he was desirous to continue this search, the king is pleased "to grant and give him . . . the governorship of any islands or mainlands he may thus discover or find afresh."[5] Armed with this patent (which, incidentally, may have offended Joao Fernandez and prompted the latter to go to England) Gaspar sailed on an expedition which seems to have reached the east coast of Greenland, sailed south around Cape Farewell and up the west coast of Greenland. There seems little doubt that both he and Joao Fernandez were at this time activated by a desire to find a northwest passage to Asia.[6] In the next year, 1501, Gaspar made another voyage from Portugal with two or three ships which departed on March 15, 1501. We have reports of this expedition from the Venetian Ambassador in Portugal, Pietro Pasqualigo, both in a report to his government and in a letter to his brothers in Venice. In his letter to the latter, dated October 19, 1501, he writes:

. . . The 8th day of this month there arrived here one of the two ships, which his Serene Majesty dispatched, under the command of Gaspar Corte-Real (Corterat), to discover lands in the north. And they claim that they discovered a land 2000 miglia from here, between northwest and west, unknown before. Along the coast of this land they sailed, possibly 600-700 miglia, without finding an end to it, therefore they believe that it is a mainland, which is connected by land with another country, which was found in the north last year, but the ships could not get to the terminus of it, because the sea was covered with ice, and there were great masses of snow. They also believed this because of the great number of rivers they found there, and which would certainly not have been so many and so large on an island.[7]

Albert Cantino also describes this voyage, writing:

First he [Gaspar] reported that after they had left the port of Lisbon, they had sailed continually for four months in the same direction and towards the same pole, and never in all that time did they see anything. In the fifth month, as they wished to continue on the same course, they said they had met with unspeakable masses of frozen snow, which floated in the sea and moved with the waves. . . . They began now to sail to the north and west, and sailed on that course for three months always in fine weather. And on the first day of the fourth month they saw land of great size between the north and west, and approached this with great pleasure. Many large rivers of fresh water ran through this land to sea, up one of which they sailed for a league (legha) into the land.[8]

We cannot know with any certainty what land or region Gaspar reached, but the meagre information given in the above accounts might suggest Labrador. The account of Cantino, especially as to the duration of the voyage, is of course unacceptable.

There can be little doubt that on his voyages, Gaspar Corte-Real followed the old Vinland course via Iceland, the east coast of Greenland, south around Cape Farewell and up the west coast, north as far as Disko Island. On the Cantino map of *circa* 1502, Greenland is shown with an inscription which must mean "end or point of Asia" (A ponta d [e Asia]). The exploration during the second voyage would seem to have been confined largely to the coast of Labrador and there is some indication that they sailed into Hamilton Inlet where they encountered many caribou, and accordingly gave it the name "Bay of Does." Then they sailed farther south and recorded finding trees too large to be used as masts for even the biggest ships. Here they encountered what were almost certainly Eskimos (some say they were Naskapi Indians), of whom they kidnapped fifty, with the intention of selling them as slaves when they reached Europe. Soon after this, very likely in the region of the Strait of Belle Isle, the expedition divided. Two vessels sailed home to Portugal, while Gaspar sailed on farther south. The king of Portugal is said to have been pleased with the results of the expedition and the prospect of obtaining slaves, but his pleasure must have been somewhat marred by the fact that nothing more was ever heard of Gaspar.[9]

The failure of Gaspar to return prompted his brother, Miguel, to ask the king for permission to go in search of him. This was granted on January 15, 1502, and Miguel seems to have reached Newfoundland with three ships in June. In the harbour of St John's, the ships separated and searched the adjoining coasts. They were to meet at St John's late in August, but Miguel's ship did not turn up and nothing further is known of his fate.[10]

These voyages, both those from Bristol and those from Portugal, were without any real result for the future exploitation or settlement of Canada. They did, it is true, supply some information which was valuable to cartographers and others interested in the geography of what was coming to be recognized not as a part of Asia but a mainland, preventing direct access to the lands of the Khan. The place names resulting from these voyages in Newfoundland and the Maritime provinces of present-day Canada lie, however, outside the scope of this work and, in any case, they have been dealt with in such detail by various scholars that anything said here would be superfluous.

It was also in 1502 that another voyage was made from Bristol, and three savages were brought back from the "newe founde launde." This is all we really know of this voyage and we do not know whether the savages came from Newfoundland, the Maritimes, or Labrador. The entry regarding them, as preserved by Richard Hakluyt, may indicate that these men were Tunnit or an intermixture of the Tunnit with the Skraelings, preserving to a great extent Nordic characteristics. It reads as follows:

> This yeere also were brought unto the king three men, taken in the new founde Iland, that before I spake of in William Purchas time, being Maior. These were clothed in beastes skinnes, and ate rawe fleshe, and spake such speech that no man coulde understand them, and in their demeanour like to bruite beastes, whom the king kept a time after. Of the which upon two yeeres past after I saw two apparelled after the manner of Englishmen, in Westminster pallace, which at that time I coulde not discern from Englishmen, till I was learned what they were. But as for speech, I heard none of them utter one worde.[11]

These Bristol voyages of 1501-1502, for which Williamson has collected all the evidence,[12] were followed by the issue of a new patent dated December 9, 1502. The grantees here were Joao Gonsalves, Francisco Fernandez, Thomas Asshehurst, and Hugh Eliot, and the patent authorizes them "to find, recover, discover and search out any islands, countries, regions or provinces whatsoever of heathens and infidels in whatsoever part of the world placed . . . provided always that they in no wise occupy themselves with nor enter the lands . . . first discovered by the subjects of our very dear brother and cousin the king of Portugal."[13]

Williamson has shown that voyages were made under this patent between 1503 and 1506 and that those taking part in them were, at least in 1506, the Company of Adventurers to the New Found Land. But these voyages, again, were without lasting results and little is known about them.[14]

It has been argued in a previous chapter that Sebastian Cabot made no voyage in search of the northwest passage in the years 1508-1509. It is not as certain that he did not have a hand in an abortive voyage in the year 1517, along with Thomas Spert, a shipowner and first master of Trinity House, although both these men may have acted only in an advisory capacity. Henry VIII evidently gave the venture some support and it was also supported by two London merchants. A fleet was equipped with John Rastell, a brother-in-law of Sir Thomas More, in command.

The goal of the voyage is not entirely clear but it seems to have been directed to Newfoundland, although the whole east coast of Canada may have been included under this name. It has also been conjectured that if Cabot was a sponsor of the expedition, a search for the northwest passage may be indicated, but there is no evidence for this. The Lord-Admiral, the Earl of Surrey, was opposed to the expedition and by various machinations he was able to delay its departure to such an extent that it reached Cork in Ireland late in the season. Here, the purser of one of the ships, John

Ravyn, threatened violence against Rastell and the two London merchants who were backing the venture and managed to abscond with part of the cargo. The leaders had to return to London where lawsuits followed, about which we know little. The venture thus collapsed, whatever its aim may have been.[15]

The same is true of certain attempts to sail to northern Canada under the auspices of Spain and Portugal. The former attempted to send out an expedition in 1511 to the New Found Land under Juan de Agramonte, but we do not know if it even sailed.[16] In 1520 Joao Alvarez Fagundes headed an expedition to the vicinity of Nova Scotia, Cape Breton, Newfoundland, St Pierre, Miquelon, and Langlade. On his return to Portugal he was given rights to these islands, and may later have tried to found a colony.[17]

In 1521 the English, under the direction of Cardinal Wolsey, tried to undertake an expedition to the New Found Land. It was at this time that the Drapers' Company made their assertion referred to above, that Sebastian Cabot, who was, it seems, to lead the expedition, had never been in the territories to which it was to sail. The merchants of London failed, for this or other reasons, to furnish financial support, and the venture came to nought.[18]

Meanwhile, both the French and the Spanish sent further expeditions to Canada. In 1524, Giovanni da Verrazano was dispatched by Francis I and, sailing north from Florida, may have reached Canadian waters.[19] In 1524-1525, Estevan Gomez, a Portuguese by birth, in the service of Spain, reached Newfoundland and sailed on to Cape Breton Island. Thence he made his way to Nova Scotia, where he allocated names to places he visited. He then sailed south to Cuba.[20] Otherwise these voyages have left no impression on Canadian history. The same is true of the expedition launched by Henry VIII in 1527. In the spring of that year, two ships, the *Samson* and the *Mary Guildford*, sailed from London to seek a passage to Asia by way of Davis Strait. The *Samson* was lost in latitude 53° N but the *Mary Guildford*, whose master was John Rut, abandoning her northward course after reaching latitude 63° N, turned southward and eventually made her way to the West Indies, where she was fired upon by the Spaniards. From there, she seems to have finally made her way back to England.[21]

English interest in these voyages continued, spurred possibly by the writings of Robert Thorne, an English merchant who spent some time in Spain and knew Sebastian Cabot. He has already been referred to as the authority for the statement that his father, also named Robert, and Hugh Eliot discovered the New Found Land.[22] Thorne's idea was to sail directly over the North Pole to China, a route he thought to be by far the shortest. Of Thorne's influence, however, we know little.[23]

In 1536, there occurred a rather mysterious and obscure voyage. We are told that two ships, the *Trinity* and the *William*, sailed in that year, with Captain Robert Hore in command, to Cape Breton and thence to southern Newfoundland where they lived on the eggs and flesh of the great auk and on bears which they managed to kill. Having exhausted their food supply, their situation got so desperate that, according to the account, they resorted to cannibalism. One man, when asked where he got the meat he was eating, replied, "If thou wouldest needes know, the broyled meate that I had was a piece of such a man's buttocke." Such as survived were finally saved by their opportune capture of a French ship well supplied with food, and they eventually made their way back to England.[24] This was a voyage which marked the end, for a space of over forty years, to the early attempts by the English to find the North-West Passage.

These voyages from 1498 to 1536 were all inspired by the desire to find Asia either by sailing down the east coast of America or by circumventing the new mainland and discovering an open passage north of it into the Pacific. Colonization as an object of these voyages is not an impossibility, but there is very little in the accounts of them that would indicate that it was an important motivation. The attempt to circumvent the mainland, as Williamson points out, whether pursued by the Bristol merchants or by the Portuguese, "died out in the ice-fields." After 1536 both peoples, for different reasons, temporarily gave up the attempt to find a short route to Asia by way of the Arctic. The English did this through frustration at receiving no return for the monies expended in fruitless ventures. The Portuguese, who already had discovered and mastered a long, arduous, but profitable sea route to Asia, ceased to try to find a shorter and easier one by way of the Arctic. Another reason for English lack of interest for the next quarter-century in a passage to Asia, either by the northwest or the northeast, was the preoccupation with the king's business, that is, Henry VIII's marital difficulties and the schism with Rome resulting from this. In the meantime, English, French, and Portuguese fishermen continued to exploit the fisheries in Canadian waters that offered such rich returns, but returns often despised in comparison with the wealth which a contact with Asia was believed to offer those who would find new routes thither.

Most of these early endeavours to discover a sea way to Asia, utilized the knowledge, often fragmentary, of the Icelandic lands in the west, which were believed to be parts of Asia or to lie off Asia. They ended in failure, and were not to be renewed until the latter part of the sixteenth and, to a greater extent, the early part of the seventeenth centuries. They were to be accompanied by a resumption of the exploitation of northern resources by the French in the St Lawrence waterway and its hinterland, and a little later by the English ventures into Hudson Bay and the northern parts of Canada.

CHAPTER 19

The Arctic Expeditions of Martin Frobisher

For the next thirty or forty years, then, except for the fisheries off Newfoundland, Canada was largely forgotten, not only by Europeans but also by the English. The English, however, retained an interest in finding a shorter route to Asia and concentrated their efforts on finding a passage by way of the northeast.[1] Although this led to increased trade with Russia, the search for the passage proved unsuccessful and, in the 1560's, attention was again directed to the possibility of finding it by the northwest. In fact, as early as 1555, Sir Humphrey Gilbert was an eloquent advocate of this and of colonizing America for its own sake. His ventures directed to the latter end, however, fall outside the scope of this volume and, as it turned out, proved in any case abortive. His ideas on the passage to Asia may have influenced others, including Sir Martin Frobisher, who was, after the attempts made in the reign of Henry VIII, the first to re-attempt a discovery of a route to Asia by the northwest. It must be remembered, too, that Michael Lok, John Dee, Richard Hakluyt, and others, no doubt influenced Frobisher's thinking on the subject of a passage.

Martin Frobisher was born about 1539 in Yorkshire and early went to sea, where he practised not only legitimate trading but also piracy.[2] He made voyages to Africa, and it is possible that his interest in a northwest passage was stimulated by Portuguese contacts made at that time, and by his knowledge of the Zeno map. He tried to interest various men of high rank in a search for the North-West Passage and finally succeeded in securing financial support, largely from Michael Lok, for an expedition which sailed in 1576 on two small ships, the *Gabriel* and the *Michael*, neither of which was over twenty-five tons.

The expedition sailed north and reached the southern tip of Greenland, which they took to be the Friesland of the Zeno map. After being buffeted by storms, they reached Baffin Island and sailed into the bay to which Frobisher gave his name. Here they encountered Eskimos in kayaks, and

Frobisher caught one of these who came near the ship and "plucked him with maine force, boate and al into his bark, out of the Sea: Whervpon when he founde himself in captiuite, for very choller and disdain he bit his tong in-twayne within his mouth: notwithstanding, he died not thereof, but liued vntill he came in Englande, and then he died, of colde which he had taken at Sea."[3]

The interest the English showed in the Eskimo was not sufficient to kindle the enthusiasm which developed for the dispatch of a second expedition: this was provided by the report that the first expedition had found unlimited quantities of gold. On his return on October 1, Frobisher brought back with him pieces of black stone, one of which by chance was thrown into the fire by one of the wives of the eighteen backers or "adventurers" of the expedition. It was found to glisten after it cooled from the effects of the fire. Michael Lok took it to some assayers in London, one of whom, an Italian named John Baptista Agnello,[4] told him that the ore was gold, although other assayers denied that this was so. Frobisher also reported that the bay which now bears his name was the passage to Asia which he and his men had been unable to explore fully through the loss of a boat and five seamen, who were presumably slain by the Eskimos. It was, however, the belief in the fabulous deposits of gold ore that enabled Lok and Frobisher to gain support for a second voyage. On March 17, 1577, Queen Elizabeth granted a charter to the backers to form the Cathay Company.[5] The Queen also gave £1,000 and a 200-ton ship named the *Aid*, which was to accompany the *Gabriel* and the *Michael*. Thirty miners, together with assayers and craftsmen, were to sail as part of the 120-man crew of the three ships. The *Aid* was to be loaded with ore, while Frobisher explored his bay westward on one of the smaller ships. Six criminals were to be landed in Greenland (Friesland) in order that they might make a report on that country and its inhabitants. After sending the *Aid* back to England with the ore, Frobisher could proceed to Cathay if he so desired.[6]

The expedition sailed on May 26, 1577, and arrived in the Orkneys on June 7. They sighted Greenland on July 4 but were unable to land and, continuing on, they reached the entrance to Frobisher Bay in the vicinity of Queen Elizabeth Foreland (Resolution Island). They immediately prepared to look for the gold and put ashore two assayers on a small island where they found no ore. They then tried other islands and found great quantities of it. To a height they bestowed the name Mount Warwick and here they met Eskimos with whom they exchanged goods. They were concerned over the fate of the five missing men[7] who in the previous year had gone ashore and been either captured or killed by the Eskimos. They tried to secure hostages from whom they could obtain information. Finally, after Frobisher had been hit by an arrow in the buttocks, they managed to

F

capture one of the Eskimos. Shortly thereafter, in a storm that came up suddenly, all three ships nearly foundered in the heavy ice.

They then explored the islands and both shores of the bay, searching for ore and bestowing names at various points. They found a dead narwhal whose horn was almost two yards in length and, because of a break near the tip, was seen to be hollow. Into the horn they put spiders which died, indicating that this was a sea unicorn, whose horn was long regarded as being an antidote to all poisons, such as that emitted by spiders.

It was at this time too, that having found quantities of gold ore, they encountered some Eskimos who fled into the mountains at their approach. Searching out the Eskimos' tents, Frobisher's men left "Kniues, Bels, and Glasses" in order to entice the natives back, and they stole a dog from them. Upon returning from the Eskimos' lodgings, they found the natives waiting for them and ready to attack. They easily repulsed the natives, some of whom leaped into the sea, while others took to the interior. The Englishmen captured two women and a child but let the older woman go and carried off only the younger one and her child. They then plundered the Eskimos' tents but were disappointed in the spoils. These encounters took place on what is described as the "West shoare, supposed firme with America." They then sailed to the "East shoare," whither Frobisher had gone before them, and anchored off an island named for the Countess of Warwick. From the beginning of August to the twenty-second, they dug about two hundred tons of the "precious" ore for which they were searching and freighted the ships with it.

Here also they met natives and Frobisher attempted again to ascertain what had happened to the five men lost the year before. The natives indicated by means of signs that three of the five men were alive and asked for pen, ink, and paper. The request is so preposterous, if we may believe the narrative, that it can only mean that some of the natives were Icelanders who had come from the European culture of Greenland and still retained some traces of this. In fact, Dionyse Settle, one of the supercargo of gentlemen who accompanied Frobisher, was driven to say in his account of the voyage that "It seemeth they have bene vsed to this trade or traffique, with some other people adioyning, or not farre distant from their Countrie."[8] It is difficult to know who this people would be, unless one supposes that remnants of the Icelanders in Greenland, or Europeans trading with Eskimos in Labrador with whom the Baffin Islanders were in contact, are meant.

Frobisher, greatly desirous of getting some news of his missing men, kept trying to make contact with the natives who, we are told, proved treacherous. At one time, while "coasting the contrie," they met with "three of the craftie villains with a white skin [who] allured vs to them." They attempted to lead Frobisher into an ambush with "craftie allurements." The encounter ended with Frobisher's ordering his men to fire on them. Some were injured, and Frobisher was unable to gain any further knowledge of the five missing men.[9]

Obviously, we are dealing here, not with so-called "pure" Eskimos, but with Icelanders who had not yet completely intermixed with Skraelings and who were, it would seem, more Icelandic than Eskimo. Nevertheless, the Icelanders seem to have adopted completely what has come to be known as the Eskimo mode of life. Settle describes them as follows in one of the earliest descriptions which we possess of the Canadian Eskimo: "They are men of a large corporature, and good proportion: their colour is not much vnlike the Sunne burnte Countrie man, who laboureth daily in the Sunne for his liuing." He says that they eat all their food raw and in case of necessity "plucke vppe, and eate, not deintily" such grass as the country provides. They do not use a table or practise any of the table manners of a European. They wear the skin of beasts and birds and their apparel has "hoods and tailes."[10]

Their houses, Settle adds, are tents made of seal skins, but he also mentions that they have other kinds of houses which, however, the members of the expedition found to be uninhabited. These were built of stones and whalebones, with a skin laid over them to withstand the rain or other weather. This sounds like a description of typical houses of the Thule Culture which, as Stefansson suggests, may still have been used but only in the winter.[11] Their weapons are described as arrow heads, some of which are made of iron, although most are of bone, and this is followed by a description of the umiak and kayak. Settle goes on to add that they have some iron "whereof they make arrowe heades, kniues, and other little instrumentes, to woorke their boates, bowes, arrowes, and dartes withal, whiche are very vnapt to doe anything withall, but with great labour."[12] He deduces from this that they had commercial relations with some other people from whom they received the iron. He then goes on to describe the nature of the country, the frost, lack of moisture, and so on. Although we cannot say with certainty that this was not Greenland, it is more likely to have been Labrador, whither, it has been conjectured, many of the inhabitants of the Eastern Settlement migrated.

Frobisher and his men, however, were not primarily interested in the natives they met but rather in the procurement of the precious ore, although Settle does say, when discussing the departure of the expedition for England, that "after wée had satisfied our mindes with frayght sufficient for our vessels, though not our couetous desires, with such knowledge of the countrie people and other commodities as are before rehearsed, the 24 thereof wée departed therehence."[13] They departed with their cargo of "gold" and ran into storms in which two men were lost overboard off the

Gabriel and the rudder of the *Aid* was broken and had to be repaired under most trying circumstances in icy water. The expedition reached England on September 17, to be received with general acclaim. Frobisher received an award of one hundred pounds from Queen Elizabeth, who named the land he had discovered south of Frobisher Bay *Meta Incognita*. It may be noticed that the Eskimos they had kidnapped and who proved a great attraction, died very shortly after the return of the expedition. Assays of the ore that was brought back varied, but it was generally thought rich enough to yield a profit of some five pounds a ton; enthusiasm for the further exploitation of the ore deposits of the newly discovered land was such that there was no difficulty in interesting men in an expedition the following year.

Accordingly, in the spring, fifteen vessels were equipped and dispatched to Meta Incognita. They were expected to bring back 2,000 tons of ore and to establish a colony of 120 souls. They left Harwich on May 31, 1578, and sailed west across the Atlantic and sighted Friesland, that is, the southern tip of Greenland, on June 20. Frobisher named it "West England." They sailed along the coast and, finding an ice-free harbour, Frobisher and some of his men went ashore. Here they found traces of a people similar to those they had met on Meta Incognita. They found kayaks, umiaks, and tents made of skins, the inhabitants of which ran away at their arrival. Thomas Ellis, "*sailer and one of* the companie," tells us that upon investigation, they found the tents to be "furnished with fleshe, fishe, skinnes, and other trifles: amongest the which was found a boxe of nailes: whereby we did coniecture, that they had either Artificers amongst them, or else a trafficke with some other nation."[14] In his account of the third voyage, Edward Sellman, "servant of Michael Lok," states that Frobisher and his men saw in the tents of the Eskimos "nayles like scupper nayles and a tryvet of yron."[15] This indicates that either there were Icelanders in Greenland who practised the ancient art of iron smelting, or there was contact with Europeans from whom iron nails could be obtained. It must be admitted that the latter is the more likely possibility, suggesting communications with Europe through Labrador. The trivet would hardly be a native product, but its presence and that of the iron nails shows that the natives of Greenland could not have suffered from a serious shortage of iron for the making of knife blades, arrow and harpoon heads, and other implements for which iron would be desired.

Frobisher, however, was not particularly interested in Greenland but rather in the gold-bearing regions farther west. Three days later, a fair wind enabled the expedition to set sail for Frobisher Bay. When they arrived at Queen Elizabeth Foreland on July 2, however, they encountered adverse weather conditions. There they "sawe so much yce, that we thought it vnpossible to get into the Streightes: yet at the last we gaue the aduenture, and entered the yce." The struggle against the ice and the contrary winds made it impossible to reach land and there were times when the members of the expedition were "looking euerie houre for death." Indeed, one of the vessels, the bark *Dionyse* which was carrying supplies for the proposed colony and materials for the building of a fort, struck an iceberg and sank, although the crew was saved. Sellman describes eloquently how the storm increased and the ice closed in, the rigorousness of the tempest and all the events of that "dismall and lamentable night" until God's providence finally saved them. Safe for the moment, they then glimpsed a "maruellous huge mountaine of yce, which surpassed all the rest that euer we sawe." So impressed was Ellis with this iceberg that he inserted in his book four drawings showing views of it from various angles. Battling against the weather, Frobisher finally made his way into a strait where he found the tides and currents surprisingly strong. This was Hudson Strait, and Frobisher would have discovered Hudson Bay, had he not turned back after sixty leagues, naming the passage Mistaken Strait. The party finally made their way to the Countess of Warwick Island, in the course of which, the *Gabriel* sailed through Gabriel Strait, proving that Queen Elizabeth Foreland (Resolution Island) was an island. The men began mining on the Countess of Warwick Island and on another island called Best's Blessing. This was done in July in spite of ice, storms, and at times scorching heat. The ships were laden with cargo and thus one object of the expedition was accomplished, but the colonization venture could not be carried out because of the loss of much of the timber when the bark *Dionyse* went down.

There was nothing to do but return. Loaded with ore, the fleet sailed, only to run into a storm which scattered the ships. Frobisher himself was caught on the *Gabriel*, instead of his own ship, the *Aid*, and had to make his voyage home on it. The *Emmanuel*, it might be said, miraculously escaped from the coast and on the way home discovered a large island in latitude 57° which was given the name of Buss, after the ship *Emmanuel*, which was of the type of vessel known as a buss. This island, which long remained on maps, turned out to be fictitious. The whole fleet managed to reach England about October 1, only to find that all its labours had been in vain. While its members had been away from England, the precious ore had been assayed and pronounced worthless. Lok was placed in debtor's prison, and the stockholders of the Cathay Company went bankrupt. Frobisher's ventures seemed to have ended in total failure. Indeed, from the financial or commercial view, this was true; Frobisher, himself, seems to have been forced to return to piracy for a time. Then, in 1588, he fought the Spanish Armada and, continuing in the service of the crown, received a fatal wound fighting the Spaniards at Brest. He died on November 22, 1594.

Yet Frobisher's voyages were not without consequence. He was the first, after the Greenland Icelanders, to make his way west beyond Greenland to the islands of the Canadian archipelago and supply to Europe geographical knowledge of Baffin Island and its environs as well as its people. He was the first to sail halfway through Hudson Strait and, although he did not reach the bay, the voyage served to stimulate the belief that a northwest passage to the fabulous lands of Asia might be found. It must also be said that Frobisher was one of the most outstanding mariners of all time, as is shown especially by his third expedition. Considering the difficulties the expedition encountered, it is amazing that only one ship deserted, only one was lost, and only some forty men died accidentally or from scurvy or the rigours of the climate. Although Frobisher added geographical knowledge of Frobisher Bay and the neighbouring regions, his voyages also created confusion in the minds of cartographers which lasted for some two centuries. This was partly a result of reliance on the Zeno map, and Frobisher himself mistook Greenland for the non-existent Friesland of the Zeno map. This resulted in Baffin Island and the neighbouring regions visited by Frobisher being shown as located on the east coast of Greenland, with Frobisher's supposed strait cutting through southern Greenland, and later as a bay on its east coast. John Davis, head navigator of the expedition, was largely responsible for this, for he believed that Frobisher, having passed Friesland, sailed west to the east coast of Greenland and that his explorations had been conducted there. Necessarily, Frobisher's Strait must therefore cut through Greenland. Misled thus, map-makers showed it there for some two centuries. Other causes contributing to the confusion were the inadequate means possessed at this time of determining longitude and the variation of the compass in northern regions. To these must be added the failure of Frobisher and his men to distinguish clearly in many cases what was land and what was simply ice and mist. The island of Buss mentioned above is a good example of this, and it bedevilled the cartography of the north Atlantic for two or three centuries. Hakluyt had reported its discovery in his *Navigations* in 1589.[16] As no one ever came across it, it was believed to have sunk and for a long time was known as the sunken island of Buss.

These geographical misconceptions led to a failure to identify correctly Frobisher's discoveries. Their location was finally established in 1862 by the American Arctic explorer, Charles Francis Hall. The Eskimos of Baffin Island told him that white men had come to their land for three years in succession. In the first year, they arrived on only one ship; in the second year, on three ships; and in the third year, on many ships. These white men dug up the ground. It is sometimes amazing how accurately the Eskimo legends have preserved the memory of certain things from the past, but such information can only be relied on if it is given spontaneously, for if leading questions are asked of the Eskimo, he will attempt to give the information which he believes the interrogator wants.[17] Hall confirmed the above stories by finding many relics of the expedition which he sent to the Smithsonian Institution in Washington and to the Royal Geographical Society in England. These relics, which attested to the location of Frobisher's mining operations, constitute a further problem: not one of them can be found, having been lost by the depositaries.

Frobisher's voyages are typical of those that follow and have therefore been described in some detail. We must now survey briefly some of the later voyages.

CHAPTER 20

The Later Search for the
North-West Passage

The failure of Frobisher only temporarily discouraged the English in their quest for the North-West Passage. Hakluyt, John Dee, Sir Humphrey Gilbert, his brother Adrian, and John Davis, all continuously urged that a passage be found and that colonies be planted in the New World. Finally they succeeded in interesting the government, particularly Secretary Sir Francis Walsingham. On February 16, 1584, a patent was issued to Adrian Gilbert to discover a passage to China and the Maluccas by either the northeast or northwest. Merchants of Exeter and London financed the project, and John Davis was placed in command of the expedition.[1]

On June 7, 1585, the expedition sailed in two ships, the *Sunshine* and the *Moonshine*. It was held up by contrary winds in the Scilly Islands and it did not leave them until June 28. Greenland was reached on July 20 and described as "the most deformed, rocky and mountainous land that we ever sawe." Davis named it the "Land of Desolation." This was the southeast coast of Greenland, and Davis sailed south along it, rounded Cape Farewell and, sailing north, entered the fjord where present-day Godthaab is located. Here the party met the Eskimos and traded with them. They then sailed northwest to latitude 66° 40′ and entered the mouth of Cumberland Sound on Baffin Island. Davis described the land as very "mountaynous, altogether without wood, grasse or earth, and is only huge mountaines of stone, but the bravest stone that we ever sawe." Davis spent the time between August 6, when he reached Cumberland Sound, and August 26, when he sailed for England, in examining the neighbourhood, its flora and fauna, and the nature of the region. He reached England on September 30, believing that he might have found the entrance to the sought-for passage.

He was able to convince the merchants of this, and another expedition was launched the next year, this time with two additional ships, the *Mermaid* and the *North Star*. They sailed for Greenland on May 7, 1586. A month later they were near Greenland in latitude 60°. The *Sunshine* and the *North Star* were sent to explore the east coast of Greenland while Davis, with the other two ships, sailed to present-day Godthaab. Here they traded again with the Eskimos, and Davis explored the neighbouring fjords, after which he sailed north to latitude 63°, where ice blocked further progress. At this time, several of his men fell sick and Davis transferred them to the *Mermaid*, which he ordered to sail home. He himself then crossed over to Baffin Island to the vicinity he had reached the year before, but he did not attempt to explore Cumberland Sound. Whether this was because of the "muskyto [which] did sting grievously" or whether he doubted that this was the passage he sought, we do not know. Instead, he sailed southward to the Labrador coast to latitude 57° N, and then farther south to, it would seem, the Strait of Belle Isle. He landed on the Newfoundland coast, and while curing fish there, two of the crew were killed by Indians. After riding out a severe storm, Davis then sailed for England, tremendously impressed with the fishing-grounds off Newfoundland, which he thought might pay for future expeditions searching for the North-West Passage. The *Sunshine* and the *North Star*, after following the ice to Iceland and sailing thence to Godthaab, where they played football and fought with the natives, finally departed for England on August 31. The *North Star* was lost in a storm, but the *Sunshine* reached England on October 6.

Although some of Davis's supporters were discouraged, a third voyage was undertaken on May 19, 1587 – this time on the *Sunshine*, the *Elizabeth*, and the *Ellen*. In spite of various misfortunes, Davis reached Godthaab on July 15. Here the natives showed animosity, and relations between them and the Europeans deteriorated. On June 21, the *Sunshine* and the *Elizabeth* left for the fishing-grounds off Labrador and Newfoundland. Davis himself sailed north on the *Ellen* and without any difficulty reached latitude 72° 12′, naming the most northerly point reached "Sanderson his Hope," in honour of William Sanderson, his greatest backer. He then turned westward and encountered the middle pack of ice in Baffin Bay, which, together with head winds, drove him back to Greenland. However, by July 19 he had crossed the strait which bears his name and reached Cumberland Sound, which this time he explored fully. Sailing south, he did not recognize Frobisher Bay, and renamed it Lumley's Inlet. The strong tides and currents at the entrance of Hudson Strait discouraged him, and he sailed past to the northern tip of Labrador, to which he gave the name, Fort Chidley. He then sailed south to the rendezvous which had been agreed upon, but finding neither of the two ships there, he made for England on August 15 and reached it on September 15.

Davis's voyages are important for several reasons. He added a great deal of new geographical knowledge concerning the regions he visited, in spite of the fact that Frobisher Bay was depicted in southern Greenland and

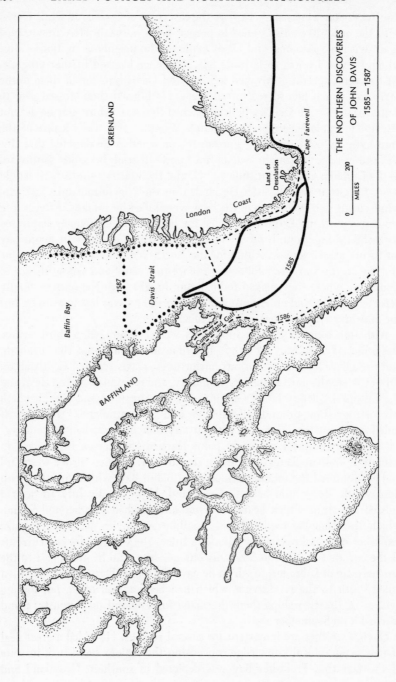

THE NORTHERN DISCOVERIES
OF JOHN DAVIS
1585 — 1587

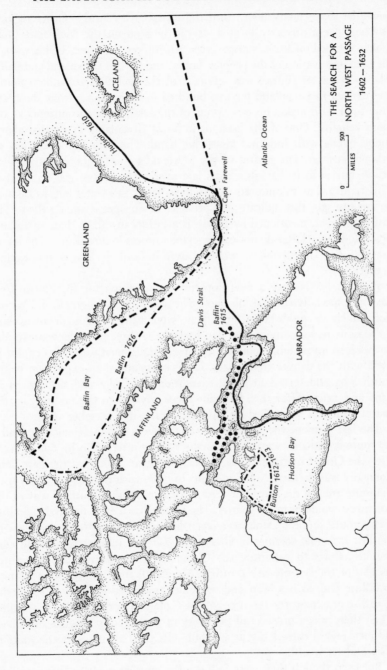

THE SEARCH FOR A
NORTH WEST PASSAGE
1602 — 1632

0   500
MILES

ICELAND

Hudson 1610

GREENLAND

Cape Farewell

Atlantic Ocean

Davis Strait

Baffin 1616

Baffin Bay

Baffin
1615

BAFFINLAND

LABRADOR

Button 1612-1613

Hudson Bay

remained so on many maps until the nineteenth century. Other regions, however, were correctly located, as can be seen on the Molyneux globe which is based on Davis's discoveries. An interesting aspect of his work is his keen observation of the peoples, fauna, and flora of Greenland and Baffin Island. Davis, of course, was ignorant of the fact that Icelandic colonies had existed in Greenland for five hundred years or more, from about the year 1000. This makes his description of the Eskimos he encountered all the more valuable. One of the Eskimos in West Greenland, as noticed above, shook hands with him and kissed his hand. This is a European, not an Eskimo, custom. The master of the *Mermaid* found a grave, with several people buried in it, having a cross laid over them – a vestigial remnant of Christianity. The Eskimos are said to have drunk salt water but, as Eskimos do not use salt, this indicates the presence of Europeans among them. The eating of grass, mentioned by Davis, is a European rather than an Eskimo practice, for the latter do not eat vegetables unless in dire straits. The use of nets by the Greenlanders, which Davis noticed, is also a non-Eskimo practice.

Further, Davis gave a new impetus to the search for the North-West Passage, especially through his book, *The Worldes Hydrographical Description*, which was published in 1595. Plans were made for a fourth voyage but, for various reasons, those who had backed the three previous ventures did not wish to invest more money; then, too, Englishmen were preoccupied in 1588 with the danger from Spain. Davis commanded an expedition to the South Seas and served in naval expeditions to Cadiz and the Azores in 1596 and 1597. After this, he made three voyages to the far east, on the last of which he was killed by Japanese pirates in December 1605.

The last years of the reign of Elizabeth saw a lull in attempts to find a sea route to India by way of the northwest, but interest in this and in trade with the Orient remained alive. In fact, it was in 1600 that the East India Company was granted exclusive rights to trade with that region. They used the route around the Cape but were fully aware that a route by way of the northwest would be much shorter. The Dutch also were interested in finding such a route, and the Danes were very desirous of establishing contact with the lost Icelandic colonies in Greenland. All this interest resulted in continuous efforts to penetrate the Canadian Arctic during the first three decades of the seventeenth century. Almost all these efforts were doomed to failure and, as has been said, were not prompted by a conscious desire to utilize or exploit the resources of the Canadian north. Only incidentally, when there was a prospect of discovery of rich deposits of gold and silver, did men regard these lands as anything else than a barrier on the route to Asia and its wealth.

But even though they were failures, the voyages made to the north had important results. The whaling industry of Spitzbergen was to a great extent the outcome of the attempt to find a northeast passage, and the whaling industry in Davis Strait and Baffin Bay was the outcome of a search for a northwest passage. And, when in the 1630's men despaired of finding the North-West Passage by way of Hudson Bay, they turned to an exploitation of the furs and other resources of the shores and hinterland of the bay. Again, these voyages to the Canadian Arctic greatly increased the knowledge of the geography of this region. Its flora and fauna became well known and the climatic and natural conditions could be assessed better on the basis of voyages made frequently – sometimes year after year. Also, it must not be forgotten that these voyages often exhibit the human being at his best, albeit sometimes at his worst. The annals of these expeditions are records of courage, perseverance, and almost incredible endurance amidst some of the harshest and most difficult natural conditions ever encountered by man. They are true tales of heroism, for the Canadian Arctic – while it is a "friendly" region to one who, like Stefansson, knows its every mood, whim, and caprice, and who is equipped mentally, physically, and materially to cope with all its conditions – can be the deadliest of all regions to those who bring little more than ignorance to the conquest of it. And this was the case with the great majority of those who, in the beginning of the seventeenth century, ventured to penetrate its ice, fog, and mists – in what can only be described as frail little barks, fitted for little more than coastal navigation or for sailing the high seas under the most favourable conditions. Surprisingly, however, the smaller vessels withstood the buffetings and ice of the Arctic seas more successfully than the larger ones. Up to 1500, the only Europeans who were acquainted with the hazards and dangers of sailing in the Arctic seas were the Icelanders in Greenland, the Thule Culture people, and possibly, to a limited extent, a few Norwegians. When one considers how completely inexperienced Englishmen and Dutchmen were in problems of voyaging in Arctic waters, it is indeed remarkable how many expeditions to the Arctic returned. Another result, therefore, of these early voyages to Greenland and the Canadian Arctic was to teach later adventurers how to cope with the ice and other hazards of the northern seas.

The voyages made between 1602 and 1632, with which we must now deal, have much in common. Most of them share a similar pattern and experience. The earliest was that led by the navigator, George Weymouth, in the service of the East India Company.[2] The avowed object of this voyage was to discover the North-West Passage. Weymouth was to be paid five hundred pounds if he discovered it; if he did not, he was to receive nothing. He had under his command two small vessels, the *Discovery* and the *Godspeed*, whose crews came principally from Devon. The expedition was not to return to England for a year, unless it discovered the passage before the year had elapsed. Weymouth and his men left England on May 2, 1602, and sighted Greenland on June 18. They sailed directly to Baffin Island and ten days later reached Frobisher Bay. It is not known exactly what regions Weymouth explored, but he may have sailed south to northern Labrador. It is almost certain that he went a short distance into Hudson Strait where, like so many others, he was impressed by the strong currents and overfall.

His crew, however, seemed to have been more impressed with the hardships they had to undergo in stormy, cold, weather, among the quantities of ice. At any rate, on the night of July 19, they mutinied. Weymouth was forced to agree to return to England and, after surviving violent storms off Labrador, they reached Dartmouth on August 5, 1602. None of the mutineers was really punished, except that the chaplain, John Cartwright, who may have instigated the mutiny, was required to return the gown which he had been given to wear at his audience with the Great Khan. Weymouth himself was freed of all blame for the failure of the voyage. Plans were made for him to lead another expedition the following year, but these were later dropped and Weymouth made no further trips.

The next English expedition to the Arctic was not until 1606, but there were three Danish expeditions to Greenland in the years 1605, 1606, and 1607. As has been said, Christian IV was eager to establish contact with the lost Icelandic colonies in Greenland. The leaders of these voyages, in varying positions of authority, were the Scot, John Cunningham, the Englishmen, John Knight and James Hall, and the Dane, Godske Lindenow.[3]

On the first voyage Hall made valuable maps of parts of the west coast as far north as Disko Island. He kidnapped four Eskimos, one of whom became so violent that he had to be shot. On Hall's return, the interest shown in the captured Eskimos was secondary to that engendered in the samples of "silver" ore which he brought back with him, and a second expedition was planned at once.

The second voyage, made in 1606, proved to be entirely fruitless. Its efforts were largely concentrated in the mining and loading of "silver" ore, which upon the return to Denmark turned out to be valueless. Contact was not, of course, made with the old Icelandic colonies, nor was the knowledge of the geography of the country increased. Five natives were captured, four of whom reached Denmark, with the purpose of training them as interpreters, but this plan fell through. Furthermore, when Hall visited Greenland in 1612 he was recognized by an Eskimo, probably a relative of one of those kidnapped, who plunged a weapon into Hall's side, pierced his liver, and brought about his death. The 1607 expedition never got beyond Iceland. The best that can be said about these expeditions is that both Hall and Knight had received valuable training in northern voyaging.

Knight had taken part in the 1605 voyage only, returning to England on its completion. There he found both the East India Company and the Muscovy Company preparing to underwrite another expedition. He was placed in command of this, along with Olivier Brunel, a veteran of the earlier Dutch ventures to the northeast. They sailed in the bark *Hopewell* on April 18, 1606, and reached Greenland about June 3. As might have been expected from the early date of their departure, they encountered very heavy ice off Greenland and had to fight their way through this to reach Labrador on June 19 in the vicinity of present-day Nain. Now a storm struck them; they almost lost their ship, but were able to ground her, half full of water. This was only the beginning of the tragedy. On June 26, Knight, Brunel, and three members of the crew rowed to an island not far distant. Brunel and another man were left behind to guard the shallop while Knight and the other two men, all well armed, started off inland. They were never seen again, but a clue as to their fate may be provided by the fact that two days later, a band of Indians appeared at the camp where Knight's men were attempting to pump out and repair the *Hopewell*. The Indians were frightened off. With emergency repairs, the expedition limped to Fogo Bay, Newfoundland, where more adequate repairs were made. It finally returned to Dartmouth on September 24, 1606.

The Muscovy Company, although deeply disappointed in the results of the Knight expedition, did not abandon its search for the passage. It now placed the experienced navigator, Henry Hudson, in command of a new expedition.[4] His instructions were to sail "by way of the northern regions, whether across to Cathay or elsewhere," that is, across the Pole. Hudson sailed from England on May 1, 1607, on the bark *Hopewell*. He reached the east coast of Greenland about latitude 70° and was able to make his way as far north as Cape Hold with Hope. Because he was stopped by ice and possibly because he was confused by the Zeno map, he turned eastward and sailed off the ice pack until he came into sight of Spitzbergen. He had at this point penetrated farther north in these regions than any man before him, to latitude 81°. Convinced that he was not on the right track, although the sea here was ice-free, Hudson turned back, passed Bear Island and, on the way, discovered the island of Jan Mayen which he named "Hudson's Touches"; from there he sailed to England. He had failed in his object but, as has been said, his glowing account of the mammal life of the northern seas gave a great impetus to the growing whale industry. In 1608, again in the services of the Muscovy Company, he attempted to find a northeast passage, but failed miserably.

If he was not already known to the Dutch East India Company, these voyages served to bring him to its attention. In 1609 the company put him in charge of their ship, the *Half-Moon*, in which he was to sail north or south of Novaya Zemlya. This he was unable to do as his crew mutinied and made him turn about. Hudson now persuaded the sailors to allow him to sail west in the more temperate region of latitude 40°, in an attempt to discover a passage through America in that vicinity. He sailed to Newfoundland, touched at Nova Scotia, then proceeded along the east coast of America to Chesapeake Bay. But nowhere could he find the passage. He then turned back and, continuing up the coast, entered the mouth of the river which now bears his name, and sailed up as far as Albany. Drawing a blank, he left on October 4 for home, arriving at Dartmouth on November 7, 1609. He immediately sent word to the Dutch East India Company of his failure. He had made, however, one of the longest voyages man had made up to this time, and the Dutch were given grounds for claiming the territory where in 1614 they founded the colony and trading-post of New Amsterdam (New York).

The Dutch geographer, Peter Plancius, had shown his friend, Hudson, the journal and log books from Weymouth's voyage of 1602, and Hudson had become desirous of attempting to find the North-West Passage. He had no trouble in obtaining support in England for this venture. On April 17, 1610, he left England with his seventeen-year old son on Weymouth's old ship, the *Discovery*, on the most tragic but by no means the last of the voyages of this most durable craft.

The important members of the crew were Robert Jouet, the mate, who had sailed with Hudson on his second and third voyages; Edward Wilson, surgeon; Habakkuk Prickett, a servant of Sir Dudley Digges (one of the backers); Robert Bylot, a naval officer; Arnold Ludlow, Michael Pierce, sailors; Thomas Woodhouse, a mathematical student; Henry Green, a protégé of Hudson's and a spendthrift and wastrel; Phillip Staffe, carpenter; and John King, quartermaster. Hudson set his course for Iceland. This indicates that he may have been relying on the sailing directions given in the treatise by Ivar Bardarson, *Description of Greenland*, which Hudson is known to have carried about with him. In any case, he followed the old Icelandic sailing course. He put in briefly at Iceland, where Green and Wilson seem to have quarrelled and Jouet got mixed up in the trouble. From Iceland Hudson sailed to the east coast of Greenland, south along the ice, rounded Cape Farewell, and reached Resolution Island by the end of June. He then entered the strait which bears his name, and encountered the strong currents which characterize the strait, and also some ice. On the first of August he entered the bay which also bears his name, in the vicinity of Digges Island – which he named in honour of Sir Dudley. He sailed south along the coast of the bay until he reached what is now James Bay. It was late in the fall and the ice was forming behind him. Stores were low, many of the crew discontented. In fact, at a sort of trial on September 10, Jouet was relieved of his duties and Bylot made first mate. The winter was a hard one, provisions ran short, and the discontent grew. The ice freed the ship about the middle of June, when about two weeks' provisions were left. Some of the men were sick. The dissatisfied felt it a waste of food to feed these. Hudson wanted to continue the search but the men wanted only to return home. On June 22, coming on deck, Hudson was surprised, seized, and bound. King and Staffe rallied to his side. The mutineers now hustled these two, Hudson and his son, Woodhouse (who was sick), and four sick sailors, into the shallop. Some guns and ammunition, some meal, and an iron kettle were given them, but nothing else. The boat was cast adrift and Hudson and his eight companions were never heard of again.

The *Discovery*, manned by the thirteen mutineers, sailed north. When they reached the strait, they stopped at Cape Digges to hunt birds and secure other provisions if possible. On July 29, Green, Wilson, Prickett, and three sailors – Motter, Thomas, and Pierce – went ashore, unarmed, to bargain with the Eskimos about provisions. Suddenly these peaceful negotiations came to an abrupt end when the natives attacked, disembowelling Thomas and Wilson, and wounding Pierce and Green. They were all, however, able to reach the boat and take off. The Eskimos sent a shower of arrows after it, killing Green on the spot and wounding Prickett and Pierce for the second time. Thomas and Wilson died in a very short time, and Pierce in a couple of days.

The nine men remaining salted birds and loaded the ship with as many of them as they could – and experienced a very hard voyage home. Provisions ran short and Jouet starved to death. On September 6, they reached Ireland. When the *Discovery* at last reached London, the case was examined, and the Masters of Trinity House agreed that the mutineers should hang. They did, however, get off free. Indeed, Bylot, who may have been a reluctant accomplice, was even hired to lead a new expedition now that the North-West Passage had, as they thought, at last been discovered.

There is no need to emphasize the greatness of Henry Hudson as a navigator. Any one of his voyages would suffice to prove that. Perseverance, courage, and stubbornness may indeed have been his outstanding traits, but through these qualities he was enabled to carry out his four great voyages, the results of which were of lasting value. In particular, he made not inconsiderable contributions to geographical knowledge, as can be seen on the map of Hessel Gerritz, 1612-1613. Probably no voyage since that of Christopher Columbus had so stirred the minds of men, kindled their enthusiasm and fired their imagination as the 1610 voyage of Hudson. Not only England but much of western Europe was desperately desirous of finding a short route to Asia across the Arctic. Now it had been found. The mutineers brought back word of a broad and navigable strait, leading into a huge body of water whose western limits were unknown but which there was every reason to believe could be none other than the fabled shores of Cathay, the goal of every merchant. Hudson's fame is deservedly commemorated in the river, strait, and bay, which bear his name.

So great was the enthusiasm aroused by Hudson's discovery that in July 1612, 288 individuals were granted a royal charter as the "Governor and Company of the Merchants of London, discoverers of the North-West Passage."[5] This was to become known as the North-West Company, and its members included all the great names in England who had any interest in the North-West Passage. The company received a monopoly of any passage in regions of Hudson Strait and westward. Even before the incorporation of this company, some who were to be its members had already dispatched another expedition designed to put the existence of the passage beyond the slightest hint of doubt. A Welsh captain, Thomas Button, was placed in charge of a large ship called the *Resolution*, and the old *Discovery* was placed under Captain John Ingram.[6] Both ships were provisioned for a year and a half. Robert Bylot and Habakkuk Prickett, their misdeeds forgotten, were to accompany Button and guide him into the strait to the sea. The Prince of Wales himself gave Button his instructions on April 5, 1612: these were, to make directly for Digges Island and, having observed from which direction the flood came, he was to sail into it; he was not to give a thought to anything except the passage.

Button experienced no difficulty in finding the strait and, as he passed into it, in honour of his ship he gave Resolution Island the name it has since borne. Although there was ice in the strait, no great impediment was encountered in reaching Digges Island. He then sailed for what proved to be the west coast of Hudson Bay, passed the southern coast of Coats Island, and reached the west coast in the vicinity of latitude 60°. His disappointment is evident in the name he gave to the spot where he landed – "Hopes Checked." Nevertheless, he continued to explore and sailed south to the mouth of the Nelson, which he named after the sailing master of the *Resolution*, and there he wintered. Some of the crew died here during the winter, and in the spring Button sailed north with the remainder of the crew in the *Discovery*, making his way as far up the coast as Roes Welcome Sound, which he seems to have thought was a bay. He sailed east along the south coast of Southampton Island, mistook Fisher Strait for a bay and reached Coats Island, which he thought was a promontory of Southampton Island. He sailed around in these waters, discovered Mansel Island and gave it its name before making for Cape Wolstenholme. Button made some useful observations on the tides in these regions, especially around Salisbury and Nottingham Islands. In September of 1613 he returned to England, where he was received with enthusiasm and was made Admiral Sir Thomas Button.

He served in the English navy until his death in April 1634. Needless to say, this voyage added many geographical details to the incomplete picture of the Canadian north. Its chief effect was to reveal the existence of western Canada as a barrier of unknown width between the Atlantic and Asia.

It should be noticed that in the same year, 1612, on April 20, James Hall commanded an expedition from Hull which sailed in two ships, the *Patience* and the *Heart's Ease*.[7] Part of its objective was to investigate whether or not there was silver ore in Greenland, in spite of the earlier denials of this. As we have seen, upon reaching Greenland, Hall was killed by one of the natives. After his death, the ore was declared worthless by a James Carlisle, a goldsmith who had been brought along to pronounce on its value. The expedition then returned to Hull, which it reached on September 17. It is of interest that William Baffin, the great navigator, accompanied this expedition upon which he seems to have begun the careful observations which were to characterize his conduct on his later voyages.

In spite of the apparent failure of both of these expeditions, so encouraging were Button's discoveries deemed by many, that in 1614 the North-West Company sent his cousin, Captain William Gibbons, in the *Discovery*, to follow up the work. He was unable to get through Hudson Strait because of ice and, in fact, was trapped on the Labrador coast for ten weeks in a place his men named "Gibbons his Hole." Thus, they returned having achieved little.

In spite of this, the North-West Company was eager to dispatch another expedition. In 1615, therefore, the company fitted and sent out the old *Discovery* for its fifth voyage, this time with Robert Bylot as Captain and William Baffin, who had risen from a lowly status to become an experienced sailor, as mate and pilot.[8] On April 19, 1615, the expedition sailed from England and, on its way to Cape Farewell, Baffin figured for the first time their position as to longitude at sea while underway. On May 10 they passed Cape Farewell and on the 27th came within sight of Resolution Island. They then set their course off the north shore of Hudson Strait. The end of the strait was reached late in June. In line with the purpose of the expedition – which was to gain further information about the tides observed by Button – they spent a month on this task in the vicinity of Salisbury and Nottingham Islands, Foxe Channel, and Southampton Island. They skirted the northeast coast of Southampton Island and in Frozen Strait concluded that they would never find any passage in these regions. They therefore turned back, stopped at Digges Island around July 29, and reached England on September 8. The expedition was not a total loss, however. Baffin became convinced of the existence of a passage but felt that it would be somewhere off Davis Strait or north of there. He also mapped in a meticulous way the geographical features of the shores, islands, and seas the expedition had visited. Again, he made the first reckonings of longitude at sea and noticed the variation of the compass. All this was a good harbinger of his later research and discoveries.

In 1616 the North-West Company sent out the *Discovery* again under Bylot as Captain and Baffin as pilot. The object of this expedition was to explore Davis Strait and discover there the elusive passage. This was to be one of the grand, exploratory voyages in the Canadian Arctic. The expedition sailed from England on March 26 and saw no further land until May 14, when the region of Sukkertoppen in west Greenland was sighted. Pushing north from there, it had reached Sanderson his Hope by May 30. Sailing north from there, Bylot and his crew landed into trouble with the middle pack; they made again for the coast of Greenland, where natives were encountered who were willing to exchange walrus, narwhal tusks, and seal skins for iron and beads. By July 1 they had freed themselves of the ice and reached latitude 75° 40'. Continuing north, Baffin named a headland in the vicinity of 76° 30' Cape Dudley Digges, and a fjord north of there Wolstenholme Sound. A fjord north of Cape Parry was named Whale Sound, for it teemed with these animals. They then crossed the head of the bay to the Canadian islands on the west side and here gave a name to Jones Sound. Skirting Devon Island, they came to what Baffin called Lancaster Sound, about latitude 74°, which Baffin failed to recognize as the only feasible northwest passage in these regions. The opportunity was missed and the expedition continued its southeasterly course off the ice until, about latitude 68°, they altered course and made for Sukkertoppen (Cockayne Sound). After treating the sick, they made for England and cast anchor there on August 30.

Baffin carefully mapped all the strands along which he sailed, but his discoveries and the extent of the voyage sounded so fantastic that people refused to believe that his narrative and maps were true. This was partially due to the fact that Purchas published only an abbreviated narrative and not Baffin's detailed log and map. It was not until Sir John Ross in 1818 traversed the same region that Baffin Bay was accepted as an actual body of water, existing north of Davis Strait.

Baffin himself concluded that there was no North-West Passage to be found in the waters north of Davis Strait. This conclusion seems to have been accepted by the North-West Company, and English ventures to the Arctic came almost to an end. There were a few, however, who would not accept this conclusion. One was Sir John Wolstenholme who, along with others contemplated an expedition for 1619, which came to nought. In 1625 another expedition was launched, in the charge of Captain William Hawkridge.[9] It sailed in June and succeeded by about the middle of July in entering Hudson Strait and sailing through it, but its endeavours there were fruitless; Hawkridge returned to England with nothing to encourage further ventures.

There was one man, however, who was not discouraged – a Yorkshireman named Luke Foxe, who had spent years in sailing to Scandinavia, the Mediterranean, and western Europe.[10] Throughout the greater part of his early life, his consuming passion seems to have been to learn what was known about the North-West Passage, and he kept urging further ventures in this direction. He had the support of Henry Briggs, who introduced the use of logarithms, a tremendous help to navigators. It is very likely that Briggs made Foxe's expedition possible. When, in December 1629, Foxe and his supporters asked Charles I for the loan of a ship, Charles consulted Sir Thomas Button, who immediately expressed approbation of the proposed venture and offered his whole-hearted help. The upshot was that a ship, the *Charles*, was placed at the disposal of Foxe in 1630. He secured the support of various other influential people, including Captain Thomas James, whom the merchants of Bristol were backing for a similar venture.[11] James proposed a merger of the two expeditions, with himself in command but with the understanding that equal credit be given to each, if any success were achieved. Foxe sailed on May 5, 1631, crossed the Atlantic without event and reached Hudson Strait on May 22. He had some difficulties with ice, both in the Strait and after his entrance into the bay. He crossed the bay, passing Southampton Island, where he bestowed some names, such as Roes Welcome, which was given to the little island in the sound that now bears that name. On August 5 he reached Churchill Bay and on the 8th, Port Nelson. He then explored all the southern shore of Hudson Bay between Port Nelson and Cape Henrietta Maria. On this tract of coast, on August 29, he met Captain James. He then made his way north into the channel and basin which have since then borne his name, and north into the basin almost as far as 67°. As sickness was attacking his men, however, he reversed his course on September 22 and returned to England. Back home, he was received with anything but enthusiasm, in spite of his having made what should have been regarded as a major voyage of exploration. The book which he wrote on his exploits and those of Button, Gibbons, and Hawkridge, was not published until 1635 and he died that same year, a disappointed man.

If North-West Foxe (self-styled) did not receive due recognition for his exploits, this was not the case with Thomas James. He sailed from England two days before Foxe, on May 3, and immediately landed in trouble crossing Davis Strait; he encountered even greater obstacles and danger in sailing through Hudson Strait. Like Foxe, he reached Churchill, on the western shore of the bay, and then sailed south to Cape Henrietta Maria, meeting Foxe on the way. After the encounter he reached the cape on September 2, whence he continued into the bay which still bears his name. After having sunk his ship in shoal water on November 29 in order to prevent her being smashed by ice, he wintered on Charlton Island, which he named Charlestown. Several of the men fell sick with scurvy and some died, but in the spring, having obtained vetches and sorrel, the sick began to mend and they were able to refloat the ship and rehang the rudder, which had been lost the previous autumn. Before they departed, James almost lost his life in a forest fire which he had ordered set in tinder-dry trees to see if it would attract any natives who might be in the vicinity, and which had got out of control.

On July 1, the company left the island, intending to continue a search for the passage. The deteriorating condition of their ship increasingly precluded this, and on August 24 they left Nottingham Island for England, which they reached on October 22. Many marvelled at how they could ever have reached Bristol Road in such a battered vessel.

James had accomplished little. He himself reached the conclusion on this voyage that there was no North-West Passage by way of Hudson Bay. Yet, in spite of the fact that Foxe had carried out his enterprise with skill, daring, courage, and success (although failing to find the passage), James, whose expedition can only be called a failure, received the accolades of his countrymen and their commiseration for the hardships he had endured – hardships which Foxe had never encountered because of his superior seamanship. Both men contributed something to an increased knowledge of the geography of the bay, but Foxe's contribution was infinitely the greater. James, however, got his book, *The Strange and Dangerous Voyage of Captain Thomas James*, a work of literary merit, into the hands of the public while Foxe was still writing his witty but tortured narrative. James's book is said to have provided much of the inspiration for Coleridge's *The Rime of the Ancient Mariner*.

The voyages of Foxe and James are the culmination of over one hundred years of English enterprise, the purpose of which was to discover a shorter sea route to Asia and one which would enable England to capture from Spain and Portugal the advantage they had gained through their prior discoveries of the commerce of Asia and America. From the time of the Cabots to the time of Foxe, England's ventures proved failures, and it was almost two hundred years until England felt again able to venture into the Arctic regions for the same purpose as had actuated her in the sixteenth and early seventeenth centuries. Nor were the other countries, who had also been actuated by the same desire in the sixteenth and early seventeenth centuries, prompted to keep up the search for this passage – although mention must be made of one final attempt by the Danes to follow the will-o'-the-wisp of the North-West Passage. This venture was one of the most tragic and yet one of the most eloquent tributes to the human spirit in the annals of Arctic exploration.

As has been mentioned, in the sixteenth and seventeenth centuries Denmark showed intense interest in the new discoveries which were being made, and desired both for commercial and for scientific reasons to share in these. Her monarch, Christian IV, who had dispatched the expeditions to Greenland in 1605, 1606, and 1607, discussed above, was passionately interested in restoring contact with the colonies of his Icelandic subjects in Greenland. He also wished to attain for Denmark a share in the new discoveries that were being made and the colonies that were being founded, although his early efforts in this direction had proved abortive. The early voyages made by the English in the years 1602-1616 in their quest for the North-West Passage aroused great interest in Denmark. Therefore, in 1619 Christian launched an expedition which seems to have been designed not primarily to re-establish contact with Greenland, but to discover the North-West Passage.

In charge of this expedition was placed one of the most colourful figures in all of Danish history. Whether he was a Dane or Norwegian is disputed, but there can be no question that Jens Munk, who was born about 1579, served Denmark most of his life and regarded himself as a Dane. On May 9, 1619, he was made captain of two naval vessels, the *Unicorn* and the *Lamprey*, with a crew of sixty-five. At the same time, two Englishmen, William Gordon, who had taken part in the Bylot and Baffin expedition in 1616, and John Watson, were made mates on the two vessels. This expedition sailed from Denmark on May 16, 1619, and from Norway on May 30. They reached Cape Farewell without incident and by July 8 had entered Frobisher Bay by mistake. Here, they at once ran into difficulties because of ice and stormy winds and did not reach Digges Island until August 20. They then sailed across Hudson Bay and made land at present-day Churchill on September 7, where they decided to winter. All went well during the early part of the winter. Provisions seemed plentiful and were supplemented by game gained in hunting. Although wine was rationed, beer was freely available. Christmas was celebrated in the wonted Nordic manner. Everything seemed to be going satisfactorily but, after the New Year, disasters accumulated in a catastrophic fashion. Scurvy appeared and, one after another, the men fell sick. By January 21, thirteen of the crew were mortally ill. A month later, twenty were dead and all except seven confined to their beds, so that it proved difficult to bury the dead. The doctor died without giving Munk any information that would enable him to administer the small store of medicine available; shortly thereafter the chaplain died also. By April 10, forty-one men were dead and only four able to leave their beds. The sick were almost helpless. One day, in brilliant sunshine, they made their way to the deck where most of them collapsed and Munk had tremendous difficulty in getting them back to their bunks. By June 4, Whit Sunday, Munk says that he was now one of the four left alive. All four were so weak that they could not help one another. They had some appetite but they were unable to chew any solid food and not one of them could arise from his bed to give the others a drink of wine. The cook's boy lay dead beside Munk's bed, and three dead men were on the deck. On the same day, Jens Munk wrote his will, asking that his body be buried and his journal forwarded to the king; it concluded with these words: "Herewith goodnight to the whole world and my soul into the hand of God."

The stench of the corpses, however, became so great in the ship that the four who lived had to make their way to land, where one more died. There, as time passed, Munk and the other two gradually regained their strength and by July 16 they were able to sail in the smaller of the ships of the expedition; although they ran into severe storms, they managed to land in Norway near Bergen on September 21, 1620.

Munk's journals and maps provided further knowledge of the bay. He himself wished to make another expedition but was unable to do so and died in 1628 during the Thirty Years' War. The Danes thereafter abandoned, to all intents and purposes, the search for the North-West Passage and, although other expeditions were made later in the seventeenth century, their purpose was the re-establishment of contact with Greenland; this, however, was not permanently achieved until the eighteenth century. Again the ties that had frayed away between Europe and the Canadian Arctic parted once more. The Eskimos, remnants of the Greenland colonies, became wholly separated from their European origins.

CHAPTER 21

Conclusion

In the foregoing pages, an attempt has been made to survey the history of Canada in the High Middle Ages and in the Age of the Great Discoveries. What has emerged? A survey that falls roughly into three divisions:

1. An early period of discovery and exploration on the part of the Icelandic discoverers of Greenland.
2. A middle period in which intermixture took place between these Icelandic settlers and the aborigines of Greenland and the Canadian Arctic – a period in which the Icelanders very gradually abandon almost unwittingly their European and Christian culture, abandon husbandry and take up a way of life which is based on fishing and the hunting of land and marine mammals, producing in the process a new culture which gradually spread from Greenland west across the entire reaches of Arctic Canada. This process is accompanied by, and to a certain extent stimulated by, a limited loss of contact with the homeland and Europe.
3. A period in which a new interest, fostered by the discovery of a New World by Columbus and his successors, led to ventures which had as their object, first, the exploitation of the fishing-grounds off the east coast of Canada and second, the desire to discover a northwest passage to Asia.

About the year 1000, when the Icelanders appear upon the scene, the northern regions of Canada were very sparsely inhabited by an aboriginal people whom we know as the Dorset Eskimos, albeit the word "Eskimos" is a misnomer. The origin of this people is obscure, and at the present time a highly controversial subject. This problem falls outside the scope of this work, but a few remarks on it may not be amiss.

Our knowledge of this people is almost entirely derived from the archæological research that has been carried out over the last thirty years in Greenland and the Canadian Arctic; it is supplemented by a few notices in the Icelandic sagas and scattered references in other mediæval literature whose sources, however, are the same as those of the Icelandic sagas – although some of this material is based on information later than that available to the saga writers. Both the archæological and saga evidence suggests, if indeed it does not postulate, an Asiatic origin for the Dorset people, the Skraelings of the sagas, and their progression from Asia along the north coast of the Canadian Arctic with a way of life based on the hunting of sea mammals and fishes. The alternative view, that the migrants from Asia crossed to Canada and then penetrated south into the interior, only later turning to the sea and adopting a marine culture, is hardly tenable on the basis of the evidence we now possess, as revealed by the archæology in the inland regions of Canada and the Dorset sites in the Arctic. In any case, it may be confidently asserted that when the Icelanders came to Greenland, the Canadian Arctic was occupied – insofar as it was occupied – by an Asiatic people and had been so from about 1000 B.C. These people had spears, lances, harpoons, knives, scrapers, and adzes made of stone or bone. They may have had soapstone lamps and certainly pots made of soapstone. They had hand sleds, possibly tents, and subterranean or semi-subterranean houses which were in most cases simply holes in the ground but which, in the case of the semi-subterranean, may have been constructed to a certain extent of stone and sod. Taylor has summarized their mode of life very well: "The people were semi-nomadic, using seasonal camps and practised a hunting economy. Available data suggest that sea-mammal hunting was the chief aspect of the food quest, although baleen whales do not seem to have been taken. Fish, land mammals, and birds were also exploited."[1]

These were the people whom the Icelanders met both in Greenland and the Arctic regions of Canada. Taylor writes: "The nature of the demise of the Dorset culture has not been determined and there are remarkably scant data bearing on this important problem."[2] This can be a problem only if studied in a historical vacuum, as it is by most scholars interested in Eskimo research. It is indeed an amazing phenomenon that, while admitting the existence of Icelandic settlements in Greenland for over five hundred years, scholars should fail completely even to attempt to assess the amount of intercourse between these Europeans and the aborigines of America. Evidence of such intercourse is usually brushed aside as having been incidental, casual, or indirect. And yet the whole nature of the Dorset Culture is changed in the years following the year 1000: it is transformed from a stone-age to an iron-age culture – the culture known as Thule.

The contention that the Thule Culture is the product of a new influx of "Eskimos" from Alaska is one of the most astounding myths in the whole of history. One is asked to believe that in the centuries preceding 1000, the bearers of a new culture migrated from Alaska, gradually moved across the Canadian Arctic and reached Greenland at about the same time as the Icelanders. One is asked to believe this without the evidence of any pre-1000 sites of the Thule Culture in the western Arctic. One is asked to believe this, although the oldest Thule sites are to be found in Greenland. And, most difficult of all, one is asked to believe this in spite of the fact that the oldest Thule sites in Greenland testify that this culture was not a stone-age but an iron-age culture. How much simpler is the explanation that may be deduced upon examination of the historical conditions in Greenland in the years following 1000. We have here, co-existing in the same land, two peoples, one an iron-age people – albeit only a few centuries removed from a stone-age culture – and a primitive people whose culture is still completely that of the stone age. We then find evidence, not only in Greenland but also in Arctic Canada, that a stone-age people and an iron-age people lived side by side. Can there be any doubt that the two met, intermixed, and in the process there evolved a stone-age – iron-age culture? Other factors in addition to this indicate that the new culture that emerged was not a recent importation from Alaska but a result of the above-mentioned inter-mixture. The Dorset people had no dogs. Suddenly in the Thule Culture we find the dog and the dog sled. We find that, whereas the Dorset people were not predominantly whalers, Thule was a great whaling culture. We find that a new and distinctively Norse type of house appears in the Thule Culture. We find hunting-installations appearing in the Thule Culture which are characteristic of stone-age Norway and persist into the iron age – installations which are unknown in any previous "Eskimo" culture. All in all, everything indicates, not the migration from Alaska of a tribe of "Eskimos" already possessed of an iron-age culture and many European features, but rather an intermingling of the bearers of a stone-age culture with the bearers of an iron-age culture.

The intermixture continued, and migrations took place to the Canadian Arctic, with a consequent loss of contact with the sources of iron and other European artifacts. Stone and bone implements increasingly replaced the iron artifacts to which one of the intermingled people had been accustomed. Contrary to Duason's statement that iron was in plentiful supply in Greenland, archæological excavations now suggest that this was not the case. At the oldest farm so far excavated in Greenland, dating from the first years of the Icelandic settlements there, stone and bone implements were already being fashioned and used side by side with the iron European ones. If this was the situation in Greenland itself, what would the circumstances be in the far distant hunting-settlements in Nordrseta, that is, northern Greenland and the Canadian Arctic archipelago? And as the migrants moved farther west and farther from the source of iron, the reliance on stone and bone would become more and more of a necessity. Crudely fashioned at first, these implements would become more refined and whereas, according to Mathiassen, the implements of the Thule Culture show a deterioration on their progress from Alaska to the east – the truth is that these implements show a greater refinement as the Thule Culture progressed from Greenland westward. Indeed, all scholars who believe, without any evidence, in the west-east progress of the Thule Culture are forced to postulate a later east-west progress of the Thule Culture. Set in its historical context, the Thule Culture presents no problem. It is the result of the inter-mingling of the bearers of the Dorset Culture and the bearers of a European iron-age culture; as European contacts were lost, there was an inevitable reversion to a stone-age culture and to what we now know as an Eskimo mode of life. This is the central feature of the mediæval history of Canada.

Up to 1500, or whenever direct contact between Europe, Greenland, and the Arctic ended, the main purpose of both the Icelanders in Greenland and Europeans who were in contact with that country, was the exploitation of the resources of the Canadian north. This was not the case in the six-teenth century, except for the fisheries off the Newfoundland banks. Men were not concerned then with the icy wastes or the icy waters, teeming though they were with fish and marine mammals. Fired by the exploits of Columbus, their one aim was to by-pass these "barren" reaches and find a way to the fabulous riches of the east. Only the occasional explorer in the fifteenth and early sixteenth century mentions the gain that might be made by the exploitation of the marine wealth to be found in Davis Strait and Baffin Bay. Only the mineral wealth, illusory as it was to prove, turned men's attention for a time to the resources of the region. It was only when French enterprise, not lured by any will-o'-the-wisp ventures seeking an easier route to Asia, had discovered the wealth in furs and pelts which the interior of Canada afforded, that men began to view the Arctic not as the location of a passage to Asia, but as another route to the riches of the hinterland.

It fell to the English and French to exploit and settle the southern and central regions of Canada. It fell to the descendants of Eric the Red and his intrepid fellow colonizers of Greenland to intermingle with the Dorset people and to bring into being one of the most viable cultures in the history of the world – viable in one of the harshest environments to be met any-where – and to produce a race unequalled for its ability to meet the cruellest climatic conditions, the bleakest of environments, with an unparalleled cheerfulness and equanimity in the face of disaster.

One cannot conclude more fittingly than by quoting Knud Rasmussen's description of his kinsmen at a salmon-fishing place on King William's Island:

Never in my life have I seen such a joyous and carefree people, full of mirth though starving, full of humour though freezing in their poor, tattered clothing. I will always remember the Samik boys, who were as joyous on the playing field as in the cold river water, clad at all times in tatters, with their feet, legs, arms and hands red and swollen from the cold, but unconscious of all this. These folk conceive of Paradise as a place where joy is unending and every day is spent in play. This ideal existence men seem to have realized in this life at this salmon fishing place, where people of every age and both sexes played at least five to six hours a day.[3]

NOTES TO CHAPTER TWO

1. Although its subject-matter lies outside the scope of this volume, reference may be made to Gutorm Gjessing, *Circumpolar Stone Age*, "Acta Arctica," fasc. II (Copenhagen, 1944).

2. On the early migrations of the ancestors of the Eskimo to Canada see J. L. Giddings, "Cultural Continuities of Eskimos," A.A. XXVII (1961), 155-173, and the works there cited.

3. On Pytheas, see Vilhjalmur Stefansson, *Ultima Thule* (New York, 1940), pp. 9-79. It is not necessary to discuss such obviously fantastic views as that the Phoenicians were to be found in Pennsylvania or that the Germans reached Oklahoma in the early centuries of our era (Frederick J. Pohl, *Atlantic Crossings Before Columbus* [New York, 1961], pp. 17-35, 45-54). For those who enjoy such fantasies, reference may be made to Charles Michael Boland, *They All Discovered America* (New York, 1961). Three Roman coins found in Iceland hardly prove the Romans visited it in the fourth century A.D. (Kristjan Eldjarn, *Gengid a reka* [Akureyri, 1948], Chap. 1).

4. On the Irish in America, see Gustav Lanctot (trans. Josephine Hambleton), *A History of Canada from its Origins to the French Royal Regime, 1663* ("History of Canada Series," Vol. I [Toronto, 1963]), for arguments in favour of their presence there.

5. On the qualities of the skin boat, see Vilhjalmur Stefansson, *Arctic Manual* (New York, 1944), pp. 383-392; *Ultima Thule*, pp. 36-43; *Greenland* (New York, 1942), pp. 23-25.

6. Dicuil, *Liber de mensura orbis terrae* (Berlin, 1870), pp. 42-44; F. Jonsson, ed., *Landnamabok* (Copenhagen, 1900), Chap. I.

7. On such fancied voyages, see Geoffrey Ashe, *Land to the West* (London, 1962). For the latest expression of the belief that the Irish were in contact with America and left some mark upon the native people, see Marcel Trudel, *Histoire de la Nouvelle-France: les Vaines Tentatives, 1524-1603* (Montreal, 1963), Chap. I.

8. Cf. Jon Johannesson, *Islendinga saga* (Reykjavik, 1956-1958), pp. 19-22.

9. Norsemen may even have visited China as early as the seventh century (C. P. Fitzgerald, *Son of Heaven* [Cambridge, 1933], p. 200), and there are many who believe that Mexico and Peru fell within the orbit of their expansion (cf. Jon Duason, *Landkonnun og landnam Islendinga i Vesturheimi* [Reykjavik, 1941-1947], pp. 120-123). Gustav Holm attempted to point out cultural similarities between the Eskimos and the Aztecs and Mayas ("Bidrag til Kjendskabet om Eskimoernes Herkomst," G.T., XI [1891-1892], pp. 15-27). All such attempts have proved futile.

10. Johannes Brondsted, *The Vikings* (London, 1960), pp. 27-42.

11. Cf. A. W. Brogger, *Ancient Emigrants* (Oxford, 1929), pp. 9-10.

12. On this, see A. W. Brogger and Haakon Shetelig, *The Viking Ships* (Oslo, 1953).

13. G. J. Marcus, "The Norse Emigration to the Faroe Islands," *English Historical Review*, LXXI (1956), pp. 59-60.

14. A term especially used in the thirteenth and fourteenth centuries.

15. See Elli and Paul Heinsius, "Hvordan seilte Vikingene med sine Bater?" *Viking*, XVII (1953), 63-67; Kristian Kielland, "Hvordan seilte Vikingene med sine Bater?" *Viking*, XVIII (1954), 227-234; H. Akerlund, "Ass och beiti-ass," *Unda Maris*, 1955-56, and "Vikingatidens skepp och sjovasen," *Svenska Kryssark klubbens Arsskrift*, 1959.

16. On the general subject of colonization, see Gudmund Hatt, "Types of European Colonization," *Greenland*, III, 1-14.

17. *Landnamabok*, Chaps. II-IX: Ari Thorgilsson, *Islendingabok*, ed. H. Hermannsson, "Islandica," XX (Ithaca, 1930), Chap. I.

18. It may be emphasized that the *Althing* was in no sense a representative body, but a Germanic folk-moot – a meeting of the folk, an *alsherjarthing*. To call it a parliament or even a "grandmother of parliaments" is both foolish and misleading.

19. These terms were used synonymously.

20. On these matters, see Jon Duason, *Rjettarstada Graenlands Nylendu Islands* (Reykjavik, 1947) and Karl von Amira, *Grundriss des germanischen Rechts* (Strasbourg, 1913); Hermann Conrad, *Deutsches Rechts-geschichte*, Vol. I (Karlsruhe, 1954).

21. A small quantity of barley was cultivated during the time of the Commonwealth.

22. On the early economy, see Johannesson, *Islendinga saga*, pp. 341-425. The export of fish became a major item in the economy only in the fifteenth century. Previous to that, wadmal was the major export article.

23. Bjorn M. Olsen estimated the population in 930 at 50,000-65,000, but the sources for accurate estimation from that time are very slim. On the other hand, they are much more abundant for the twelfth century. Here Olsen arrived at the figure of 77,520, which Johannesson thinks may be too high. It may, however, be confidently asserted that the population at the beginning of the twelfth century was at least 60,000. See Olsen, *Um Skattbaendatal 1311 og manntal a Island i fram ad theim tima*, Safn til sogu Islands, IV (Copenhagen, 1911) and Johannesson, *Islendinga saga*, I, 46-49.

24. I need hardly say that I feel free to use the sixteenth-century term *novus mundus*, even though it then betokened a land, parts of which had been well known to northern Europe for five centuries, but usually regarded as parts of east Asia.

25. The matter is thoroughly discussed by Steingrimur Jonsson in his review of V. Stefansson's *Greenland*, in *Skirnir*, CXVII (1943), 205-206; J. Kr. Tornoe, "Hvitserk og Blaserk," N.G.T., V (1934-1935); and cf. E. G. R. Taylor, *The Haven-Finding Art* (London, 1956), p. 79.

26. *Landnamabok*, pp. 27, 34, 48, 147-150. They cannot be located with certainty but are likely either the tips of mountains on the east coast of Greenland or islands off Angmagssalik.

27. The only reason Gunnbjorn is mentioned in this connection is that the skerries were named for him.

28. Possibly in or north of Scoresby Sound.

29. *Landnamabok*, pp. 48-51, 173-174. It is interesting to compare the events on this voyage with those on the voyage of Freydis to Vinland (*Graenlendinga saga*, ed. Matthias Thordarson, *Islenzk fornrit*, IV (Reykjavik, 1935), 264-267.

30. The sources for the career of Eric the Red, which is detailed in the following pages, are Ari Thorgilsson, *Islendingabok*, pp. 51-52; *Landnamabok*, pp. 34-36; *Eiriks saga rauda*, ed. Matthias Thordarson, *Islenzk fornrit*, IV (Reykjavik, 1935), and *Graenlendinga saga*.

31. Both *Eiriks saga rauda* (p. 197) and *Graenlendinga saga* (p. 241) say that Thorvaldr and his son Eric came to Iceland from Norway, but both are obviously based in this instance on *Landnamabok* (pp. 34-36). On the other hand, *Islendingabok*, which is the most trustworthy source, says only that Eric was from Breidafjord in Iceland. The whole matter hinges on the date of Thorvaldr's settlement in Iceland. Duason (*Landkonnun*, pp. 72-77) has argued convincingly that Thorvaldr came to Iceland *circa* 926 and that Eric must have been born there. It is not reasonable, he says, to suppose that Eric was sixty or more years old when he

settled in Greenland. Leifr Eiriksson was dead by 1025. If he died *circa* 1020, at what may be called the ripe age of sixty, he would have been born *circa* 960. If Eric the Red was born *circa* 926 (and Thorvaldr must have come to Iceland before the end of the Age of Settlement when all free land was gone, i.e., 930), then he would have been thirty-four when Leifr was born. On the other hand, if he took part in the homicides committed by his father in Norway, he must have been at least twelve years old (the age at which men might be tried for homicide) when he came to Iceland. I pursue the matter no further.

32. All Eric's farms were on the west coast of Iceland and all were very small and poor.

33. Some MSS say he wintered near the centre of what was to become the Eastern Settlement on the present-day island of Igdlotalik.

34. Cf. Jon Duason, *A Island ekkert rettartilkall til Graenlands?* (Reykjavik, 1953), pp. 122-124.

35. The other ships were either lost or driven back to Iceland. This is a reminder that, in spite of the seaworthiness of the ships of the Icelanders at this time, the sea voyage to Greenland could be a hazardous one, by reason of the east Greenland ice pack and the difficulty in stormy weather of maintaining a true course in the days before the compass.

36. Bjorn Jonsson, in his seventeenth-century *Graenlands annall* (A. M. 769 4to), copied from a very old manuscript the information that there were 190 farmsteads in the Eastern Settlement and 90 in the Western (G.h.M. III, 228). Archæological work has revealed that this figure is too low. There have now been excavated 383 Norse ruin sites in Greenland. Of these, 71 are

farmsteads in the Western Settlement and 207 are farmsteads in the Eastern and Middle Settlements (Michael Wolfe, "Norse Archeology in Greenland since World War II," A.S.R., XLIX [1961], 391-392. Cf. also Aage Roussell, *Farms and Churches in the Mediæval Norse Settlements of Greenland*, M.o.G., LXXXIX, No. 1 [Copenhagen, 1941], p. 11, and Sigurd Grieg, "Nordmenn pa Gronland, i Mellomalderen," N.T.V.K.I., XXXIII [1957], p. 22).

|37. Christen Leif Vebaek, "Mellembygden," *Gronland*, 1956, pp. 92-98. It is usually assumed that this was an outlying part of the Eastern Settlement. The farmsteads are in the Frederikshaab district (from Tigsaluk to Ameralikfjord).

38. The population is difficult to estimate because of the paucity of information concerning Nordrseta.

39. Leaf knives found in farm ruins attest the presence of such foliage. (See, e.g., M.o.G., LXXXVIII, No. 2, p. 111).

40. E.g., the byres at the North farm at Brattahlid seem to have accommodated about 30 cattle (*ibid.*, No. 1, pp. 86-7) and at the River farm, 12 (*ibid.*, p. 90). There were two large stable complexes at Sandnes, housing not only cows but also sheep, goats, and pigs (*ibid.*, No. 2, pp. 36-54). Cf. also *ibid.*, LXXXIX, No. 1.

41. *Ibid.* LXXXVIII, No. 1, 149-155.

42. *Ibid.* No. 3, p. 1. Magnus Degerbol writes on animal bones found on the inland farms of the East Settlement: "To judge from this material the Norsemen lived as much on hunting seals and reindeer as on animal husbandry" (*ibid.*, XC, No. 1, 114).

43. *Ibid.*, LXXXVIII, No. 3, 7. At Gardar numerous walrus skulls were interred in the churchyard (*ibid.*, LXXVI, No. 1, 114).

44. See *ibid.*, LXXXVIII, No. 3, 7-13.

NOTES TO CHAPTER THREE

1. One of the great needs of Vinland research is, however, an exhaustive and detailed study of the two. The author may say that on the whole he prefers

the version given in the *Graenlendinga saga* and hopes to present his arguments for this in the near future.

2. *Landnamabok*, pp. 35, 124, 156.

3. A day's sailing might be the distance covered in twelve or twenty-four hours, but usually the latter is meant when sailing on the open sea is involved. How many miles a merchant ship could cover in a day is disputed, but 150 miles is a reasonable estimate and, with favourable winds and currents, 200 miles might be covered (see Duason, *Landkonnun*, pp. 37-42).

4. *Graenlendinga saga*, pp. 244-247.

5. Cf. Halldor Hermannsson, *The Problem of Wineland* ("Islandica," XXV [Ithaca, 1936]), 35-36: "Such things do not happen in our workaday world, they only happen in fairy tales and lying sagas."

6. Cf. Sigurdur Gudjonsson, "Ferd Bjarna Herjolfssonar," *Vikingur*, 1958, pp. 162-167. The weightiest arguments against its authenticity are two: (1) The *Graenlendinga saga* itself suggests that interest in the lands sighted by Bjarni was not aroused for at least fifteen years, and (2) the *Eiriks saga rauda* does not mention Bjarni, nor, for that matter, does any other work dealing with the saga age.

7. Hermannsson, *The Problem of Wineland*, p. 36.

8. Or in some year between 1000 and 1014, the years in which Earl Eirikr ruled in Norway.

9. Here the saga adds that Greenland was by this time Christian but that Eric the Red had died before the adoption of the new faith.

10. Here the saga equates Straumfjord with Vinland.

11. Fridtjof Nansen's translation, *In Northern Mists* (London, 1911), II, 27-28. Another translation (Hjalmar R. Holand, "Vinland visited 1050," *A.S.R.*, XXXVII [1949], 18) reads: "Far and wide they were driven from the coast of Vinland, and were cast on the ice

of the uninhabitable regions, needing food and clothing. Evil fate may overtake one so that he dies early."

12. An attempt has been made (*ibid.*, pp. 19-25) to identify the young man as Thrandr Halfdanarson, the nephew of King Harold Hardrada. He incurred the enmity of his uncle and fled to Greenland. This conjecture is rather a bold one, for the saga does not give his father's name, nor state that he was a nephew of King Harold. Moreover, it states only that he spent several years in Greenland and has nothing to say of his death (*Flateyjarbok* [Christiana, 1860-1868], III, 314-316). On the Honen runes, see also R. Hennig, *Terrae Incognitae* (Leiden, 1944-1956), II, 368-373.

13. Adam of Bremen, *History of the Archbishops of Hamburg-Bremen*, trans. Francis J. Tschan (New York, 1959), p. 219. Adam here relates also that King Harold Hardrada "lately attempted this sea. After he had explored the expanse of the Northern Ocean in his ships, there lay before their eyes at length the darksome bounds of a failing world, and by retracing his steps he barely escaped in safety the vast pit of the abyss." Nothing further is known of this expedition (see Hennig, *Terrae Incognitae*, II, 365-368, and the works there cited).

14. It was to King Sveinn Ulfsson that Audunn presented his famous polar bear (cf. T. J. Oleson, "Polar Bears in the Middle Ages," *C.H.R.* XXXI [1950], 52-53).

15. Hermansson, *The Book of the Icelanders*, p. 64.

16. Pp. 129, 198.

17. *Kristni saga*, in *Biskupa sogur*, I (Copenhagen, 1858), p. 20.

18. *Islandske Annaler indtil 1578*, ed. G. Storm (Christiania, 1888); *Annalar og Nafnaskra*, ed. Gudni Jonsson (Reykjavik, 1948).

19. The *Leidarvisir* is sometimes ascribed to Abbot Nikulas Saemundsson of Thingeyri (e.g., S. Runciman, "Some re-

G

marks on the image of Edessa," *C.H.J.*, III, 238 ff.; see, however, Francis P. Magoun, Jr., "The Pilgrim-Diary of Nikulas of Munkathvera," *Mediæval Studies*, VI, 314; Duason, *Landkonnun*, p. 89).

20. *Alfraedi Islensk*, ed. Kr. Kalund (Copenhagen, 1908), p. 12. Other similar passages are found in other fourteenth-century works (see C. C. Rafn, *Antiquitates Americanae* [Copenhagen, 1837], pp. 278-300).

NOTES TO CHAPTER FOUR

1. On these see Duason, *Landkonnun*, pp. 81-97, 1413, 1414; Edmundo O'Gorman, *The Invention of America* (Bloomington, 1961), pp. 51-69.
2. *Eiriks saga*, p. 222.
3. *Graenlendinga saga*, p. 255.
4. Cf. *Eiriks saga*, p. 210 (*Eyrbyggja saga, Islenzk fornrit*, IV [Reykjavik, 1935], 137-139).
5. "Aldur Graenlendinga sogu," *Nordaela* (Reykjavik, 1956), pp. 153-156. An English translation of this article will shortly appear in the *Saga Book of the Viking Society*.
6. G. Storm, ed., *Monumenta historica Norvegiae* (Oslo, 1880), p. 76.
7. *Eiriks saga*, pp. 211-212.

8. *Ibid.*, p. 212. In 1961, the ruins of this church and its graveyard were discovered by accident in Greenland at Brattahlid, Eric the Red's farm. See Jorgen Meldgaard, "Fra Brattahlid til Vinland," *N.V.* (1961), pp. 353 ff.; Michael Wolfe, "Thjodhild's Church," *A.S.R.*, LI (1963), 55-66.
9. Unlike Baffin Island and Labrador, Ellesmere does not appear to have been settled by the Thule Culture Eskimos, but rather to have been visited by Icelandic hunters and the bearers of the Thule Culture. See Moreau S. Maxwell, "The Movement of Cultures in the Canadian High Arctic," *Anthropologica*, N.S., II (1960), 177-189.

NOTES TO CHAPTER FIVE

1. Cf. Gunnar and Fridtjov Isachsen, "Hvor langt mot nord kom de norrone Gronlendinger?" *N.G.T.*, IV (1932-1933), 75-92; Duason, *Landkonnun*, pp. 426-455.
2. *G.h.M.*, III, 242-244.
3. See Duason, *Landkonnun*, pp. 426-429.
4. *G.h.M.*, III, 250-260.
5. Cf. Oleson, "Polar Bears," pp. 47-55.
6. Duason, *Landkonnun*, pp. 436-442.
7. William Thalbitzer, "Two Runic Stones from Greenland and Minnesota," Smithsonian Miscellaneous Collections, CXVI, No. 3 (Washington, 1951).
8. *Skraelingerne i Gronland* (Copenhagen, 1935), pp. 48-49.
9. Sir George Strong Nares, *Narrative of a Voyage to the Polar Sea during 1875* (London, 1878), I, 88, 162.

10. See Isachsen, "Hvor langt mod nord," p. 78.
11. Edward L. Moss, *Shores of the Polar Sea* (London, 1878). Jorgen Meldgaard has seen fit to question the identification of these little stone structures as eiderduck nests and has suggested that they are probably fireplaces dating as far back as the Dorset Culture. This suggestion hardly merits mention. "Om de gamle Nordboer og deres Skjaebne," *Gronland* (1961), p. 95.
12. Gunnar Isachsen, "Nordboernes faerder til Norderseta," *N.G.S.A.*, XVIII (1906-1907), 20-32.
13. *G.h.M.*, III, 842-843.
14. Duason, *Landkonnun*, pp. 436-442, and the works there cited.

NOTES TO CHAPTER SIX

1. Hermansson, *The Book of the Icelanders*, p. 64.
2. *Eirik the Red*, trans. Gwyn Jones (London, 1961), pp. 150-153.
3. Edward F. Gray, *Leif Eriksson: Discoverer of America A.D. 1003* (New York, 1930), pp. 59-61.
4. *Historia Norwegiae*, pp. 75-76.
5. R. Collinson, *The Three Voyages of Martin Frobisher* (Hakluyt Society: London, 1867), p. 35.
6. Adolf Eric Nordenskiold, *Facsimile Atlas to the Early History of Cartography* (Stockholm, 1889), p. 95.
7. Axel Anthon Bjornbo, *Cartographia Groenlandica*, M.o.G., XLVIII, No. 1 (1911), 285-286.
8. H. Zimmer, "Brendans Meerfahrt," *Zeitschr. f. deutsches Altertum*, XXXIII (1889), p. 138.
9. G. Storm, "Et brev til pave Nicolaus den 5te om Norges beliggenhad og undre," N.G.S.A., X (1898-1899), p. 5.
10. G. Storm and K. H. Karlsen, "Finmarkens Beskrivelse af Erkebiskop Erik Walkendorf," N.G.S.A., XII (1900-1901), pp. 12-13.
11. *Qualiscunque descriptio Islandiae*, ed. Fr. Burg (Hamburg, 1928), p. 32.
12. A. A. Bjornbo and Carl S. Petersen, *Der Dane Claudius Clausson Swart* (Innsbruck, 1909), p. 144.
13. *Von der Moscouiten Bottschaft* (Strasbourg, 1534).
14. Ove C. L. Vangensten, *Michel Beheims Reise til Danmark og Norge i 1450* (Christiania, 1909), p. 18.
15. Pierre François Xavier de Charlevoix, *Histoire de la Nouvelle France* (Paris, 1744), I, 17.
16. H. Rink, *Eskimoiske Eventyr og Sagn* (Copenhagen, 1866-1871), pp. 313-314. Cf. Knud Rasmussen, *Myter og Sagn fra Gronland* (Copenhagen, 1921), III, 246-247.
17. Duason, *Landkonnun*, pp. 493-510, and especially pp. 521-537.
18. *Ibid.*, pp. 537-538.
19. *Ibid.*, p. 537.
20. *Ibid.*, p. 538.

NOTES TO CHAPTER SEVEN

1. "A New Eskimo Culture," G.R., XV (1925), pp. 428-437. Therkel Mathiassen for some years denied that the Dorset Culture was independent of the Thule Culture. On the whole history, see William E. Taylor, "Review and Assessment of the Dorset Problem," *Anthropologica*, N.S., I (1959), 24-46, and H. B. Collins, "Recent Developments in the Dorset Culture Area," A.A., XVIII, No. 3, Part 2 (January 1953), 32-39.
2. Cf. W. E. Taylor, "Dorset Problem," pp. 24-46.
3. Therkel Mathiassen, *The Sermermiut Excavations 1955*, M.o.G., CLXI, No. 3 (1958): Helge Larsen and Therkel Mathiassen, *Paleo-Eskimo Cultures in Disko Bugt, West Greenland*, M.o.G., CLXI, No. 2 (1958).
4. Meldgaard, "Dorset Kulturen," *Kuml* (1955), pp. 158-177.
5. Collins, "The Origin and Antiquity of the Eskimo," A.R.S.I., 1950 (1951), p. 427.
6. Duason, *Landkonnun*, pp. 515-517.
7. Lawrence Oschinsky, "Two Recently Discovered Human Mandibles from Cape Dorset Sites on Sugluk and Mansel Islands," *Anthropologica*, N.S., II (1960), 212-227.
8. Duason, *Landkonnun*, pp. 521-537.
9. V. Stefansson, *The Three Voyages of Martin Frobisher* (London, 1938), I, 64-65.
10. T. Mathiassen, *Contributions to the Archæology of Disko Bay*, M.o.G., XCIII, No. 2 (1934), 135-136.
11. Cf. Duason, *Landkonnun*, pp. 768-781.

NOTES TO CHAPTER EIGHT

1. The literature is conveniently summarized in Duason, *Landkonnun*, pp. 736-767.
2. Meldgaard, "Dorset Kulturen," pp. 171, 176.
3. Duason, *Landkonnun*, p. 737.
4. Franz Boas, "The Central Eskimo," *Sixth A.R.B.E.* (1888), pp. 634-636.
5. Cf. Duason, *Landkonnun*, pp. 761-762.
6 E. W. Hawkes, *The Labrador Eskimo* (Ottawa, 1910), pp. 143-150.
7. Quoted in T. Mathiassen, *Archæology of the Central Eskimos*, II (Copenhagen, 1927), 187.
8. Duason, *Landkonnun*, p. 744.
9. *Ibid.*, pp. 757-759.
10. *Ibid.*, p. 766.

NOTES TO CHAPTER NINE

1. Cf. Collins, "The Origin and Antiquity of the Eskimo" and "Recent Developments in the Dorset Culture Area"; W. E. Taylor, "Dorset Problem." On all these cultures see Collins, *Arctic Area* (Mexico, 1954), pp. 67-87.
2. See Mathiassen, *Archæology of the Central Eskimos*.
3. Eric Holtved, *Archæological Investigations in the Thule District*, M.o.G., CXLI, No. 1 (Copenhagen, 1944); Helge Larsen, "Archæology in the Arctic, 1935-60," A.A., XXVII (1961).
4. H. B. Collins, *Archæological Investigations on Southampton and Walrus Islands, Northwest Territories*, National Museum of Canada, Bulletin No. 147 (Ottawa, 1956), and other works by Collins cited therein. See also, Collins, "Archæological Work in Arctic Canada," A.R.S.I. (Washington, 1957), "Recent Developments in the Dorset Culture Area," and *Arctic Area*.
5. Mason, "Excavations of Eskimo Thule Culture Sites," pp. 383-394.
6. Cf. Collins, *Arctic Area*, pp. 75-77; "The Origin and Antiquity of the Eskimo," pp. 428-429. See Taylor, "Hypotheses on the Origin of Canadian Thule Culture," where the present views on the relation of the Birnirk and Thule Cultures are discussed.
7. Collins, "Recent Developments in the Dorset Culture Area," p. 35.
8 Nansen, *In Northern Mists*, II.
9. V. Stefansson, *Greenland*.
10. *The Mediæval Norse Settlements in Greenland*, M.o.G., LXXXIX, No. 2 (1942), 79-80.
11. Collins, "Recent Developments in the Dorset Culture Area," p. 35. Edward Weyer, "Eskimo Prehistory in Perspective," *Polar Notes*, I (1959), 75, emphasizes trade in iron between the Eskimos and the Norse, and the consequent employment of meteoric iron in northern Greenland.
12. *Ibid.*, pp. 32-39.
13. Mathiassen, *Inugsuk: a Mediæval Eskimo Settlement in Upernivik District, West Greenland*, M.o.G., LXXVII (1930), 291.
14. Cf. Collins, "The Origin and Antiquity of the Eskimo," p. 427.
15. J. Alden Mason, "Excavations of Eskimo Thule Culture Sites at Point Barrow, Alaska," *Proceedings of the 23rd International Congress of Americanists* (New York, 1930).

NOTES TO CHAPTER TEN

1. Mathiassen, *Archæology of the Central Eskimos*, II, 6.
2. *Ibid.*, pp. 196-201.
3. *Ibid.*, pp. 285-287.
4. On this whole matter, see Duason, *Landkonnun*, pp. 768-781, and the works there cited.
5. Mathiassen, *Archæology of the Central*

Eskimos, II, 145. Mathiassen regards the Cape York type of house, sometimes referred to as pear-shaped or clover-leaf shaped, as a local derivative of the round whale-bone house of the Thule Culture, but Steensby believed the Cape York house to have evolved from a four-sided house.

6. *Ibid.*, pp. 128-130.

7. Mathiassen, *Ancient Eskimo Settlements in the Kangamiut Area*, M.o.G., XCI, No. 1 (1931), 33.

8. Duason, *Landkonnun*, p. 782.

9. Mathiassen, *Archæology of the Central Eskimos*, II, 129-130.

10. Duason, *Landkonnun*, pp. 794-798.

11. F. and G. Isachsen, "Hvor langt mot nord," p. 78. Cf. Duason, *Landkonnun*, pp. 801 ff.

12. Nares, *Narrative of a Voyage*, I, 88.

13. George Palmer Putnam, "The Putnam Baffin Island Expedition," G.R., XVIII (1928), 5.

14. V. Tanner, "Ruinerna paa Sculpin Island," G.T., XLIV (1941).

15. Gathorne-Hardy, "A Recent Journey to Northern Labrador," G.J., LIX (1922), p. 164.

16. Putnam, "The Putnam Baffin Island Expedition," pp. 5, 6.

17. T. Mathiassen, "Norse Ruins in Labrador," *American Anthropologist*, XXX (1928), 577.

18. Mathiassen, *Archæology of the Central Eskimos*, II, 130.

19. Cf. Knud Rasmussen, *Fra Gronland til Stillehavet* (Copenhagen, 1925-1926), II, 199.

20. G. M. Asher, *Henry Hudson, the Navigator* (London; Hakluyt Society, 1860), p. 107.

21. George Francis Lyon, *A Brief Narrative of an Unsuccessful Attempt to Reach Repulse Bay* (London, 1825), p. 58.

22. Ed. L. M. Larson (New York, 1917), p. 145. Cf. Magnus Degerbol, *Animal Remains from the West Settlement in Greenland*, M.o.G., LXXXVIII, No. 3 (Copenhagen, 1936).

23. Oleson, "Polar Bears."

24. F. and G. Isachsen, "Hvor langt mot nord," Cf. Duason, *Landkonnun*, pp. 812-828.

25. *Ibid.*, pp. 768-933.

26. See *ibid.*, pp. 754-766.

27. Mathiassen, *Archæology of the Central Eskimos*, II, 123. Cf. Duason, *Landkonnun*, pp. 945-946.

NOTES TO CHAPTER ELEVEN

1. Nansen, *In Northern Mists*; Stefansson, *Greenland*; Duason, *Landkonnun*.

2. Poul Norlund, *Buried Norsemen at Herjolfsnes*, M.o.G., LXVII (1924).

3. *Ibid.*

4. *The Mediæval Norse Settlements in Greenland*, p. 79.

5. K. Broste and K. Fischer-Moller, *The Mediæval Norsemen at Gardar*, M.o.G., LXXXIX, No. 3 (Copenhagen, 1944), 58.

6. On this subject, see Otto Pettersson, *Klimatforandringar i historisk och forhistorisk Tid* (Stockholm, 1913); F. Nansen, "Klimat-Vekslinger i Nordens historie" (Det norske Videnskaps-Akademis Avhandl., I, Mat.-Nat. Klasse, 1925, No. 3); Thorvaldur Thoroddsen, "Arferdi a

Islandi i thusund ar" (Copenhagen, 1916-17); Jon Eythorsson, "Um loftlagsbreytingar a Islandi og Graenlandi," *Skirnir*, C (1926). The popular and widely prevalent view that there was a deleterious change in the climate of Greenland after 1300 is well set forth in James L. Dyson, *The World of Ice* (New York, 1962), pp. 182-184, but his remarks on the graveyard at Herjolfsnes should be compared with Duason, *Landkonnun*, pp. 617-645; cf. pp. 615-617.

7. Odd Nordland, "Oya med Giftarmals-Vanskane," *Viking*, XVII (1953), 87-107.

8. Cf. Wolfe, "Norse Archeology in Greenland," p. 384.

9. Corrado Gini, *On the Extinction of*

the Norse Settlements (Bergen, 1958), p. 9.

10. *Ibid.*, pp. 13-24.

11. Gisli Oddsson, *Annalium in Islandia Farrago,* "Islandica," X (Ithaca, 1917), p. 2. Bishop Gisli wrote in the seventeenth century (hence his use of America), but scholars are agreed that he was drawing his information from old manuscripts in the archives of the cathedral of Skalholt in Iceland.

12. *The Mediæval Norse Settlements in Greenland,* p. 80.

13. G.h.M., III, 238-245.

14. Duason, *Landkonnun,* pp. 1144-1145, and the works there cited.

15. G.h.M., III, 513-516.

16. V. Stefansson, *The Three Voyages,* II, 56.

17. *Ibid.*, p. 22.

18. *Ibid.*, I, 125.

19. Albert Hastings Markham, *Voyages and Works of John Davis the Navigator* (London: Hakluyt Society, 1880), LIII, 8.

20. *Ibid.*, p. 18; LIX, 41.

21. G.h.M., III, 688-689.

22. *Bericht von Gronland* (Hamburg, 1674), II, Chap. 5, 42.

23. *Beschreibung der Muscowitischen . . . und Persianische* (Schleswig, 1656), p. 167.

24. Hans Egede, *Relationer fra Gronland,* 1721-1736, ed. L. Bobé, M.o.G., LIV Copenhagen, 1925), p. 36.

25. David Cranz, *Historie von Gronland* (Leipzig, 1765), I, 178.

26. Louis de Poincy, *Histoire naturelle & morale des Iles Antilles de l'Amérique* (Rotterdam, 1658), Chap. 18, pp. 194-195.

27. V. Stefansson, *The Three Voyages,* I, 166.

28. *Ibid.*, II, 19.

29. *Ibid.*, I, CVIII-CIX.

30. Duason, *Landkonnun,* pp. 1162-1164.

31. A place name appearing on Newfoundland, stemming from the voyages of Joao Alvarez Fagundes around 1521. (Cf. Bernard G. Hoffman, *Cabot to Cartier* [Toronto, 1961], index *sub voce.*)

32. Damiao de Goes, *Chronica do Felicissimo Rei Dom Emanuel* (Lisbon, 1566), fol. 65.

33. Cited in William Gilbert Gosling, *Labrador* (London, 1910), p. 38.

34. Charlevoix, *Histoire et description générale de la Nouvelle France* (Paris, 1744), II, 178-179.

35. Joseph François Lafitau, *Les Moeurs des sauvages Amériquains* (Paris, 1724), I, 56.

36. Charlevoix, *Histoire et description générale de la Nouvelle France,* I, 17-18.

37. A. W. Greely, "The Origin of Stefansson's Blond Eskimo," N.G.M., XXIII, 1912.

38. V. Stefansson, *My Life with the Eskimo* (New York, 1913), pp. 180 ff.

39. Eilert Sundt, *Egedes Dagbok i Udtag* (Oslo, 1860), pp. 160-2.

40. *Nordvest-Passagen* (Christiania, 1907), p. 86. Cf. pp. 129, 137, 148.

41. L. T. Burwash, "Across Arctic Canada, 1925-1926," G.J., LXXIV (1929), 560.

42. Rasmussen, *Fra Gronland til Stillehavet,* II, 19-20, 220, 261-262.

43. Diamond Jenness, *The Life of the Copper Eskimo* (Ottawa, 1922-1923), Part A, pp. 191-217.

44. Collins, "Stefansson as an Anthropologist," *Polar Notes,* IV (1962), pp. 8-13.

45. Jenness, "The 'Blond' Eskimos," *American Anthropologist,* N.S., XXIII (1921), 257-267; *The Copper Eskimos,* part B, pp. 46B-B.65.

46. Mason, "Excavations of Eskimo Thule Culture Sites," pp. 383-394.

47. Bruce Chown and Marion Lewis, "Blood Groups in Anthropology," Bulletin of the National Museum of Canada, No. 167 (Ottawa, 1958), pp. 66-79.

48. *Landkonnun,* pp. 1025-1037.

49. *The Eskimo Skeleton,* M.o.G., CXLVI, No. 2 (1953).

50. "Facial Flatness and Cheekbone Morphology in Arctic Mongoloids," *Anthropologica,* N.S., IV (1962), 349-377 (especially p. 364); see also the same

scholar's "Two Recently Discovered Human Mandibles" and "A Short Note on Upper Lateral Incisor Tooth Crowding among the Eskimos" (*Anthropologica*, N.S., III [1961]), and Lawrence Oschinsky and Roy Smithurst, "On Certain Dental Characters of the Eskimo of the Eastern Canadian Arctic" (*Anthropologica*, N.S., II [1960]). Cf. also, Collins, "The Origin and Antiquity of the Eskimo," p. 453, and Arne Hoygaard, *Studies on the Nutrition and Physio-Pathology of Eskimos* (Oslo, 1941), p. 13.

51. Oddsson, *Annalium in Islandia Farrago*, p. 2.

52. *Qualiscunque descriptio Islandiae*, p. 21.

53. Quoted from the manuscript, A.M. 192 B. 4to, Chap. 4, by Duason, *Landkonnun*, p. 674. Cf. p. 1023.

54. *Efterretning om Rudera eller Levninger af de Gamle Normaends og Islaenderes Bygninger paa Gronlands Vester-Side* (Copenhagen, 1776).

55. Jorgen Meldgaard, *Eskimo Skulptur* (Copenhagen, 1959), pl. 25A; H. Ingstad, *Landet under Leidarstjernen* (Oslo, 1959), pl. 41, No. 1. Cf. Weyer, "Eskimo Prehistory," p. 76.

56. "Dorset Kulturen."

57. Meldgaard, *Eskimo Skulptur*, pl. 25B, 26.

58. Cf. *ibid.*, pl. 22, 23, 24A, 24B.

NOTES TO CHAPTER TWELVE

1. Duason, *Landkonnun*, pp. 1042-1046 and the works there cited.

2. *Ibid.*, pp. 1047-1053.

3. *Ibid.*, p. 1055.

4. E. B. Tylor, "Old Scandinavian Civilization Among the Modern Esquimaux," *J.A.I.G.B.I.*, XIII (1884), 351.

5. Cf. Duason, *Landkonnun*, pp. 1062-1077.

6. *Ibid.*, pp. 920-923.

7. *Ibid.*, pp. 1081-1087 and the works there cited.

8. Markham, *Voyages and Works of John Davis*, pp. 8, 41.

9. Duason, *Landkonnun*, pp. 786-793. Mathiassen and others have noticed, without fully realizing its significance, the contrast between burial customs in the early Thule Culture and those in its later stages and among the modern Eskimo (Mathiassen, *Archæology of the Central Eskimos*, II, 130-131).

10. Cf. V. Stefansson, *My Life with the Eskimo*, pp. 353-367; *The Friendly Arctic* (New York, 1921), pp. 104-105.

11. *Efterretning om Rudera*, here cited from V. Stefansson, *Greenland*, pp. 173-174.

12. Duason, *Landkonnun*, pp. 112-114.

13. *Ibid.*, pp. 114-121.

14. *Historie von Gronland*, p. 261.

15. *Ibid.*, pp. 254-255.

16. Herein cited from Duason, *Landkonnun*, p. 1123. *Norske Register*, 1723, pp. 19-20.

17. Duason, *Landkonnun*, cites the relevant sources, pp. 1125-1127.

18. *Ibid.*, pp. 1127-1128.

19. Nansen, *Eskimo liv* (Oslo, 1890), pp. 216-249; Duason, *Landkonnun*, pp. 1129-1134.

20. *Ibid.*, pp. 1134-1140.

NOTES TO CHAPTER THIRTEEN

1. Aage Roussell, *Sandnes and the Neighbouring Farms*, M.o.G., LXXXVIII, No. 2 (Copenhagen, 1936), pp. 34, 106-107; Johs. Iversen, "Et botanisk Vidne om Nordboernes Vinlandsrejser," *Naturhistorisk Tidende*, No. 8 (October 1938).

2. Adam of Bremen, *History of the Archbishops*, p. 218.

3. *The Book of the Icelanders*, p. 64.

4. *Annalar og Nafnaskra*, sub anno 1121.

5. On reproductions of these maps, see Theo E. Layng, ed., *Sixteenth-Century Maps Relating to Canada* (Ottawa, 1956), pp. 1-3.

6. See Ashe, *Land to the West* and the works there cited.

7. *G.h.M.*, III, 428.

8. T. J. Oleson, "Giraldus Cambrensis and Iceland," *Icelandic Canadian*, XII, No. 4 (1954), 31.

9. E. G. R. Taylor, "A Letter dated 1577 from Mercator to John Dee," *Imago mundi* (1956), p. 59.

10. *G.h.M.*, III, 260.

11. *The Art of Falconry* (Stanford, 1955).

12. Here quoted from Duason, *Landkonnun*, pp. 302-303.

13. Oleson, "Polar Bears," p. 54.

14. *The Book of Ser Marco Polo*, ed. Yule (London, 1871), I, 237, 240.

15. *Ibid.*, p. 238; E. G. Ravenstein, *Martin Behaim* (London, 1908), p. 91. Both Yule and Ravenstein believe that Bargu is Barguchen Turgum or Barguti in Asia.

16. Cf. Nansen, *In Northern Mists*, pp. 226-231.

17. Cf. *ibid.*, p. 267.

18. See Storm, "Et brev."

19. Cf. Nansen, *In Northern Mists*, I 326; II, 29, 61.

20. Ed. G. Storm, p. 76.

21. Duason, *Landkonnun*, pp. 300-302.

22. Nansen, *In Northern Mists*, p. 191 .

23. Bjornbo and Petersen, *Claudius Clausson Swart*; Joseph Fischer, *The Discoveries of the Norsemen in America* (London, 1903), pl. 1-6.

24. *Ibid.*, p. 144.

25. Johann Schoner, *Luculentissima quaedam terre totius descriptio* (Nürnberg, 1515).

26. Roger Bacon, *Opus majus* (Oxford, 1897-1900), I, 290. Cf. Duason, *Landkonnun*, pp. 280-281.

27. Cf. T. J. Oleson, "Inventio fortunata," *Timarit Thjodraeknisfelags Islendinga*, XLIV (1963).

28. Fischer, *The Discoveries of the Norsemen*, pp. 83-85.

29. Konrad Miller, *Mappae mundi* (Stuttgart, 1895-1898), III, 22.

30. A. E. Nordenskiold, *Periplus* (Stockholm, 1897), p. 15.

31. Miller, *Mappae mundi*, I, 35.

32. *Ibid.*, IV, 27.

33. Nordenskiold, *Periplus*, p. 159.

34. Bjornbo and Petersen, *Claudius Clausson Swart*, p. 234.

35. K. Kretschmer, "Eine neue mittelalteriche Weltkarte der vatikanischen Bibliothek," *Zeitschr. d. Gesellschaft für Erdkunde z. Berlin*, XXVI (1891), 208.

36. Sophus Ruge, *Geschichte des Zeitalters der Entdeckungen* (Berlin, 1881), pp. 78-79.

37. Nordenskiold, *Periplus*, XXXIX.

38. Cf. Nansen, *In Northern Mists*, p. 212. I have altered the translation slightly.

39. C. C. Rafn, *Antiquitates Americanae* (Copenhagen, 1837), p. 448.

40. Nordenskiold, *Periplus*, X.

41. Duason, *Landkonnun*, p. 299.

42. Bjornbo, *Claudius Clausson Swart*, p. 144.

43. Fischer, *The Discoveries of the Norsemen*, p. 86.

44. Ravenstein, *Martin Behaim*.

NOTES TO CHAPTER FOURTEEN

1. Boland, *They All Discovered America*, p. 251. Cf. William S. Godfrey, Jr., "The Archæology of the Old Stone Mill," *A.A.*, XVII (1951).

2. Zella Armstrong, *Who Discovered America?* (Chattanooga, 1950); Pohl, *Atlantic Crossings*, pp. 171-175; Thomas Stephens, *Madoc* (1893).

3. Ashe, *Land to the West*, pp. 16-119.

4. *Ibid.*, pp. 123-156.

5. Lanctot, *A History of Canada from its Origins to the Royal Régime*, Chap. III.

6. Pohl, *Atlantic Crossings*, p. 15; Ashe, *Land to the West*, pp. 195-220.

7. *Eiriks saga rauda*, p. 234.

8. *Ibid.*, pp. 233-234.

9. *G.h.M.,* I, 154.

10. *Eyrbyggja saga,* pp. 176-180.

11. Holand has conveniently summarized his previous writings and added some new material in his recent book, *A Pre-Columbian Crusade to America* (New York, 1962).

12. *Ibid.,* p. 41; cf. p. 27.

13. *Annalar og Nafnaskra,* p. 123.

14. H. R. Holand, *Westward from Vinland* (New York, 1940), p. 143.

15. *Annalar og Nafnaskra, sub annis* 1343, 1347.

16. *Ibid., sub anno* 1347.

17. Holand, *A Pre-Columbian Crusade,* p. 115.

18. *Ibid.,* p. 41.

19. Thalbitzer's translation, "Two Runic Stones."

20. Holand, *A Pre-Columbian Crusade,* p. 185.

21. Holand, *Westward from Vinland,* pp. 244-251.

22. Eric Wahlgren, *The Kensington Stone* (Madison, 1958).

23. Holand, *A Pre-Columbian Crusade,* pp. 103-119.

24. Ingstad, *Landet under Leidarstjernen,* p. 475.

25. "Ein Nordpolsekspedisjon ar 1360," *Syn og Segn,* LXIV (1958), 417.

26. *Tudor Geography* (London, 1930), p. 3.

27. *Winnipeg Tribune,* December 22, 1962.

28. Richard Hakluyt, *The Principal Navigations, Voyages, Traffiques & Dis-coveries of the English Nation* (Glasgow, 1903-1905), I, 303.

29. *Loc. cit.*

30. E. G. R. Taylor, "A Letter," p. 67.

31. Oleson, "Inventio fortunata."

32. J. A. Williamson, *The Cabot Voyages and Bristol Discovery under Henry VII* (Cambridge: Hakluyt Society, Sec. Ser. CXX, 1962), p. 212.

33. See Oleson, "Inventio fortunata" for these references.

34. *Ibid.,* p. 76.

35. Cf. E. G. R. Taylor, "A Letter," pp. 56-61.

36. *His Exercises Containing Eight Treatises . . . to the Furtherance of Navigation* (London, 1613), p. 760.

37. Hjalmar R. Holand, *Explorations in America before Columbus* (New York, 1956), p. 246.

38. Frederick J. Pohl, *The Sinclair Expedition to Nova Scotia in 1398* (Pictou, Nova Scotia, 1950).

39. *Ibid.,* pp. 14-15.

40. Pohl, *Atlantic Crossings,* pp. 226-290.

41. *Ibid.,* pp. 279-287.

42. Fred W. Lucas, *The Annals of the Voyages of the Venetian Brothers Nicolo and Antonio Zeno in the North Atlantic Ocean* (London, 1898).

43. *Annalar og Nafnaskra, sub annis.*

44. C. T. Currelly, "Viking Weapons Found Near Beardmore, Ontario," *C.H.R.,* XX (1939). Cf. *Globe and Mail,* Nov. 30, 1956.

45. Boland, *They All Discovered America,* pp. 231-232.

NOTES TO CHAPTER FIFTEEN

1. *G.h.M.,* III, 251.

2. Cf. Nansen, *In Northern Mists,* pp. 111-112.

3. Bjorn Thorsteinsson, "Islandsverzlun Englendinga a fyrra hluta 16. aldar," *Skirnir,* CXXIV (1950), 84.

4. On all this, see Thorsteinsson, *Islenzka Skattlandid* (Reykjavik, 1956), and Johannesson, *Islendinga saga,* II. Extant documents of trade between Iceland, England, and Germany are to be found in *Diplomatarium Islandicum* (Copenhagen and Reykjavik, 1857), XVI.

5. *Ibid.,* IV, 523-525.

6. Bjornbo, *Claudius Clausson Swart,* p. 144.

7. See Duason, *Landkonnun,* pp. 581-610, and for a contrary view, Johannesson, "Reisubok Bjarnar Jorsalafara," *Skirnir,* CXIX (1945).

8. On this letter, see the works cited in Duason, *Landkonnun*, pp. 548-549.

9. Cf. Carl V. Solver, *Imago mundi* (Copenhagen, 1951), pp. 29-31.

10. *Ibid.*, pp. 35-36.

11. A pursuivant was an attendant on the heralds. He served seven years before becoming himself a herald. (See Sofus Larsen, *The Discovery of North America Twenty Years before Columbus* [Copenhagen and London, 1924], p. 19.)

12. *Ibid.*, pp. 16-20.

13. *Ibid.*, *passim*; Duason, *Landkonnun*, pp. 1271-1287; Solver, *Imago mundi*, pp. 46-48.

14. Louis Bobé, "Aktstykker til Oplysn-

ing om Gronlands Besejling, 1521-1607," *Dansk Magazin*, Series 5, VI (1909), 304 ff.

15. *Historia general de las Indias* (Saragossa, 1552-1553), Chap. 37.

16. G.h.M., III, 479-480.

17. *Ibid.*, pp. 475-476.

18. *Diplomatarium Norvegicum* (Oslo, 1849-1915), XVII, 1131.

19. See Duason, *Landkonnun*, pp. 1316-1332; for a different viewpoint, see Williamson, *The Cabot Voyages*, pp. 98-101; 116-117; 120-121; 310-311.

20. Duason, *Landkonnun*, p. 1289.

21. Norlund, *Buried Norsemen*, pp. 251-252.

NOTES TO CHAPTER SIXTEEN

1. Thorsteinsson, *Islandsverzlun Englendinga*, *passim*.

2. Duason, *Landkonnun*, pp. 1429-1440.

3. *Ibid.*, pp. 1440-1450.

4. Williamson, *The Cabot Voyages*, pp. 19-20.

5. *Ibid.*, p. 23.

6. *Ibid.*, p. 228.

7. *Ibid.*, p. 213.

8. *Ibid.*, pp. 26-32.

9. Nordenskiold, *Facsimile Atlas*, p. 53a.

10. Williamson, *The Cabot Voyages*, pp. 33-44.

11. *Ibid.*, p. 204.

12. *Ibid.*, p. 48.

13. *Landkonnun*, pp. 1481-1482.

NOTES TO CHAPTER SEVENTEEN

1. Williamson, *The Cabot Voyages*, p. 204.

2. *Ibid.*, p. 216.

3. *Ibid.*, p. 207.

4. *Ibid.*, pp. 209-211.

5. *Ibid.*, pp. 56-57; 25-25; 57-58. It is to be noted that the eighth legend says that Prima Terra Vista had near it a large island which Cabot named Saint John. This may suggest Labrador or Newfoundland. The description of the people suggests Eskimos, and the adjective "sterile" used of the land suggests large portions of Labrador. That it can have been Cape Breton or even Newfoundland is contradicted by the fact that according to the legend "there are many white bears" and "very large stags like horses," for the polar bear is an infrequent visitor south of the Strait

of Belle Isle, and the caribou is not found in great numbers in Newfoundland. The reference to fish and birds could apply to either Labrador or Newfoundland, although the reference to black hawks would seem to suggest Labrador, where the black gerfalcon is today a rare bird, but may have been more plentiful in the past.

6. *Ibid.*, pp. 266-268.

7. *Ibid.*, pp. 272-273.

8. *Ibid.*, p. 274.

9. These accounts are quoted in *ibid.*, pp. 275-278. Cf. pp. 152-158.

10. *Ibid.*, p. 278.

11. Henry Percival Biggar, *The Precursors of Jacques Cartier* (Ottawa, 1911), p. 136. Cf. Williamson, *The Cabot Voyages*, p. 150.

12. Cf. Contarini's report to the Venetian Senate in 1536 (ibid., p. 270).

13. Ibid., p. 164.

14. Ibid., p. 170.

15. Loc. cit.

16. W. F. Ganong, "Crucial Maps in the early Cartography and Place-nomenclature of the Atlantic Coast of Canada," T.R.S.C., 1929-1937, V, 159.

17. Williamson, The Cabot Voyages, pp. 12, 95, 169.

18. Ibid., pp. 95-96.

19. Ibid., pp. 226-227.

20. Cf. ibid., pp. 59-60, 65, 81-82.

21. Ibid., pp. 113-115.

NOTES TO CHAPTER EIGHTEEN

1. Williamson, The Cabot Voyages, p. 235.

2. Theo E. Layng, "Charting the Course to Canada," Actas, Congresso Internacional Dos Descobrimentos (Lisbon, 1961), II, 1-22.

3. Loc. cit.

4. Williamson, The Cabot Voyages, p. 237. Williamson (ibid., pp. 117-118), relying on S. E. Morison, Portuguese Voyages to America in the Fifteenth Century (Cambridge, Mass., 1940), argues that Fernandez could have made no voyage of discovery before 1500, but Layng has shown that Morison's arguments do not necessarily point to this conclusion.

5. Biggar, The Precursors of Jacques Cartier, p. 35.

6. Williamson, The Cabot Voyages, pp. 118-120.

7. Cf. ibid., p. 229.

8. Cf. Biggar, The Precursors of Jacques Cartier, p. 63.

9. Williamson, The Cabot Voyages, pp. 121-122. Cf. Ernest S. Dodge, Northwest by Sea (New York, 1961), pp. 21-22.

10. Loc. cit.

11. Cf. Williamson, The Cabot Voyages, p. 222.

12. Ibid., pp. 125-132.

13. Ibid., pp. 250-251.

14. Ibid., pp. 134-140.

15. Dodge, Northwest by Sea, pp. 28-29.

16. Williamson, The Cabot Voyages, p. 148.

17. Biggar, The Precursors of Jacques Cartier, pp. xxiv-xxv. Cf. Hoffman, Cabot to Cartier, pp. 33-35.

18. Ibid., p. xxv.

19. Loc. cit.

20. Ibid., pp. xxv-xxix.

21. Ibid., pp. xxix-xxxi.

22. Williamson, The Cabot Voyages, p. 202.

23. Ibid., pp. 26-29.

24. Dodge, Northwest by Sea, pp. 33-34.

NOTES TO CHAPTER NINETEEN

1. In the 1540's Roger Barlowe proposed voyages to the north, but nothing came of this. (V. Stefansson, Three Voyages, pp. lxxix-lxxx.)

2. The best recent work on Martin Frobisher is the one referred to in the above note.

3. Ibid., I, 50.

4. Ibid., II, 84-93.

5. Ibid., pp. 103-105.

6. Ibid., I, cxii-cxiii.

7. Ibid., pp. 52-71.

8. Ibid., II, 18.

9. Ibid., pp. 18-19.

10. Ibid., pp. 19-20.

11. Ibid., p. 21.

12. Ibid., pp. 21-22.

13. Ibid., p. 25.

14. Ibid., I, cxv, 36.

15. Loc. cit.

16. Ibid., II, 56.

17. C. C. A. Gosch, Danish Artcic Expeditions, 1605 to 1620 (London: Hakluyt Society, 1897), I, 164-202.

18. On the fact of the relics, see V. Stefansson, Three Voyages, II, 240-248.

NOTES TO CHAPTER TWENTY

1. The standard work on John Davis is Albert Hastings Markham, *Voyages and Works of John Davis the Navigator* (London: Hakluyt Society, 1880).
2. Weymouth's voyage is dealt with in T. Rundall, *Narrative of Voyages towards the North-West, in Search of a Passage to Cathay and India, 1496-1631* (London: Hakluyt Society, 1849).
3. The standard work on these voyages is C. C. A. Gosch, *Danish Arctic Expeditions, 1605 to 1620* (London: Hakluyt Society, 1897). On Knight's later voyage, see C. R. Markham, *Sir James Lancaster* (London: Hakluyt Society, 1877).
4. On Hudson's voyages, consult Asher, *Henry Hudson, the Navigator*. On Hudson's fate, see T. James, *The Strange and Dangerous Voyage of Captain Thomas James* (London, 1633).
5. C. R. Markham, *William Baffin, 1612-1622* (London: Hakluyt Society, 1881).
6. On this voyage see C. R. Markham, *William Baffin*, and A. H. Markham, *Voyages and Works of John Davis*.
7. C. R. Markham, *William Baffin*.
8. *Op. cit.*
9. M. Christy, "Captain William Hawkeridge and his Voyage in Search of a North-West Passage in 1625," *The Mariner's Mirror*, XIII (1927).
10. M. Christy, *The Voyages of Captain Luke Foxe of Hull and Captain Thomas James of Bristol in Search of a Northwest Passage in 1631-32* (London: Hakluyt Society, 1894).
11. Gosch, *Danish Arctic Expeditions, 1605 to 1620*. A new edition of Jens Munk's *Navigatio Septentrionalis* was published in Copenhagen in 1962.

NOTES TO CONCLUSION

1. Taylor, "The Dorset Problem," p. 39.
2. *Loc. cit.*
3. Rasmussen, *Fra Gronland til Stillehavet*, II, 95-96.

ABBREVIATIONS

A.N.O.H.: *Aarboger for Nordiske Oldkyndighed og Historie.*
A.A.: *American Antiquity.*
A.S.R.: *American Scandinavian Review.*
A.R.B.E.: *Annual Report of the Bureau of Ethnology.*
A.R.S.I.: *Annual Report of the Smithsonian Institution.*
C.H.J.: *Cambridge Historical Journal.*
C.H.R.: *Canadian Historical Review.*
G.T.: *Geografisk Tidskrift.*
G.J.: *Geographical Journal.*
G.R.: *Geographical Review.*
G.h.M.: *Gronlands historiske Mindesmaerker.*
J.A.I.G.B.I.: *Journal of the Anthropological Institute of Great Britain & Ireland.*
M.o.G.: *Meddelelser om Gronland.*
N.h.T.: *Norsk historisk Tidsskrift.*
N.G.M.: *National Geographic Magazine.*
N.V.: *Naturens Verden.*
N.G.S.A.: *Norsk Geografisk Selskabs Aarbok.*
N.G.T.: *Norsk Geografisk Tidsskrift.*
N.T.V.K.I.: *Nordisk Tidskrift for Vetenskap Konst och Industrei.*
T.R.S.C.: *Transactions of the Royal Society of Canada.*

BIBLIOGRAPHY

ADAM OF BREMEN. History of the Archbishops of Hamburg-Bremen. Translated by Francis J. Tschan. New York, 1959.

AKERLUND H. "Ass och beiti-ass," Unda Maris, 1955-56.

—— "Vikingatidens skepp och sjovasen," Svenska Kryssark klubbens Arsskrift, 1959.

AMIRA, KARL VON. Grundriss des germanischen Rechts. Strasbourg, 1913.

AMUNDSEN, ROALD E. G. Nordvest-Passagen. Christiania, 1907.

ARI THORGILSSON. Islendigabok (The Book of the Icelanders), ed. H. Hermannsson ("Islandica," Vol. XX), Ithaca, 1930.

ARMSTRONG, ZELLA. Who Discovered America? Chattanooga, 1950.

ASHE, GEOFFREY. Land to the West. London, 1962.

ASHER, G. M. Henry Hudson, the Navigator. London: Hakluyt Society, 1860.

BACON, ROGER. Opus majus. Oxford, 1897-1900.

BARDARSON, IVAR. Det gamle Gronlands Beskrivelse, ed. F. Jonsson. Copenhagen, 1930.

BIDDLE, R. A Memoir of Sebastian Cabot. London, 1832.

BIGGAR, HENRY PERCIVAL. The Precursors of Jacques Cartier. Ottawa, 1911.

BIRKET-SMITH, KAJ. The Eskimos, New York, 1960.

BJORNBO, AXEL ANTHON. Anecdota Cartographica Septentrionalis. Copenhagen, 1908.

—— Cartographia Groenlandica, M.o.G., Vol. XLVIII, No. 1 (1911).

BJORNBO, AXEL ANTHON, AND PETERSEN, CARL S. Der Dane Claudius Clausson Swart, Innsbruck, 1909.

BLUNDEVILLE, THOMAS. His Exercises Containing Eight Treatises . . . to the Furtherance of Navigation. London, 1613.

BOAS, FRANZ. "The Central Eskimo," Sixth A.R.B.E., 1888.

—— "Eskimo of Baffin Land and Hudson Bay," Bulletin of the American Museum of Natural History, Vol. XV (1907).

BOBÉ, LOUIS. "Aktstykker til Oplysning om Gronlands Besejling, 1521-1607," Dansk Magazin, Series 5, Vol. VI (1909).

—— "Om Carsten Grip," ibid., Series 6, Vol. 1 (1913).

—— "Gronlands Genopdagelse og James Halls Rejser," Gronl. Selskabs Aarskrift 1916 (1917).

BOGARAS, WALDEMAR. The Chukchee ("Memoirs American Museum of Natural History, Vol. 2), 1904-1909.

—— "Early Migrations of the Eskimo between Asia and America," Twenty-first International Congress of Americanists. Goteborg, 1925.

BOLAND, CHARLES MICHAEL. They All Discovered America. New York, 1961.

The Book of the Icelanders, See Ari Thorgilsson.

BROGGER, A. W. Ancient Emigrants. Oxford, 1929.

BROGGER, A. W., AND SHETELIG, HAAKON. Vikingeskipene. Oslo, 1950. (English translation, The Viking Ships, Oslo, 1953).

BRONDSTED JOHANNES. The Vikings. London, 1960.

—— "Norsemen in North America Before Columbus," A.R.S.I., Washington, 1954.

BROSTE, K., AND FISCHER-MOLLER, K. The Mediæval Norsemen at Gardar. M.o.G., Vol. LXXXIX, No. 3. Copenhagen, 1944.

BURWASH, L. T. "Across Arctic Canada, 1925-1926," G.J., Vol. LXXIV (1929).

CHARLEVOIX, PIERRE FRANÇOIS XAVIER DE. Histoire et description générale de la Nouvelle France. Paris, 1744.

CHOWN, BRUCE, AND LEWIS, MARION. "Blood Groups in Anthropology," The National Museum of Canada, Bulletin No. 167. Ottawa, 1958.

CHRISTY, M. The Voyages of Captain Luke Foxe of Hull and Captain Thomas James of Bristol in Search of a Northwest Passage in 1631-32. London: Hakluyt Society, 1894.

—— "Captain William Hawkeridge and his Voyage in Search of a North-West Passage in 1625," The Mariner's Mirror, Vol. XIII (1927).

COLLINS, H. B. Arctic Area, Mexico, 1954.

—— "Archæological Investigations on Southampton and Walrus Islands,

Northwest Territories," The National Museum of Canada, Bulletin No. 147. Ottawa, 1956.

—— "Outline of Eskimo Prehistory," Smithsonian Misc. Coll., Vol. C, 533-592 (1940).

—— "The Origin and Antiquity of the Eskimo," A.R.S.I., 1950 (1951), pp. 423-467.

—— "Recent Developments in the Dorset Culture Area," A.A., XVIII, No. 3, Part 2 (January, 1953).

—— "Eskimo Archæology and its Bearing on the Problem of Man's Antiquity in America," Amer. Philosophical Soc. Proceedings, LXXXVI, No. 2 (1943), 220-35.

—— "Archæological Research in the Northern American Arctic," Arctic, Vol. VII (1955).

—— "Archæological Work in Arctic Canada," A.R.S.I., Washington, 1957.

—— "Stefansson as an Anthropologist," Polar Notes, IV (1962), 8-13.

—— "Vanished Mystery Men of Hudson Bay, N.G.M., Vol. CX (1956).

—— "The Present Status of the Dorset Problem," Proceedings of the Thirty-second International Congress of Americanists, Copenhagen, 1958.

COLLINSON, R. The Three Voyages of Martin Frobisher. London: Hakluyt Society, 1867.

CONRAD, HERMANN, Deutsches Rechtsgeschichte, Vol. 1, Karlsruhe, 1954.

COSTA, B. F. DE. Sailing Directions of Henry Hudson. Albany, 1869.

—— "Arctic Exploration," Journal of the American Geographical Society of New York, Vol. XII (1880).

CRANZ, DAVID. Historie von Gronland. Leipzig, 1765.

CURRELLY, C. T. "Viking Weapons Found Near Beardmore, Ontario," C.H.R., Vol. XX (1939).

DEGERBOL, MAGNUS. "Animal Bones from the Norse Ruins at Brattahlid," in Poul Norlund, Brattahlid.

—— Animal Remains from the West Settlement in Greenland. M.o.G., Vol. LXXXVIII, No. 3. Copenhagen, 1936.

—— Animal Bones from the Norse Ruins at Gardar. M.o.G., Vol. LXXVI (1930).

DICUIL. Liber de mensura orbis terrae. Berlin, 1870.

Diplomatarium Islandicum. Copenhagen and Reykjavik, 1857-.

Diplomatarium Norvegicum. Oslo, 1849.

DODGE, ERNEST S. Northwest by Sea. New York, 1961.

DUASON, JON. Landkonnun og landnam Islendinga i Vesturheimi. Reykjavik, 1941-1947.

—— Rjettarstada Graenlands Nylendu Islands. Reykjavik, 1947-.

—— A Island ekkert rjettartilkall til Graenlands? Reykjavik, 1953.

DYSON, JAMES L. The World of Ice. New York, 1962.

EGEDE, HANS. Relationer fra Gronland 1721-1736, ed. L. Bobé. M.o.G., Vol. LIV. Copenhagen, 1925.

Eirik the Red. Translated by Gwyn Jones. London, 1961.

Eiriks saga rauda. See Thordarson.

ELDJARN, KRISTJAN. Gengid a reka. Akureyri, 1948.

EYTHORSSON, JON. "Um loftlagsbreytingar a Islandi og Graenlandi," Skirnir, Vol. C (1926).

Eyrbyggja saga, ed. Einar O. Sveinsson. Islenzk fornrit, Vol. IV, Reykjavik, 1935.

FISCHER, JOSEPH. The Discoveries of the Norsemen in America. London, 1903.

FISCHER-MOLLER, K. The Mediæval Norse Settlements in Greenland. M.o.G., Vol. LXXXIX, No. 2 (1942). See also Broste and Fischer-Moller.

FITZGERALD, C. P. Son of Heaven. Cambridge, 1933.

Flateyjarbok. Christiania, 1860-1868.

FREDERICK II. The Art of Falconry being the De Arte Venandi cum Avibus, Stanford, 1955.

GANONG, W. F. "Crucial Maps in the early Cartography and Place-nomenclature of the Atlantic Coast of Canada," T.R.S.C., 1929-1937, Vols. 23-31 of Sect. II.

GATHORNE-HARDY, G. M. The Norse Discoverers of America. Oxford, 1921.

—— "A Recent Journey to Northern Labrador," G.J., Vol. LIX (1922).

—— "Om Eyktarstadr peilingen paa Leifs Vinlandsreise," Maal og Minne, 1924.

Gronlands historiske Mindesmaerker. Copenhagen, 1838-1845.

GIDDINGS, J. L. "Cultural Continuities of Eskimos," A.A., Vol. XXVII (1961).

GINI, CORRADO. *The Location of Vinland.* Bergen, 1960.
—— *On the Extinction of the Norse Settlements.* Bergen, 1958.
GJESSING, GUTORM. *Circumpolar Stone Age.* Acta Arctica, fasc. II. Copenhagen, 1944.
GODFREY, WILLIAM S., JR. "The Archæology of the Old Stone Mill," A.A., Vol. XVII (1951).
—— "Answer to 'Plaster under the Tower'," A.A., XIX (1954), 277-279.
GOES, DAMIAO DE. *Chronica do Felicissimo Rei Dom Emanuel.* Lisbon, 1566.
—— *Chronica do Principe Dom Joam.* Lisbon, 1567.
GOMARA, FRANCESCO LOPEZ DE. *Historia general de las Indias.* Saragossa, 1552-1553.
GOSLING, WM. GILBERT. *Labrador.* London, 1910.
GOSCH, C. C. A. *Danish Arctic Expeditions, 1605 to 1620.* London: Hakluyt Society, 1897.
GRAAH, WILHELM AUGUST. *Undersogelsesrejse til Ostkysten af Gronland.* Copenhagen, 1832.
Graenlendinga saga. See Thordarson.
GRAY, EDWARD F. *Leif Eriksson, Discoverer of America A.D. 1003.* New York, 1930.
GREELY, A. W. "The Origin of Stefansson's Blond Eskimo," N.G.M., Vol. XXIII (1912).
GRIEG, SIGURD. "Nordmenn pa Gronland i Mellomalderen," N.T.V.K.I., Vol. XXXIII (1957).
Greenland, Copenhagen, 1928-1929.
GUDJONSSON, SIGURDUR. "Ferd Bjarna Herjolfssonar," Vikingur, 1958.
HAKLUYT, RICHARD. *The Principal Navigations, Voyages, Traffiques & Discoveries of the English Nation.* Glasgow, 1903-1905.
HALL, CHARLES F. *Arctic Researches and Life among the Esquimaux.* New York, 1865.
HALLIDAY, E. "John Davis and the North-West Passage," *Geographic Magazine,* Vol. XXXIX (9) (1962).
HAMMERICH, L. L. "The Origin of the Eskimo," *Proceedings of the 32nd International Congress of Americanists 1956* (1958), 640-44.
HARP, ELMER, JR. *The Archæology of the Lower and Middle Thelon, Northwest*

Territories. (Arctic Institute of North America Technical Paper No. 8). Montreal, 1961.
—— "An Archæological Survey in the Strait of Belle Isle Area," A.A., Vol. XVI (1951).
—— Archæological Research in Arctic North America," *Anthropologica,* N.S., Vol. II (1960).
HARRISSE, H. *The Discovery of North America.* London, 1892.
HATT, GUDMUND. "Types of European Colonization," *Greenland,* III, 1-14.
HAWKES, E. W. *The Labrador Eskimo.* Ottawa, 1910.
HEINSIUS, ELLI AND PAUL. "Hvordan seilte Vikingene med sine Bater?" *Viking,* XVII (1953), 63-77.
HENCKEN, HUGH. "The 'Irish Monastery' at North Salem, New Hampshire," *The New England Quarterly,* Vol. XII (1939).
HENNIG, R. *Terrae Incognitae.* Leiden, 1944-1956.
HERMANNSSON, HALLDOR. *The Northmen in America: 982-c.1500* ("Islandica," Vol. II). Ithaca, 1909.
—— *The Problem of Wineland* ("Islandica," Vol. XXV). Ithaca, 1936.
—— *The Vinland Sagas* ("Islandica," Vol. XXX). Ithaca, 1944.
HILDERBRANDSSON, HUGO HILDEBRAND. *Sur le prétendu changement du climat Européens en temps historique* (Nova Acta Regiae Societatis Scientiarum Upsaliensis, Ser. IV, 4, No. 5). Uppsala, 1915.
Historia Norwegiae. See G. Storm, *Monumenta historica Norvegiae.*
HOFFMAN, BERNARD G. *Cabot to Cartier.* Toronto, 1961.
HOLAND, HJALMAR R. *Westward from Vinland.* New York, 1940.
—— *Exploration in America Before Columbus.* New York, 1956.
—— *A Pre-Columbian Crusade to America.* New York, 1962.
—— "Vinland visited 1050," A.S.R., Vol. XXXVII (1949).
HOLM, GUSTAV. "Bidrag til Kjendskabet om Eskimoernes Herkomst," G.T., Vol. XI (1891-1892), 15-27.
HOLTVED, ERIK. *Archæological Investigations in the Thule District.* M.o.G., Vol. CXLI, No. 1. Copenhagen, 1944. See also Mathiassen, Therkel.
HOVGAARD, WILLIAM. *The Voyages of*

the Norsemen to America. New York, 1914.

HOYGAARD, ARNE. *Studies on the Nutrition and Physio-Pathology of Eskimos.* Oslo, 1941.

INGSTAD, H. *Landet under Leidarstjernen,* Oslo, 1959.

—— "Discovery of Vinland," *Arctic Circular,* XI (1963).

ISACHSEN, FRIDTJOV, AND ISACHSEN, GUNNAR. "Hvor langt mot nord kom de norrone Gronlendinger?" *N.G.T.,* Vol. IV (1932-1933).

ISACHSEN, GUNNAR. "Die Wanderungen der ostlichen Eskimo nach und in Gronland," *Petermanns Mitteilungen,* Vol. XLIX (1903).

—— "Om opdagelsen af Svalbard," *N.G.S.A.,* Vol. XVII (1906-1907).

—— "Nordboernes faerder til Norderseta," *ibid.,* 20-32.

Islandske Annaler indtil 1578. See Storm, G.

IVERSEN, JOHS. "Et botanisk Vidne om Nordboernes Vinlandsrejser," *Naturhistorisk Tidende,* No. 8, October 1938.

JAMES, T. *The Strange and Dangerous Voyage of Captaine Thomas James.* London, 1633.

JENNESS, DIAMOND. *The Life of the Copper Eskimo and Physical Characteristics of the Copper Eskimo.* (Report of the Canadian Arctic Expedition, 1913-18, Vol. XII, Pts. A and B.) Ottawa, 1922-1923.

—— *The People of the Twilight.* New York: Macmillan Co., 1928.

—— "The Problem of the Eskimo," *The American Aborigines,* ed. D. Jenness, Toronto, 1933.

—— "The 'Blond' Eskimos," *American Anthropologist,* N.S., Vol. XXIII (1921).

—— "A Geographical Description of Southampton Island and Notes upon the Eskimo," *Bull. of the American Geographical Society,* Vol. XLII (1910).

JOHANNESSON, JON. *Islendinga saga.* Reykjavik, 1956-1958.

—— "Reisubok Bjarnar Jorsalafara," *Skirnir,* Vol. CXIX (1945).

—— "Aldur Graenlendinga sogu," *Nordaela,* Reykjavik, 1956.

JONSSON, BJORN. *Grænlands annall,* A. M. 769 4to.

JONSSON, GUDNI (ed.). *Annalar og Nafnaskra.* Reykjavik, 1948.

JONSSON, STEINGRIMUR. Review of V. Stefansson, *Greenland,* in *Skirnir,* Vol. CXVII (1943).

JORGENSEN, JORGEN BALSLEV. *The Eskimo Skeleton.* M.o.G., Vol. CXLVI, No. 2 (1953).

JOUIUS, PAULUS VON NOUOCOMEN. *Von der Moscouiten Bottschafft.* Strasbourg, 1534.

KALUND, KR. (ed.). *Alfraedi Islensk.* Copenhagen, 1908.

KARLSSON, K. H. See Storm, G.

KIELLAND, KRISTIAN. "Hvordan seilte Vikingene med sine Bater?" *Viking,* XVIII (1954), 227-234.

The King's Mirror. See F. Jonsson.

KNUTH, EIGIL. "An Outline of the Archæology, of Peary Land," *Arctic,* Vol. V (1952).

—— "Archæology of the Farthest North," *Proceedings of the Thirty-second International Congress of Americanists,* Copenhagen, 1958.

KONUNGSSKUGGSJA. See F. Jonsson, Copenhagen, 1920-31. (English translation, L. M. Larson, *The King's Mirror,* New York, 1917.)

KRETSCHMER, K. *Die Entdeckung Amerikas.* Berlin, 1892.

—— "Eine neue mittelalterliche Weltkarte der vatikanischen Bibliothek," *Zeitschr. d. Gesellschaft für Erdkunde z. Berlin,* Vol. XXVI (1891).

—— "Die Katalanische Weltkarte der Biblioteca Estense zu Modena," *ibid.,* Vol. XXXII (1897).

LAFITAU, JOSEPH FRANÇOIS. *Les Moeurs des Sauvages Amériquains.* Paris, 1724.

LANCTOT, GUSTAV. *A History of Canada from its Origins to the Royal Régime, 1663.* ("History of Canada Series," Vol. I.) Toronto, 1963.

LANDNAMABOK. See F. Jonsson, Copenhagen, 1900.

LARSEN, HELGE. *Dodemandsbugten, An Eskimo Settlement on Clavering Island.* M.o.G., Vol. CII, No. 1 (1934).

—— *Archæological Investigations in Knud Rasmussen's Land.* M.o.G., Vol. CXIX, No. 8 (1938).

—— "Recent Developments in Eskimo Archæology," *Actes du IVe Congrès Internationale des Sciences Anthropologiques et Ethnologiques,* Vienna, 1952. Vienna, 1955.

—— "Eskimokulturen," *Gronland,* 1960.

—— "Eskimo Archæological Problems in Greenland," *Circumpolar Conference in Copenhagen, 1958.* Acta Arctica, fasc. XII. Copenhagen, 1960.

—— "Paleo-Eskimo in Disko Bay, West Greenland," *Men and Cultures, Selected Papers of the Fifth International Congress of Anthropological and Ethnological Sciences.* Philadelphia, 1960.

—— "Archæology in the Arctic, 1935-60," A.A., Vol. XXVII (1961).

LARSEN, HELGE, AND MATHIASSEN, THERKEL. *Paleo-Eskimo Cultures in Disko Bugt, West Greenland.* M.o.G., Vol. CLXI, No. 2 (1958).

LARSEN, SOFUS. *The Discovery of North America Twenty Years before Columbus.* Copenhagen and London, 1924.

—— "Danmark og Portugal i det 15. aarhundrede, A.N.O.H., 1919.

LAYNG, THEO. E. "Charting the Course to Canada," *Actas, Congresso Internacional De Historia Dos Descobrimentos,* II, 1-22. Lisbon, 1961.

—— (ed.). *Sixteenth-Century Maps Relating to Canada,* Ottawa, 1956.

LEWIS, MARION. See Chown, Bruce.

LUCAS, FRED W. *The Annals of the Voyages of the Venetian Brothers Nicolo and Antonio Zeno in the North Atlantic Ocean.* London, 1898.

LYON, GEORGE FRANCIS. *A Brief Narrative of an Unsuccessful Attempt to Reach Repulse Bay.* London, 1825.

MAGOUN, FRANCIS P., JR. "The Pilgrim-Diary of Nikulas of Munkathvera," *Mediæval Studies,* Vol. VI (1944).

MAJOR R. H. *The Voyages of the Venetian Brothers Nicolo and Antonio Zeno.* London: Hakluyt Society, 1873.

MARCUS, G. J. "The Norse Emigration to the Faroe Islands," *English Historical Review,* Vol. LXXI (1956).

MARKHAM, ALBERT HASTINGS. *Voyages and Works of John Davis the Navigator.* London: Hakluyt Society, 1880.

MARKHAM, C. R. *The Voyages of Sir James Lancaster.* London: Hakluyt Society, 1877.

—— *The Voyages of William Baffin, 1612-1622.* London: Hakluyt Society, 1881.

MASON, J. ALDEN. "Excavations of Eskimo Thule Culture Sites at Point Barrow, Alaska," *Proceedings of the 23rd International Congress of Americanists.* New York, 1930.

MATHIASSEN, THERKEL. *Archæology of the Central Eskimos, II: The Thule Culture and its Position within the Eskimo Culture.* Copenhagen, 1927.

—— *Eskimoerne's Nutid og Fortid.* Copenhagen, 1929.

—— *Inugsuk, a Mediæval Eskimo Settlement in Upernivik District, West Greenland.* M.o.G., Vol. LXXVII (1930).

—— *Ancient Eskimo Settlements in the Kangamiut Area.* M.o.G., Vol. XCI, No. 1 (1931).

—— *Prehistory of the Angmagssalik Eskimos.* M.o.G., Vol. XCII, No. 4 (1933).

—— *Contributions to the Archæology of Disko Bay.* M.o.G., Vol. XCIII, No. 2 (1934).

——*Skraelingerne i Gronland.* Copenhagen, 1935.

—— *The Sermermiut Excavations 1955.* M.o.G., Vol. CLXI, No. 3 (1958).

—— "Southampton Island og dens oprindelige Beboere," G.T., Vol. XXX (1927).

—— "Traek af Iglulik Eskimoernes materielle Kultur," *ibid.,* pp. 72-88.

—— "Nordboruiner i Labrador?" G.T., Vol. XXXI (1928).

—— "Norse Ruins in Labrador," *American Anthropologist,* XXX (1928).

—— "Arkaeologiske Undersogelser i Uperniviks District i Sommeren 1929," G.T., Vol. XXXIII (1930).

—— "Det vingede Naalehus," G.T., Vol. XXXII (1929), 15-22.

—— Sporgsmaalet om Eskimokulturens Oprindelse," *ibid.*

—— "The Question of the Origin of the Eskimo Culture," *American Anthropologist,* Vol. XXXII (1930).

—— "An Old Eskimo Culture in West Greenland: Report of an Archæological Expedition to Upernivik," G.R., Vol. XX (1930).

—— "Sporgsmaalet on Eskimokulturens Oprindelse. Et Gensvar," G.T., Vol. XXXIII (1930). See also Larsen, Helge.

MATHIASSEN, THERKEL, AND HOLTVED, ERIK. *The Eskimo Archæology of Julianehaab District.* M.o.G., Vol. CXVIII, No. 1 (1936).

MAUSS, M., AND BEUCHAT, H. "Essai sur les Variations Saisonnières des Sociétés

Eskimos," *L'Année Sociologique*. Vol. IX (1904-1905) [1906].

MAXWELL, MOREAU S. "An Archæological Analysis of Eastern Grant Lands, Ellesmere Island, Northwest Territories," National Museum of Canada, Bulletin No. 170. Ottawa, 1960.

—— "The Movement of Cultures in the Canadian High Arctic," *Anthropologica*, N.S., II (1960).

MELDGAARD, JORGEN. *Eskimo Skulptur*. Copenhagen, 1959.

—— "A Paleo-Eskimo Culture in West Greenland," A.A., Vol. XVII (1951-52).

—— "Dorset Kulturen," *Kuml*, 1955.

—— "Eskimoiske Stenalderkultur i Arktisk Canada," *Polarboken*, 1955.

—— "Gronlaenderne i tre Tusinde ar," *Gronland*, 1958.

—— "Prehistoric Culture Sequences in the Eastern Arctic as Elucidated by Stratified Sites at Igloolik," *Men and Cultures. Selected Papers of the Fifth International Congress of Anthropological and Ethnological Sciences*. Philadelphia, 1960.

—— "Om de gamle Nordboer og deres Skjaebne," *Gronland*, 1961.

—— "Hvor la Markland og Vinland?" N.V., 1961.

—— "Fra Brattahlid til Vinland," N.V., 1961.

—— "Sarqaq-folket ved Itivinera," *Gronland*, 1961.

MILLER, KONRAD. *Mappae Mundi*, Stuttgart, 1895-1898.

MJELDE, M. M. "The Norse Discoveries of America, the Eyktarstadr Problem," *Saga Book of the Viking Society*, X (1928-1929), 57-68.

MORISON, S. E. *Portuguese Voyages to America in the Fifteenth Century*. Cambridge, Mass., 1940.

MOSS, EDWARD L. *Shores of the Polar Sea*. London, 1878.

MUNK, JENS. *Navigatio Septentrionalis*. Copenhagen, 1962.

MURDOCH, J. "Ethnological Results of the Point Barrow Expedition," *Ninth A.R.B.E.*, 1892.

NANSEN, FRIDTJOF. *Eskimoliv*. Christiania, 1890.

—— *Paa Ski over Gronland*. Christiania, 1890.

—— *In Northern Mists*. London, 1911.

—— *Nansen's Rost*. Oslo, 1942.

—— "Klimat-vekslinger i Nordens historie" (Det norske Videnskaps-Akademis Avhandl. I, Mat.-Nat. Klasse, 1925, No. 3).

—— "Svalbard," N.G.T., Vol I (1926-1927).

NARES, SIR GEORGE STRONG. *Narrative of a Voyage to the Polar Sea during 1875*. London, 1878.

NIELSEN, NIELS. *Evidence on the Extraction of Iron in Greenland by the Norsemen*. M.o.G., Vol. LXXVI (1930).

—— *Evidence of Iron Extraction at Sandnes, in Greenland's West Settlement*. M.o.G., Vol. LXXXVIII, No. 4 (1936).

NORDENSKIOLD, ADOLF ERIK. *Facsimile-Atlas to the Early History of Cartography*. Stockholm, 1889.

—— *Periplus*. Stockholm, 1897.

—— *Bidrag til Nordens aldsta Kartografi*. Stockholm, 1892.

—— "Broderna Zenos Resor," *Studier och forskninkgar*. Stockholm, 1884.

NORDLAND, ODD. "Oya med Giftarmals-Vanskane," *Viking*, Vol. XVII (1953).

NORLUND, POUL. *Buried Norsemen at Herjolfsnes*. M.o.G., Vol. LXVII (1924).

—— *Viking Settlers in Greenland and their Descendants during Five Hundred Years*. London, 1936.

—— "Kirkegaarden paa Herjolfsnes," N.h.T., Ser. 5, Vol. VI (1927).

—— "Nordboproblemet i Gronland," G.T., Vol. XXXI (1928).

NORLUND, POUL, AND STENBERGER, MARTIN. *Brattahlid*. M.o.G., Vol. LXXXVIII, No. 1. Copenhagen, 1934.

ODDSSON, GISLI. *Annalium in Islandia Farrago*. ("Islandica," Vol. X.) Ithaca, 1917.

O'GORMAN, EDMUNDO. *The Invention of America*. Bloomington, 1961.

OLAUS, MAGNUS. *Historia de gentibus septentrionalibus*. Rome, 1555.

OLEARIUS, ADAM. *Beschreibung der Muscowitischen und Persischen . . .* Schleswig, 1656.

OLESON, T. J. "Giraldus Cambrensis and Iceland," *Icelandic Canadian*, XII, No. 4 (1954).

—— "Inventio fortunata," *Timarit Thjodraeknisfelags Islendinga*, Vol. XLIV (1963).

—— "Polar Bears in the Middle Ages," C.H.R., Vol. XXXI (1950).

OLSEN, BJORN M. *Um skattbaendatal 1311 og manntal a Island i fram ad theim tima* (Safn til sogu Islands, Vol. IV). Copenhagen, 1911.

OSCHINSKY, LAWRENCE. "Two Recently Discovered Human Mandibles from Cape Dorset Sites on Sugluk and Mansel Islands," *Anthropologica*, N.S., Vol. II (1960).

OSCHINSKY, LAWRENCE AND SMITHURST, ROY. "On Certain Dental Characters of the Eskimo of the Eastern Canadian Arctic," *Anthropologica*, N.S., Vol. II (1960).

OSCHINSKY, LAWRENCE. "A Short Note on Upper Lateral Incisor Tooth Crowding among the Eskimos," *Anthropologica*, N.S., Vol. III (1961).

—— "Facial Flatness and Cheekbone Morphology in Arctic Mongoloids," *Anthropologica*, N.S., Vol. IV (1962).

PETERSEN, CARL S. See Bjornbo, A. A.

PETTERSSON, OTTO. *Klimatforandringar i historisk och forhistorisk Tid* (Kungl. Svenska Vetenskapsakademiens Handlingar, Vol. LI, No. 2). Stockholm, 1913.

—— "Climatic Variations in Historic and Prehistoric Times," *Svenska Hydrografisk-Biologiska Kommissionens Skrifter*, Vol. V (1914).

PEYRERE, ISAAC DE LA. *Bericht von Gronland*. Hamburg, 1674.

POHL, FREDERICK J. *The Sinclair Expedition to Nova Scotia in 1398*. Pictou, Nova Scotia, 1950.

—— *Atlantic Crossings Before Columbus*. New York, 1961.

POINCY, LOUIS DE. *Histoire naturelle & morale des Iles Antilles de l'Amérique*. Rotterdam, 1658. (2nd ed., 1681.)

PORSILD, MORTEN P. "On Eskimo Stone Rows in Greenland formerly supposed to be of Norse Origin," *G.R.*, Vol. X (1920).

PUTNAM, GEORGE PALMER. "The Putnam Baffin Island Expedition," *G.R.*, Vol. XVIII (1928).

QUINN, D. B. "Edward IV and Exploration," *The Mariner's Mirror*, Vol. XXI (1935).

—— "The Argument for the English Discovery of America between 1480 and 1494," *G.J.*, Vol. CXXVII (1961).

RAFN, C. C. *Antiquitates Americanae*. Copenhagen, 1837.

RAMUSIO, GIOVANNI BATTISTA. *Navigationi et Viaggi*. Venice, 1563.

RASMUSSEN, KNUD. *Myter og Sagn fra Gronland*. Copenhagen, 1921.

—— *Fra Gronland til Stillehavet*. Copenhagen, 1925-1926.

—— *Intellectual Culture of the Hudson Bay Eskimos*. Copenhagen, 1929.

—— *Myndeudgave*. Copenhagen, 1934-1935.

—— *Gronland langs Polhavet*. Copenhagen, 1919.

—— "The Fifth Thule Expedition, 1921-24," *G.J.*, LXVII (1926), 123-142.

—— "Eskimos and Stone Age Peoples," *G.T.*, XXXII (1929), 201-206.

RAVENSTEIN, E. G. *Martin Behaim*. London, 1908.

REED, A. W. "John Rastell's Voyage in 1517," *The Mariner's Mirror*, Vol. IX (1923).

RINK, H. *Om Monopolhandelen paa Gronland*. Copenhagen, 1852.

—— *Gronland geografisk og statistisk beskrevet*. Copenhagen, 1857.

—— *Eskimoiske Eventyr og Sagn*. Copenhagen, 1866-1871.

—— *Tales and Traditions of the Eskimo*. Edinburgh and London, 1875.

—— "Om Eskimoernes Herkomst," *A.N.O.H.*, 1871, pp. 269-302.

ROUSSELL, AAGE. *Sandnes and the neighbouring Farms*. M.o.G., Vol. LXXXVIII, No. 2. Copenhagen, 1936.

—— *Farms and Churches in the Mediæval Norse Settlements of Greenland*. M.o.G., Vol. LXXXIX, No. 1. Copenhagen, 1941.

ROWLEY, GRAHAM. "The Dorset Culture of the Eastern Arctic," *American Anthropologist*, Vol. XLII (1940).

RUGE, SOPHUS. *Geschichte des Zeitalters der Entdeckungen*. Berlin, 1881.

RUNCIMAN, S. "Some remarks on the image of Edessa," *Cambridge Historical Journal*, Vol. III.

RUNDALL, T. *Narrative of Voyages Towards the North-West, in search of a Passage to Cathay and India, 1496-1631*. London: Hakluyt Society, 1849.

SCHONER, JOHANN. *Luculentissima quaedam terre totius descriptio*. Nurnberg, 1515.

SCHOOLCRAFT, H. R. *The Indian Tribes of the United States*, ed. F. S. Drake. Philadelphia, 1891.

SELMER, CARL. *Navigatio Sancti Brendani Abbatis.* Notre Dame, Indiana, 1960.

SHETELIG, H. See Brogger, A. W.

SIXTEENTH-CENTURY MAPS RELATING TO CANADA. See Theo. E. Layng.

SMITHURST, ROY. See Oschinsky, Lawrence.

SOLVER, CARL V. *Imago mundi.* Copenhagen, 1951.

—— "Leidarsteinn: The Compass of the Vikings," *Oldlore Miscellany,* Vol. X, part VII (1945-1946).

STEENSBY, H. P. *The Norsemen's Route from Greenland to Wineland.* Copenhagen, 1917. (Reprinted from M.o.G., Vol. LVI.)

STEFANSSON, SIGURDUR. *Qualiscunque Descriptio Islandiae,* ed. Fr. Burg. Hamburg, 1928.

STEFANSSON, VILHJALMUR. *My Life with the Eskimo.* New York, 1913.

—— *Prehistoric and Present Commerce Among the Arctic Coast Eskimo.* Ottawa, 1914.

—— *The Friendly Arctic.* New York, 1921.

—— "Man in Greenland," G.R., Vol. XX (1930).

—— *Hunters of the Great North.* New York, 1922.

—— ed., *The Three Voyages of Martin Frobisher.* London, 1938.

—— *Unsolved Mysteries of the Arctic.* New York, 1939.

—— *Ultima Thule.* New York, 1940.

—— *Greenland.* New York, 1942.

—— *Arctic Manual,* New York, 1944.

STEINNES, ASGAUT. "En Nordpolsekspedisjon ar 1360," *Syn og Segn,* Vol. LXIV (1958).

STENBERGER, MARTIN. See Norlund, Poul.

STEPHENS, THOMAS. Madoc. 1893.

STORM, G. (ed.). *Monumenta historica Norvegiae.* Oslo, 1880.

—— (ed.). *Islandske Annaler indtil 1578.* Christiania, 1888.

—— *Samlede Skrifter af Peder Clausson Friis.* Christiania, 1881.

—— *Afgifter fra den norske Kirkeprovins til det apostoliske Kammer og Kardinalkollegret 1311-1523.* Christiania, 1897.

—— "Om Kilderne til Lyschanders' Gronlandske Chronica," A.N.O.H., 1888.

—— "Den danske geograf Claudius Clavus eller Nicolaus Niger," *Ymer,* 1889-91.

—— "Ginnungagap," *Archiv f. nord. Filologi,* Vol. VI (1890).

—— "Om Zeniernes reiser," N.G.S.A., Vol. II (1890-1891).

—— "Columbus paa Island og vore forfaedres opdagelser i det nordvestlige Atlanterhav," *ibid.,* Vol. IV (1892-1893).

—— "Nye Efterretninger om det gamle Gronland," N.h.T., Series 3, Vol II (1892).

—— "Sjofareren Johann Scolvus og hans Rejse til Labrador eller Gronland," *ibid.,* Ser. 2, Vol. V (1886).

—— "Studier over Vinlandsrejserne," A.N.O.H., 1887.

—— "Et brev til pave Nicolaus den 5te om Norges beliggenhed og undre," *Norsk Geogr. Selskabs Aarbok,* X (1898-1899), 1-13.

STORM, G., AND KARLSEN, K. H. "Finmarkens Beskrivelse af Erkebiskop Erik Walkendorf," N.G.S.A., Vol. XII (1900-1901).

—— "Sjofaren Johannes Scolvus og hans Rejse til Labrador eller Gronland," N.h.T., Ser. 2, Vol. V (1886).

SUNDT, EILERT, *Egedes Dagbok i Udtag* Oslo, 1860.

SVERDRUP, O. *Nyt land,* Oslo, 1903 (English translation by Ethel H. Hearn, London, 1904).

SWANTON, JOHN R. *The Wineland Voyages,* Smith. Misc. Coll., Vol. CVII, No. 12. Washington, 1947.

TANNER, V. "Ruinerna paa Sculpin Island," G.T., Vol. XLIV (1941).

TAYLOR, E. G. R. *The Haven-Finding Art.* London, 1956.

—— *Tudor Geography.* London, 1930.

—— "Master Hore's Voyage of 1536," G.J., LXXVII (1931), pp. 469-470.

—— "A Letter dated 1577 from Mercator to John Dee," *Imago mundi* (1956).

—— "John Dee and the Map of North-East Asia," *ibid.* (1955).

TAYLOR, WILLIAM E., JR. "A Description of Sadlermiut Houses Excavated at Native Point, Southampton Island, N. W. T." (National Museum of Canada, Bulletin No. 162.) Ottawa, 1960.

—— "Review and Assessment of the Dorset Problem," *Anthropologica,* N.S., Vol. I (1959).

—— "Hypotheses on the Origin of

Canadian Thule Culture," A.A., Vol. XXVIII (1963).

THALBITZER, WILLIAM. "Cultic Games and Festivals in Greenland," XXIe Congrès international des Américanistes. Goteborg, 1925.

—— "Two Runic Stones from Greenland and Minnesota." Smith. Misc. Coll., Vol. CXVI, No. 3. Washington, 1951.

THORARINSSON, SIGURDUR. The Thousand Years Struggle against Ice and Fire. London, 1956.

THORDARSON, MATTHIAS. The Vinland Voyages. New York, 1930.

—— (ed.). Eiriks saga rauda. Islenzk fornrit, IV. Reykjavik, 1935.

—— (ed.). Graenlendinga saga. Islenzk fornrit, IV, Reykjavik, 1935.

THORHALLASON, EGILL. Efterretning om Rudera eller Levninger af de Gamle Normaends og Islaenderes Bygninger paa Gronlands Vester-Side. Copenhagen, 1776.

THORODDSEN, THORVALDUR. "Islands Jokler i Fortid og Nutid," G.T., XI (1891-1892), 111-146.

—— Landfraedisaga Islands. Copenhagen, 1898-1904.

—— Lysing Islands. Copenhagen, 1908-1911.

—— "Endnu nogle Bemaerkninger om Islands Klima i Oldtiden," G.T., Vol. XXIII (1915-16).

—— Arferdi a Island i thusund ar. Copenhagen, 1916-17.

—— "Um vedrattu og landkosti a Islandi i fornold," Andvari, Vol. XLI (1916).

—— "Islands Klima i Oldtiden," G.T., Vol. XXII (1914).

THORSTEINSSON, BJORN. Islenzka Skattlandid. Reykjavik, 1956.

—— "Islandsverzlun Englendinga a fyrra hluta 16. aldar," Skirnir, Vol. CXXIV (1950).

—— "Henry VIII and Iceland," Saga-Book of the Viking Society, Vol. XV (1957-59).

TORNOE, J. KR. "Hvitserk og Blaserk," N.G.T., Vol. V (1934-1935).

TRUDEL, MARCEL. Histoire de la Nouvelle France: les Vaines Tentatives 1524-1603. Montreal, 1963.

TYLOR, E. B. "Old Scandinavian Civilization among the Modern Esquimaux," J.A.I.G.B.I., Vol. XIII (1884).

VANGENSTEN, OVE C. L. Michel Beheims Reise til Danmark og Norge i 1450. (Skrifter udgivne af Videnskabs-Selskabet i Christiania 1908, Hist-Filos. Kl.) Christiania, 1909.

VEBAEK, CHRISTEN LEIF. Inland Farms in the Norse East Settlement. M.o.G., Vol. XC, No. 1 (1943). Copenhagen, 1943.

—— "Nationalmuseets etnologiske Undersogelser i Gronland," Gronland, 1955, pp. 20-26.

—— "Mellembygden," ibid., 1956, pp. 92-98.

VIGNERAS, L. A. "New Light on the 1497 Cabot Voyage to America," Hispanic American Hist. Rev., Vol. XXXVI (1956).

—— "The Cape Breton Landfall: 1494 or 1497," C.H.R., Vol. XXXVIII (1957).

WAHLGREN, ERIK. The Kensington Stone. Madison, 1958.

WEYER, EDWARD, JR. The Eskimos: Their Environment and Folkways. New Haven, 1932.

—— "Eskimo Prehistory in Perspective," Polar Notes, I (1959).

WILLIAMSON, J. A. The Cabot Voyages and Bristol Discovery under Henry VII. Cambridge (Hakluyt Society, Sec. Ser. CXX), 1962.

WINTEMBERG, W. J. "Eskimo sites of the Dorset Culture in Newfoundland," A.A., Vol. V (1939-40).

WOLFE, MICHAEL. "Thjodhild's Church," A.S.R., Vol. LI (1963).

—— "Norse Archeology in Greenland since World War II," ibid., Vol. XLIX (1961).

WRIGHT, J. K. The Geographical Lore of the Time of the Crusades. New York, 1925.

YULE-OLDHAM, HENRY. The Book of Ser Marco Polo. London, 1871.

ZIMMER, H. "Brendans Meerfahrt," Zeitschr. f. deutsches Altertum. Vol. XXXIII (1889).

APPENDIX A

LIST OF PERSONS TAKING PART
IN THE VINLAND VOYAGES

EIRIKR THORVALDSSON (Eric the Red). Birthplace and date uncertain but likely Iceland *ca.* 930-950. After exploring the west coast of Greenland for three years, he settled there at Brattahlid in 986. He died sometime during the first decade of the eleventh century.

BJARNI HERJULFSSON. Son of one of the original settlers of Greenland, Herjulfr Bardarson. Sailing from Iceland to Greenland to join his father, he was driven off course and became the first European to sight the shores of America.

LEIFR EIRIKSSON. Son of Eric the Red. Discoverer of Helluland (Baffin Island), Markland (Labrador), and particularly Vinland (Cape Cod?). He died *ca.* 1020-1025.

THORVALDR EIRIKSSON. Son of Eric the Red. Killed by American aborigines on an expedition to Vinland in 1006.

THORSTEINN EIRIKSSON. Son of Eric the Red. Led an abortive expedition to Vinland. Died in 1008 during a plague in Greenland.

FREYDIS. Illegitimate daughter of Eric the Red. Led a bloody expedition to Vinland. Her husband was named Thorvaldr.

THORFINNR THORDARSSON. Better known by his nickname Karlsefni (meaning likely to be a man). An Icelander who came to Greenland *ca.* 1009 and soon thereafter married Gudridr, the daughter of the Icelander, Thorbjorn Vifilsson, and widow of Thorsteinn Eiriksson, mother of Snorri Thorfinnsson, the first white child to be born in America. Thorfinnr led an expedition to Vinland, the object of which was to colon-ize the country. The expedition spent either two or three years somewhere on the east coast of America and then returned to Greenland possibly because of the hostility of the aborigines. Thorfinnr, his wife, and son, then settled in Iceland.

HELGI AND FINNBOGI. Two brothers of unknown Icelandic parentage. Joined Freydis on her Vinland expedition and were murdered at her instigation.

THORHALLR THE HUNTER. A trusted retainer of Eric the Red who possibly acted as guide during the early stages of Thorfinnr's expedition to Vinland. Fell out with Thorfinnr and left the expedition with a number of companions. Driven off course to Ireland where he died after being ill-treated.

HAKI AND HEKJA. A Scots couple who are said to have discovered the grapes of Vinland although the account strains one's credulity.

TYRKR. An incredible German who is said to have been almost a foster father to Leifr when he was a child. Said to have discovered the grapes of Vinland the Good.

THORGUNNA. A woman Leifr is said to have met in the year 999 in the Hebrides and on whom he begat a son, Thorgils. Thorgunna later went to Iceland, where she brought up her son and later sent him to Leifr in Greenland. The story is likely a romantic concoction with no basis in fact.

THJODHILDR. Wife of Eric the Red and mother of his sons. Erected the first Christian church in the western hemisphere at Brattahlid *ca.* 1001-1002.

202

APPENDIX B

CHRONOLOGY OF THE EARLY VOYAGES
TO GREENLAND, VINLAND, AND THE CANADIAN ARCTIC

NOTE: The chronology of the Vinland voyages is, as explained in the text, difficult to establish except with a margin of error of, in some cases, five to ten years. The dates assigned are thus often only approximate.

ca. 900	Gunnbjorn Ulfsson sights skerries off the east coast of Greenland.
980-981	Hrolfr Thorbjarnarson and Snaebjorn Holmsteinsson winter on the east coast of Greenland.
986	Bjarni Herjulfsson sights America.
999-1000	Leifr Eiriksson is at the court of King Olaf Tryggvason in Norway.
1001-1002	Leifr buys Bjarni's ship and discovers Helluland, Markland, and Vinland.
1004-1006	Leifr's brother, Thorvaldr, sails to Vinland and is slain there.
1007	Leifr's brother Thorsteinn attempts to reach Vinland but fails.
1008	Death of Thorsteinn. His widow Gudridr is befriended by Leifr.
1009	Thorfinnr Karlsefni comes to Greenland from Iceland and marries Gudridr.
1011	Thorfinnr Karlsefni sails to Vinland on a colonization venture. His son Snorri born in Vinland.
1012	Thorhallr the Hunter deserts Thorfinnr's expedition.
1011-1013	Thorfinnr Karlsefni explores Vinland and neighbouring regions.
1013	Thorfinnr returns to Greenland.
1014	Thorfinnr sails to Norway.
1015	Thorfinnr settles in Iceland.
1013	Two Icelandic brothers, Helgi and Finnbogi, arrive in Greenland from Norway.
1014	Leifr's half-sister Freydis joins Helgi and Finnbogi in an expedition to Vinland.
1015	Freydis slays the brothers and returns to Greenland.
1121	Bishop Eirkir Gnupsson sets out in search of Vinland and disappears.
1342	The inhabitants of the Western Settlement emigrate *en masse* to the Canadian Arctic and continental America.
1347	Greenlanders seeking Markland are driven to Iceland.
ca. 1470-1476	Two Portuguese emissaries sail to Greenland and America on the ships of the Danish king, with the Icelandic Johannes Scolvus as pilot.
1492-94	Joao Fernandez and Pedro Barcellos visit Greenland on a Danish ship.
ca. 1480-1496	Bristol merchants send ships west across the Atlantic to search for the island of Brazil and possibly discover parts of the east coast of Canada or islands lying off it.
1497	John Cabot discovers the New Found Land.
1498	John Cabot makes a second voyage from which he does not seem to have returned.
1500	Gaspar Corte-Real sails north along the east coast of America as far north as Greenland.

1501	Gaspar Corte-Real makes second voyage touching Labrador and regions south of it but fails to return himself, although two ships of the expedition return to Portugal.
1502	Miguel Corte-Real sets out to find his brother, reaches Newfoundland but fails to return, although two of his three ships reach Portugal.
1517	John Rastell heads abortive expedition to America.
1524	Giovanni da Verrazano sails from France and visits various parts of the east coast of North America.
1525	Estevan Gomez sails to Cape Breton and south along the east coast of America.
1527	John Rut reaches Labrador and Newfoundland and returns to England by way of the West Indies.
1536	Richard Hore sails to Newfoundland.
1576	Martin Frobisher sails to Greenland and Baffin Island.
1577	Second voyage of Martin Frobisher to the same region.
1578	Third voyage of Martin Frobisher to the same region.
1585	John Davis sails to the regions surrounding the strait which now bears his name.
1586	Second voyage of John Davis to Greenland and Baffin Island and also Labrador and Newfoundland.
1587	Third voyage of John Davis to Greenland and Labrador.
1602	George Weymouth sails to Greenland and Baffin Island.
1605	James Hall and John Knight head Danish expedition to Greenland.
1606	John Knight heads English expedition which reaches Labrador, where he and three of his men disappear.
	James Hall heads abortive Danish expedition.
1607	Henry Hudson, on an English ship, reaches the east coast of Greenland and Spitzbergen and discovers Jan Mayen.
1609	Hudson, in the service of the Dutch, discovers the river which bears his name.
1610-11	Hudson, in the service of the English, sails through Hudson Strait and into Hudson and James Bays. He winters in the latter and is set adrift in an open boat and disappears.
1612-13	Thomas Button explores the western shore of Hudson Bay.
1612	James Hall is slain on the west coast of Greenland.
1615	Robert Bylot, with William Baffin as pilot, explores Hudson Strait and Southampton Island.
1616	Robert Bylot and William Baffin explore the bay which bears the latter's name.
1619-20	Jens Munk, in command of Danish expedition, winters at Churchill.
1625	William Hawkeridge sails through Hudson Strait.
1631	Luke Fox explores the western and southern shore of Hudson Bay and the basin which now bears his name.
1631-32	Thomas James explores the west coast of Hudson Bay and the bay which bears his name.

APPENDIX C

PLATE 1 An illustration from Frederick II's *The Art of Falconry.*

PLATE 2 *Above:* Crozier, carved from walrus tusk, found at Gardar, probably from the thirteenth century.
Below: Plates, made from wood, and used for serving food.

PLATE 3 *Above:* Crucifix from Sandnes in the Western Settlement of Greenland.
Below: Kingigtersuak stone, providing evidence for penetration of North Greenland by the Icelanders.

PLATE 4 Artifacts of the Thule Culture of ivory, bone, antler, and slate. The larger harpoon heads with drilled perforations and the harpoon end-blades of rubbed slate show something of the contrast between Thule and Dorset Culture equipment. The ivory object, third from left at bottom, was used to hold thimbles made of sealskin.

PLATE 5 Cape Dorset culture artifacts. *Row 1:* harpoon heads. *Row 2:* so-called shaman's teeth, ornament, fish spear, needle. *Row 3:* flint knife, points, and scraper. Dorset Culture tools are marked by cuts or gouged holes, for this culture did not know the bow drill. The weapons usually have blades of chipped flint. *Row 4:* Combs of bone from Sandnes in the Western Settlement of Greenland.

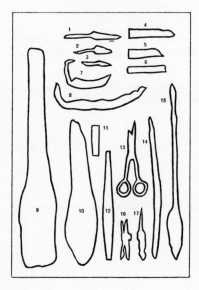

PLATE 6 1, 2, 3. Iron knives.

4. Iron knife with handle of antler.
5, 6. Knife handles of tusk ivory.
7. Leaf knife of iron.
8. Iron sickle.
9, 10. Moulding presses for horn spoons.
11, 12. Tally sticks.
13. Iron scissors.
14. Harpoon head of bone.
15. Iron hunting spear.
16. Wooden clamp held together by iron nail.
17. Iron awl with wood handle.

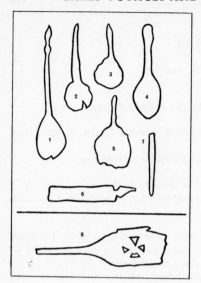

PLATE 7 1-5. Wooden spoons.
6. Knife with antler handle.
7. Thread winder.
8. Wooden stirrer.

PLATE 8 Clothes from the Churchyard at Herjolfsnes, these garments represent the only clothing of the common people of the Middle Ages that has been preserved.

PLATE 9 *Top row:* Bone button; game piece; ivory tusk pawn; steatite doll; wooden pawn; bone chess piece.
Middle row: Man of walrus ivory with a European-type collar; two women of walrus ivory with Germanic hair top; wood carving of an Icelander in Greenland.
Bottom row: Toys; carving from West Greenland; doll.

PLATE 10 Drawings of ships in Norwegian church. It is believed that the *knorr*, which carried the colonists to Greenland and America, was likely such a ship.

PLATE 11 The Gokstad ship (*above*) and the Oseberg ship (*below*) were longships, and not used for voyages to Iceland or Greenland.

PLATE 12 Henry Hudson.

PLATE 13 Sir Thomas Button.

PLATE 14 Sir Martin Frobisher.

PLATE 15 Thomas James.

PLATE 16 An old painting of Eskimos brought from Godthaab fjord to Denmark in 1654.

THE
CANADIAN
CENTENARY
SERIES

A HISTORY OF CANADA IN SEVENTEEN VOLUMES

The Canadian Centenary Series is a comprehensive history of the peoples and lands which form the Dominion of Canada.

Although the series is designed as a unified whole so that no part of the story is left untold, each volume is complete in itself. Written for the general reader as well as for the scholar, each of the seventeen volumes of *The Canadian Centenary Series* is the work of a leading Canadian historian who is an authority on the period covered in his volume. Their combined efforts have made a new and significant contribution to the understanding of the history of Canada and of Canada today.

W. L. Morton, Head of the Department of History and Provost of University College, University of Manitoba, is the Executive Editor of *The Canadian Centenary Series*. A graduate of the Universities of Manitoba and Oxford, he is the author of *The Kingdom of Canada; Manitoba: A History; The Progressive Party in Canada; One University: A History of the University of Manitoba;* and other writings. He has also edited *The Journal of Alexander Begg and Other Documents Relevant to the Red River Resistance.* He holds the honorary degree of Doctor of Laws from the University of Toronto and has been awarded the Tyrrell Medal of the Royal Society of Canada and the Governor General's Award for Non-Fiction.

D. G. Creighton, Professor of History, University of Toronto, is the Advisory Editor of *The Canadian Centenary Series*. A graduate of the Universities of Toronto and Oxford, he is the author of *John A. Macdonald: The Young Politician; John A. Macdonald: The Old Chieftain; Dominion of the North; The Empire of the St. Lawrence,* and many other works. He has received honorary Doctorates from the Universities of Manitoba, McGill, Queen's, New Brunswick, Saskatchewan, and British Columbia. Twice winner of the Governor General's Award for Non-Fiction, he has also been awarded the Tyrrell Medal of the Royal Society of Canada, the University of Alberta National Award in Letters, and the University of British Columbia Medal for Popular Biography.

PRINTED IN ENGLAND BY
WILLMER BROTHERS AND HARAM LIMITED
AND
BOUND IN CANADA BY
T. H. BEST PRINTING CO. LIMITED